Praise for *The Future Workplace Experience*

"Meister and Mulcahy have done a fantastic job laying out a detailed road map for how organizations can construct and—more importantly—execute an optimal future workplace experience that drives employee engagement and materially improves organizational outcomes. This book is required reading for your entire HR team as well as senior business leaders as you explore how to expand the scope and impact of HR and in the process create a compelling experience for both employees and customers."

—DAVID ALMEDA
SVP, Chief People Officer, Kronos, Inc.

"The workspace is an opportunity for a company to have a visible manifestation of their culture. Meister and Mulcahy make the case that in order to create compelling experiences through the physical environment you need to reach into the hearts, minds and souls of your company's talent. The Five Functions of Workspaces is not only the new outline for creating great engaging environments, it's a call to action for designers and shapers of space to listen to employees and create a place where they want to come to be a part of a community, do their best work, and can have fun in the process."

—BRYAN BERTHOLD
Managing Director of Workplace
Strategy & Change Management,
Cushman & Wakefield

"A must read for all those charged with leadership in this age of a changing and dynamic workforce. This book reminds us that 'Generational Intelligence' is a core competency in management for both today and tomorrow. It helps us recognize we must infuse mutligenerational strategies into our workforce practices throughout the entire employee lifecycle including talent acquisition, learning, development, engagement, and retention. Meister and Mulcahy have created a comprehensive road map that is an invaluable tool and resource."

—DONNA BONAPARTE
Vice President Human Resources, Babson College

"Engaging, practical, and insightful—Meister and Mulcahy have produced the definitive how-to guide for successfully navigating the future world of work. For any leader, the message is clear—'agility' will be the essential determinant of future success. To produce results and engage others, future leaders must be transparent, accountable, inclusive, and future focused."

—DR. SIMON BOUCHER
Chief Executive, Irish Management Institute

"The pace of change in the business world is incredible, and having a road map is needed. Meister and Mulcahy not only give organizations a tangible direction to follow; they capture the reality that *the evolution of work affects all companies—not just the giant ones.* Noting the importance of agility and activism for the leaders of today and tomorrow was refreshing, on point, and necessary."

—STEVE BROWNE
Executive Director of HR, LaRosa's, Inc.

"Meister and Mulcahy capture the craving the modern workforce has of an organization and its leaders. Namely, to work in a transparent (honest), connected (team-oriented) and option-filled environment (personalization). Rule #3, Be an Agile Leader, captures the need of balancing transparency with enabling trust. Organizations that can rise successfully to this challenge will end up with very engaged employees, indeed. Our mission as talent professionals has to be to drive the engagement agenda as well as flexibly motivate in an accelerated world."

—GILLIAN DAVIS
Head of Global Talent Acquisition, Havas Media Group

"In an era of unprecedented change in how we live, learn, and work, Meister and Mulcahy have documented the growing importance of investing in learning to increase productivity and competitiveness in the global marketplace. You will want to share this book with your entire learning and development team!"

—DON DUQUETTE
Executive Vice President, GP Strategies

"In *The Future Workplace Experience*, Meister and Mulcahy paint a compelling picture of navigating the trends that are reshaping the future work environment and redefining learning. This book challenges leaders to disrupt their current learning models and create learning on-demand solutions that are dynamic, innovative, and personalized. In today's highly competitive global environment, creating a continuous learning environment is critical for attracting, retaining, and engaging your workforce."

—SHIREEN DONALDSON
Vice President Human Resources, Keysight Technologies

"'Be an Agile Leader' is a lesson all of us can and should understand. Increasingly, diverse experiences, skills, and points of view are simply the price of admission to the executive table. Learning agility is a critical differentiator that separates the 'ho-hum' contributor from the 'wow' conversation leader."

—CHRIS EDMONDS-WATERS
Head of Human Resources, SVB, Silicon Valley Bank

"*The Future Workplace Experience* is a must-read and a must-act for innovative HR leaders and CEOs alike who are focused on developing people strategies that will attract and retain the talent required to lead their organizations into the future. Agile leaders who can both produce results and engage the next generation of employees will be the key to our future workplaces—the battle for talent will be one for the record books, and agile leaders will be the champions. Meister and Mulcahy share invaluable insights from leading organizations that provide a road map for continually evolving the workplace experience through their 10 Rules to Navigate the Future Workplace."

—STEPHANIE FRANKLIN
Senior Vice President, Global Human Resources,
Nuance Communications

"Mobility and choice are the new change masters, and employees are in charge of where and how they work. Meister and Mulcahy make the case that the time is now to rethink the workspace to match the fluid demands of a global workforce. It's not enough to read this book; you will want to act now to reimagine your company's approach to workplace and policy."

—MARK GILBREATH
CEO and Founder, LiquidSpace

"As work evolves away from the tangible elements of place, time and location, to the less tangible areas of identity, mindset and motivation, Meister and Mulcahy do a remarkable job articulating a framework for leaders and organizations to harness and succeed within this paradigm shift."

—BRIAN JONES
Vice President, Human Resources, American Eagle Outfitters

"Now that speed counts and organizations are flatter, Meister and Mulcahy illustrate the framework that is needed to provide great experiences and continuous development for leaders and teams of all sizes. This book is a valuable resource and reference point, as learning organizations need to adapt to these rapid changes and partner with other functional areas to solve for these ubiquitous realities."

—JAY MOORE
Global Learning Leader, GE Crotonville

"*The Future Workplace Experience* is a necessary, compelling, and actionable plan for companies in any industry, of any size, at any point in their journey toward creating a holistic experience for employees. The 10 Rules to Navigate the Future Workplace address topics such as creating seamless experiences beyond the 'trophy perks' and adopting greater transparency among leaders. These are critical topics for both HR professionals and business leaders."

—ANDREA NEWMAN
Director, HR Strategy Office, Intel

"I LOVE this book! Finally, a holistic perspective that reaches across the table to beckon HR, real estate, and IT to come together and cocreate an authentic employee experience, aligning the physical and virtual space with the culture of an organization. Our workspace is the biggest billboard our organization has to communicate culture, and this book offers a road map on 'how to' intentionally make it come alive."

—KATE NORTH
Vice President, Workplace Innovation,
PlaceValue and Global Chair,
Workplace Evolutionaries (WE)

"Companies must offer an experience for their employees that compels them to stay. The authors' 10 rules for creating the future workplace are imperatives and they make a compelling case for Rule #1: Make the Workplace an Experience. By curating the employee experience to insure innovation, freedom, movement, and connection to each other and the company, employees will stay and thrive!"

—SANDY REZENDES
Chief Learning Officer, Citizens Financial Group, Inc.

"Meister and Mulcahy provide an illuminating vision of what's next for the workplace. *The Future Workplace Experience* highlights the need to reinvent the employee value proposition. This book presents a strong case for the adaptability required not only by the HR profession, but by the business world."

—BARBARA RUNYON
Vice President and Chief Human Resources Officer,
La-Z-Boy Incorporated

"The valuable insights provided in *The Future Workplace Experience* are coupled with practical guidance from practitioners who are already actively engaged around the future of work. This book is a most valuable and insightful addition to the debate on this critical topic. It is destined to be seen as a valuable resource and reference work for business leaders, human resources professionals, academics, and students alike."

—NIALL SAUL, MSC, FCIPD
VP Organisational Capability and People, Asavie Technologies

"Meister and Mulcahy's research has clearly identified a road map to help organizations to develop an agile workplace that is able to anticipate, adapt, and act to leverage marketplace changes. Their 10 Rules to Navigate the Future Workplace have tremendous implications for the HR function to be a major force for driving and enabling the execution of organizational strategy.

—KELLY SAVAGE
Chief Human Resources Officer, Amway

"*The Future Workplace Experience* is much more than a research tome on future workplace trends. It is a compelling synthesis of original research, real-world case studies, and practical tools, *The Future Workplace Experience* is really a road map for navigating the twenty-first century world of uncertainty, exponential change, and disruption that business and HR leaders face today. Read this book and you will learn how to be a workplace activist and make the change happen in your organization."

—ERIC SEVERSON
National Advisory Council on
Innovation & Entrepreneurship,
Former Co-CHRO, Gap Inc.

"Right from the initial vivid description of a futuristic workday, *The Future Workplace Experience* paints a striking picture of changes that organizations face. The authors' call for urgent action is timely and their advice welcome. Their principles of 'Agile Leadership' capture the essence of leadership needed in the digital era. The 10 rules and insightful case studies will provide you with a clear framework to succeed in the rapidly transforming world we face. This is a much needed book!"

—DR. VISHAL SHAH
Vice President, Leadership & People Sciences,
Wipro Technologies

"Leaders responsible for developing talent in their organizations are grappling with new ways to do learning which is on demand, engaging, and aligned to the strategic business priorities of the company. *The Future Workplace Experience* argues the time is now to reimagine learning and embed ongoing development into each employee's experience at work."

—MARTHA SOEHREN, PHD
Chief Talent Development Officer
and Senior Vice President, Comcast

THE
FUTURE
WORKPLACE
EXPERIENCE

THE
FUTURE
WORKPLACE
EXPERIENCE

10 RULES FOR MASTERING
DISRUPTION IN RECRUITING
AND ENGAGING EMPLOYEES

JEANNE C. MEISTER
KEVIN J. MULCAHY

New York   Chicago   San Francisco   Athens   London
Madrid   Mexico City   Milan   New Delhi
Singapore   Sydney   Toronto

1 2 3 4 5 6 7 8 9   DOC   21 20 19 18 17 16

ISBN   978-1-259-58938-6
MHID   1-259-58938-2

e-ISBN 978-1-259-58939-3
e-MHID   1-259-58939-0

This publication is designed to provide accurate and authoritative information in regard to the subject matter covered. It is sold with the understanding that neither the author nor the publisher is engaged in rendering legal, accounting, securities trading, or other professional services. If legal advice or other expert assistance is required, the services of a competent professional person should be sought.

> —*From a Declaration of Principles Jointly Adopted*
> *by a Committee of the American Bar Association*
> *and a Committee of Publishers and Associations*

McGraw-Hill Education books are available at special quantity discounts to use as premiums and sales promotions or for use in corporate training programs. To contact a representative, please visit the Contact Us pages at www.mhprofessional.com.

For my family, Bob, Danielle, Deborah, and Matt, my loving supporters.
Thank you, everything is possible with all of you by my side!

Jeanne

For my wife Diane . . . for sharing all the best life experiences.

Kevin

And for the members of the Future Workplace Network,
for generously sharing your challenges and opportunities
in preparing for the future of work.

Jeanne and Kevin

CONTENTS

FOREWORD

There was a time when successful onboarding meant that new hires learned what they needed to learn, filled out the forms they needed to complete, and met their manager on their first day. That was the functional lens. Yet turn it around and look at the same scene through the lens of the employee—and ask, is this iconic?

To my dismay, at IBM, the answer was no. We had architected a flawless HR process, but many of our new hires were underwhelmed during their first few days. It became clear that it would take a redesigned cross-functional effort—with security for badges, IT for collaboration software and device connectivity, and real estate for workspace—to get it right. And it took design thinking to create the disruptive ideas needed to reinvent the experience, making it iconic from end to end.

This book turns the world of corporations on its side and looks at it from the standpoint of the experiences we create—for employees and ultimately customers.

Thirty years ago, companies were reengineering themselves around processes, standardizing and outsourcing them for higher levels of efficiency. *Reengineering the Corporation: A Manifesto for Business Revolution* by Michael Hammer and James Champy became the guidebook for leaders who shaped these organizations of the 1990s.

The Future Workforce Experience serves as an equally indispensable guidebook for the next wave of corporate reinvention—experience design. Meister and Mulcahy describe how companies today are being radically reimagined around the experiences they create—either intentionally or by default. The authors distill the new rules of the road for leaders to transform organizations around the compelling experiences that will engage their people and drive business success in the digital age.

Each chapter takes the reader on a guided tour of the profound changes going on inside corporate America today. We see the impact of the new workforce generation, reared on Facebook, Netflix, Instagram, and Snapchat. Unlike prior generations, millennials wield considerable labor market power, and as they are digital natives, their expectations are driving a sea change inside corporations.

We are shown how organizational boundaries made porous by the Internet are now transparent in the age of social computing, hastening the demise of the hierarchical workplace and democratizing information and power. We learn about the newer enterprises such as Airbnb, Glassdoor, and Rackspace that have provoked established competitors to rethink their business models, organization paradigms, and talent strategies. And we get inside the companies that are pivoting to the future—such as Cisco, IBM, Microsoft, and SunTrust.

One thing that is becoming clear is that organizations built in the industrial era are ripe for disruption. They were built on the concepts of hierarchy, functional expertise, and jobs. But what replaces these iconic artifacts of classic organizations? Meister and Mulcahy describe new types of leaders, new ways of working and staffing, and new forms of corporate infrastructure that are starting to appear in the corporate landscape. They provide a new architectural blueprint to reshape our organizations.

Creating a compelling workplace experience means going well beyond corporate mission statements to forging emotional connections. Agile leadership is a form of servant leadership and not just a methodology for coders. And managing workspace goes well beyond eliminating cubicles and offices to promoting conviviality, wellness, and chance collisions.

Much has already been made of the consumerization of the workplace experience and the impact on the human resources function. Recruitment was the first area to change, borrowing heavily from digital marketing. With big data analytics and mobile and social technologies, HR is becoming less process-bound, simplifying the employee experience and making it much more personalized.

But we would be missing the point if HR professionals stopped at making the workplace experience more consumer-grade. As this book lays out, the experience lens changes the mission and purpose of the HR function and blends its edges with real estate, internal communications, and IT. In my view, HR is an artifact of the industrial age—and if it is not reshaped and reinvented, it will end up on the sidelines of the most important changes affecting people in their organizations in our lifetimes. Ultimately, as suggested in this book, HR can use the power of crowdsourcing, cognitive computing, and social sentiment analysis to build a more transparent and democratic organization where employees are not simply consumers but cocreators of the organization and their careers.

This book is more than a guidebook; it is a call to action. The authors mine a lot of data to make a compelling business case for change, including over 30 studies from Aon Hewitt, Deloitte, PwC, Towers Watson, McKinsey, and professors at Harvard, London Business School, MIT, Oxford, and Wharton, among others. Embrace the future they describe, and create competitive advantage. Ignore it at your peril.

DIANE J. GHERSON

Chief Human Resource Officer

IBM

10 RULES TO NAVIGATE THE FUTURE WORKPLACE

> Lots of companies don't succeed over time. What do they fundamentally do wrong? They usually miss the future.
>
> —*Larry Page, CEO, Alphabet (Google)*

Understanding the Future Workplace: Today's Core Competency

The future is happening now. It's not waiting for you or your organization. In times of constant and accelerated change, organizations that do not adapt, that do not anticipate the future and take action, are in danger of irrelevancy—or worse, extinction. Consider that 52 percent of Fortune 500 organizations have merged, been acquired, or gone bankrupt since 2000.[1] The global business landscape will continue to experience constant change and turmoil. New circumstances require fresh solutions—and superior business results reward organizations that deliver them. Collectively, the Fortune 500 employ 28 million people and generate over $12.5 trillion in global revenue. The fastest growing, those most responsive to their business environment and who financially outperform their peers, are intense learning machines. They are led by agile leaders, consider technology as both an enabler and a disruptor, and are manically focused on satisfying their customers and engaging their employees globally. Most importantly, they encourage employees to be workplace activists, propagating changes to reinvent the experience of their global workplace to drive business results.

The Future Workplace Experience challenges most of the conventional wisdom about work, employees, human resource practices and the very nature of a job itself to help you anticipate and adapt to a new world of work! As we scan the workplace of today, and of the future, we see that everything we take for granted about work—what we expect from our work, where we work, how we work, when we work, and with whom we work—is being disrupted. Think of this: "Freelancing in America," a report issued by the Freelancers Union, states that gig economy workers (independent workers who are not employees and work when and where they need to) now account for 54 million people and contributed over $7 billion to the U.S. economy in 2015.[2] These changes in what, where, how, when, and who works will only accelerate as every organization in every category will be impacted by a new set of workplace expectations. To be ready for this massive change, you will need to anticipate the future, take action, become "a workplace activist," and advocate for change in your organization. This book will show you how.

Why We Wrote This Book

The Future Workplace Experience revolves around the premise that workers of all generations and cultures will increasingly come to expect a workplace that mirrors their personal lives, one that is transparent, connected, personalized, and offers choices. Understanding this future workplace experience will be a core competency of both business and human resource leaders. We went beyond hypothesizing about these changes. We interviewed over 100 senior HR and business executives at companies successfully navigating the trends reshaping the future workplace experience. We also conducted the Future Workplace Forecast, a global survey of human resource and business leaders.

Our interviews and survey uncovered a confluence of disruptive forces that leaders are grappling with today, from the experiences workers expect in the workplace, to the myriad of current and next-generation technologies transforming how and where we work, to the diversifying composition of workers, representing multiple generations and cultures, in addition to various segments of workers such as breadwinner moms, boomers on the grid, and independent workers. We synthesized the results of our research into 10 rules to guide you, your team, and your organization to master disruption in recruiting and engaging employees in the future workplace.

The 10 rules illustrate through interviews and real-world examples the accelerated pace of change and how organizations are proactively positioning for the future workplace. As the world has become more interconnected, so too has the workplace. Traditional hierarchies have given way to the democratization of work and radical new solutions for employees and customers. We share how Cisco created an HR Breakathon to "break" HR silos and create new solutions to enhance the employee experience and how DBS Bank in Singapore launched a "hackathon" for bankers to develop new digital financial service solutions for their clients.

The Future Workplace Experience takes a bold step toward the future, serving as a road map for organizations of all sizes to rethink, reimagine, and reinvent the employee experience. Our 10 rules will help your organization compete more effectively in a global talent marketplace, defined by changing expectations, transformative technologies, and a shifting composition of the workforce. We feature companies of all types, including companies with growing populations of younger workers like Airbnb, Cognizant Technologies, IBM, LinkedIn, Glassdoor, and GE Digital that are on the leading edge of shaping future global employment practices.

As coauthors, we each bring a set of unique experiences that shape our worldview of the future workplace. We are both partners in Future Workplace, an HR executive network and research firm dedicated to working with organizations to anticipate and plan for disruptive changes in their companies, industries, and geographic markets.

Jeanne has consulted with organizations on preparing them for the future of learning and working for over 25 years, both through her own consulting firm and with Accenture. As the author of three previous books and a contributor to *Forbes*, Jeanne consults and speaks with hundreds of organizations on how build the talent capabilities of their organization, reinvent Human Resources, and prepare for the future of work.

Kevin has consulted to executives on business strategies to respond to change across multiple industries and geographies for over two decades. He has led the delivery of business insights, facilitated business planning and strategy, and led a global start-up. He coaches on leadership effectiveness at the Harvard Business School and promotes entrepreneurial thought and action as an adjunct faculty member at Babson College.

Both of us are engaged daily in thinking about how individuals, teams, and organizations can best prepare for the future of work. We operate the Future Workplace Network, a peer membership community for senior HR leaders to regularly come together in person and online to discuss, debate, and share "next" practices to thrive in the future workplace. This book extends our members-only dialogue on the future workplace experience to a broader audience of leaders that we have not yet met. We purposefully use the word *dialogue*, because expectations of the workplace experience, applications of technology, and the composition of the workforce will continue to evolve. We invite you to join our conversation as we collaborate together to empower you to enhance your future workplace experience and take action to master disruption in recruiting and engaging employees.

What You Will Find in This Book

Our intent in writing *The Future Workplace Experience* is to weave a story of how the workplace is changing and to profile the new practices that organizations are implementing at work. We organized these practices into three areas: What workers expect from work, how technology transforms the workplace, and the changing composition of the workforce. We have synthesized our insights into 10 rules that you can apply to rethink and reimagine your future workplace.

The Future Workplace Experience combines extensive interviews and research with reflective questions that you can use to guide yourself, your team, and your organization to best prepare for and navigate the future workplace. The key features of our book include:

- Insights on new practices by organizations adapting to the future workplace, developed through over 100 personal interviews with HR and business leaders from a cross section of organizations, including Airbnb, Cisco,

Cognizant Technologies, Credit Suisse, Fidelity Investments, GE Digital, Genentech, Glassdoor, IBM, JetBlue, La-Z-Boy, LinkedIn, Rackspace, SunTrust, and Verizon Wireless, to name just a few. These organizations are leading the way in the use of innovative practices for recruiting, developing, and engaging talent for their future workplace.

- Key findings from our Future Workplace Forecast, a global survey of 2,147 human resource and business leaders across 7 countries and representing 10 industries. Our findings identify a segment of "winning organizations," which operate differently from—and better than—the rest. Their employees are likely or very likely to recommend their organization for employment to a friend or family member, they financially outperform industry peers over a three-year period, and they have been recognized on one of a number of "Best Places to Work" lists. Essentially, they have a different operating model for running their organization; they are adaptive learning organizations obsessed with providing exceptional levels of service to their customers and designing compelling workplace experiences for their employees.

- Questions ending each chapter for exploring what you, your team, and your organization could do to deliver a compelling workplace experience.

- Advice on how you can become a workplace activist and anticipate the expected and unexpected outcomes of making the changes you see needed in your workplace.

The 10 rules, each of which forms the basis of a chapter, are shown in Figure I.1. Our 10 rules paint a picture of how organizations are responding to constant disruption and shifting business goals to reimagine their workplaces and workforces. In the past, most of us could spend our entire working lives at the same organization, tapping into the skills we learned in school, college, or graduate school to further our career. This is no longer the case, as the knowledge cycle is growing shorter and shorter. Louis Ross, former vice chairman of Ford Motor Co., said, "In your career, knowledge is like milk . . . if you're not replacing everything you know . . . your career is going to turn sour fast."[3]

It's not just employees who must continually change and update skills; this need for constant reinvention also applies to organizations that have to pre-

Figure I.1   *Ten rules to navigate the future workplace*

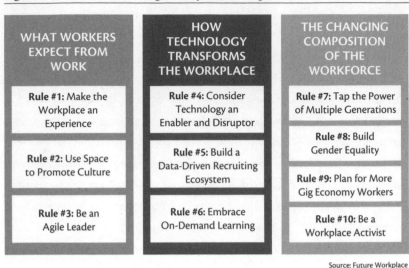

WHAT WORKERS EXPECT FROM WORK	HOW TECHNOLOGY TRANSFORMS THE WORKPLACE	THE CHANGING COMPOSITION OF THE WORKFORCE
Rule #1: Make the Workplace an Experience	**Rule #4:** Consider Technology an Enabler and Disruptor	**Rule #7:** Tap the Power of Multiple Generations
		Rule #8: Build Gender Equality
Rule #2: Use Space to Promote Culture	**Rule #5:** Build a Data-Driven Recruiting Ecosystem	**Rule #9:** Plan for More Gig Economy Workers
Rule #3: Be an Agile Leader	**Rule #6:** Embrace On-Demand Learning	**Rule #10:** Be a Workplace Activist

Source: Future Workplace

pare for changing customer and employee needs. As an executive at a leading global bank observed, "When we look at the pace at which digital native companies operate and launch new capabilities, that's something that doesn't really happen in large enterprises."[4] This is becoming a new operating model for organizations to thrive in the twenty-first century.

Our rules will guide you as you lead your organization's path forward to more confidently navigate the future workplace.

10 Rules to Navigate the Future Workplace

Rule #1: Make the Workplace an Experience

Today, we live in the experience economy. This term was coined by Joseph Pine and James Gilmore in their *Harvard Business Review* article in 1988 to refer to the movement among companies to orchestrate memorable events for their customers, which was increasingly becoming the "product" they were selling.[5] The experience economy was considered at the time to be the main underpinning for customer experience management.

Fast-forward to the workplace of the twenty-first century. Companies are now creating employee experiences to keep workers engaged, happy, and loyal to the organization. We call this new movement the Future Workplace Experience. It is driven by employees who come to expect a workplace that mirrors the quality of experiences they have when they consume, transact, or communicate outside their workplace.

Airbnb, profiled in Rule #1: "Make the Workplace an Experience," is an example of a company explicitly committed to building a future workplace experience where all the elements of work—the emotional, the intellectual, the physical, the technological, and the cultural—are carefully orchestrated to create a compelling employee experience.

On an organizational level, companies that are on a journey to create the workplace as an experience will operate outside traditional silos and assemble intact teams charged with creating this experience for employees. In many cases this means the lines within organizations, such as HR, IT, real estate, marketing, and internal communications, are blurring. And this means more partnerships among disparate groups and sometimes even new reporting lines between these functions.

For the workplace as an experience to become a reality, you must consider how your organization can go beyond providing today's "trophy perks"— such as massages, gyms, free food, game rooms, and yoga classes—to creating tomorrow's memorable employee experiences, which fully tap the emotional, intellectual, physical, technological, and cultural aspects of a job in today's new world of work.

Rule #2: Use Space to Promote Culture

Workspace shapes culture. Increasingly, companies as different as Apple and La-Z-Boy have redesigned their workspaces to better align with their core values, attract the right talent, and encourage serendipitous personal encounters. As reported by Walter Isaacson, author of *Steve Jobs*, Jobs fixated on every detail of the physical layout of his offices including where to locate the bathrooms so as to allow for more possible "points of collision." In fact, Korn

Ferry, an organizational and people advisory firm, acknowledges the importance of space by proposing in "The Future of Work: A Meeting of Minds," that "people who work in real estate should be evaluated based not on how many more people can be crammed into smaller offices but much more on how the physical space affects day-to-day collaboration."[6]

Before organizations can redesign their workspaces to support achieving their goals, business leaders and HR professionals must have a vision for the power of the workspace to motivate a community of employees to drive business results. Ben Waber, CEO of Humanyze, a Boston-based company founded out of MIT's Media Lab, makes "sociometric badges" that capture interaction, communication, and location information for the employees wearing them. The data is then analyzed to determine the types of experiences employees are having during the day. Privacy, of course, is key here, and employees must opt in to wear the badges. But what Waber has been able to demonstrate is that face-to-face interactions and a sense of community are increasingly important in workspaces of the future.

This rule highlights new ways to think about workspace and raises new questions about how space is used to support organizational values and culture while creating more opportunities for collaboration and unplanned yet productive collisions between employees.

Rule #3: Be an Agile Leader

New times require new leadership skills. In the future workplace, a new generation of managers will need to learn to lead differently to be effective. What distinguishes winning organizations in our Future Workplace Forecast study is how they demonstrate transparency by being open and communicating and regularly sharing information. The majority of our winning organizations (6 out of 10) rated their organization as transparent, compared with less than half of our survey population.

Why is greater transparency so critical at this time? Transparency enables trust, and trust plays an important role in the workplace and affects the engagement and motivation of employees. According to the American Psychological

Association, a quarter of U.S. workers claim to not trust their employer. And a staggering half do not believe their boss is open with them.[7] This lack of trust in the workplace should be a wake-up call for employers.

We asked employers about what they expected of the Agile Leader of the Future. Our results indicate that the agile leader is one who is focused on the ability to produce results by being transparent, accountable, intrapreneurial, and future focused. And this leader is also focused on the ability to engage people, meaning being team intelligent, inclusive, and a great people developer. We expand on each of these desired capabilities in depth. We provide examples of how leaders in companies like Adobe, Amway, AT&T, Cisco, DBS Bank, and Telstra are putting these capabilities into practice in their organizations. Finally, we recommend model behaviors for you to apply in yours.

Developing agile leadership skills in the workplace will be critical to recruiting and engaging the best talent. Ask yourself: Do we have a leadership pipeline that understands the power of successfully balancing the ability to produce results with the ability to engage people? What could our organization do to further develop agile leadership among our leaders?

Rule #4: Consider Technology an Enabler and Disruptor

Technology has become more critical to business than ever before. Employees must master new technologies to work. In a 2016 Cognizant study, 30 percent of executives cited a "serious" digital skills gap in their organization, mostly due to inadequate supply of both digital and sector knowledge.[8]

Being able to use technology as an enabler to get work done more effectively will be a core competency of working in the twenty-first century. We will need to be able to use cloud based services like Dropbox and Box for file storage; Yammer, Slack, Spark, and Google Hangouts for collaboration; Google Docs and Analytics to run the business; Workboard and BetterWorks for online goal setting; HipChat for team collaboration; and Basecamp for online project management, as well as a host of cognitive computing services that apply data analytics to our work flows.

Technology will also disrupt current business practices; businesses that were once managed by "gut" will now have access to streams of data. This new era of cognitive computing presents us with a unique opportunity to apply data to make better business decisions. Those making decisions without the benefit of analyzing data will quickly feel as if they are stumbling around in the dark compared with their competitors. This applies to the HR department more than anywhere else, where the way we use data to find and develop our employees will create competitive advantages.

Technology is irreversibly transforming how we work regardless of our job role. This rule describes how to respond to the technology impacting the workplace. We see that some jobs will certainly be automated by technology (think telemarketers and paralegals), others will be created by technology (data scientists and learning experience managers), and still others will be reimagined to incorporate artificial intelligence into job roles. In response, we need to understand the impact of technology for us personally, our teams, and our organizations and map a strategy for how to best incorporate technology into our future workplace practices.

Rule #5: Build a Data-Driven Recruiting Ecosystem

Conventional wisdom in recruiting is that a small percentage of people are active job seekers and the rest are passive candidates, happily employed people who aren't actively looking for a new job—but who could be convinced to take a new job under the right circumstances.

Today that distinction no longer applies. Now that job hopping is as easy as swiping right on apps such as Switch and Anthology or passively receiving job suggestions from LinkedIn and Glassdoor, everyone is a continual job seeker. So the question becomes, how does recruiting evolve to acknowledge that job seekers are always on the hunt for new gigs, whether full time or freelance? Forward-looking companies are starting with the realization that recruiting the best talent must begin with building a strong employer brand so candidates seek out the employer as a desirable company to work for.

Next, while using social media—including Facebook, Twitter, LinkedIn, Pinterest, Instagram, Snapchat, and more—was in an experimental stage for much of the last few years, companies are now leveraging these social sites to source candidates, turn customers into employees and candidates into customers. The key is to continue to leverage social media for recruiting while devising a strategy to turn a company's own employees into brand ambassadors. According to LinkedIn, socially engaged companies are 58 percent more likely to attract top talent and 20 percent more likely to retain them.[9]

The key for companies is to apply a marketing mindset to sourcing talent as they recruit various employee segments.

Rule #6: Embrace On-Demand Learning

Continual learning is now a requirement to stay employable. A recent study by Deloitte, a consultancy firm, found that the rapid pace of technological change in the workplace is leading to a skills half-life of only 2.5 years,[10] while IBM believes that the shelf life of knowledge in some industries is as short as 13 months.[11]

Whatever estimate you believe, the conclusion is the same: being able to stay on top of your field and adjacent fields by continually learning will be crucial for you and your organization to win in the future workplace. To stay competitive, organizations will need to go beyond paying lip service to the importance of being a continual learner. They will need to create opportunities for learners to become serial learners, providing access to all forms of learning available on demand, and encouraging learners to become intellectually curious in looking beyond their immediate job to possible new ways of working.

Companies can start down the path of serial learning by offering employees opportunities to access learning from a wide array of sources, both internal and external to the organization. Will on-demand learning replace formal learning programs? Not immediately. But companies and their learning leaders should begin to question where their budgets and resources are going, and whether they are being deployed in the most effective and efficient way possible.

Satya Nadella, Microsoft's CEO, recently spoke about his passion for and commitment to continual learning and improvement, even with the increased responsibilities and demands of his new role. Says Nadella, "What defines me [is that] . . . I'm a lifelong learner." Nadella continued, during the Q&A following his appointment, "I get energized when I see people achieve standards. That's the thing that gets me going."[12]

Corporate learning departments need to think and act in new ways to deliver on the promise of on-demand learning. The department must move from controlling learning inside the four walls of the organization to allowing—even encouraging—learning to happen in any number of ways, including MOOCs (massive open online courses), TED Talks, and podcasts. We must offer new ways for our learners to become serial learners. It's time for corporate learning leaders to relinquish control and give it to learners!

Rule #7: Tap the Power of Multiple Generations

We believe age is a mindset rather than a number. As older generations continue to stay in the workforce longer, we see multiple generations working side by side.

What unfolds can either drive creative thinking or lead to generational conflict. And this becomes very interesting when the tables are turned and older workers increasingly find themselves managed by younger workers. Younger bosses—already prevalent in industries like IT, professional services, and accounting—will likely become more common as companies promote millennials (aged 24–35) into leadership positions.

In the end, the key is to develop what we call generational intelligence, or the ability to understand the expectations, similarities, and differences of each generational cohort and think of the positive benefits of how working across the generations can lead to diversity of thought. How organizations successfully develop generational intelligence will be a key factor in attracting, engaging, and retaining top talent.

Rule #8: Build Gender Equality

The research is in: companies that put into practice an inclusive workplace out-perform their peers. McKinsey calls this the diversity dividend. Companies in the top quartile for gender diversity are 15 percent more likely to have financial returns above their respective national industry medians.[13]

If we can make the business case for inclusion, how are we doing against this goal? According to LeanIn and McKinsey's survey of 30,000 men and women at 118 North American companies, women hold 45 percent of entry-level jobs at the companies surveyed. However, their ranks thin out sharply as you go higher in the organization. Only 27 percent of vice presidents at those companies are women, followed by 23 percent of senior vice presidents and 17 percent of C-suite executives.

This decline in female leadership is occurring at the same time that women are rising in educational achievement. In the United States, women comprise almost 60 percent of the annual university graduates and more than 70 percent of 2012 high school valedictorians. Research by EY has found that a majority of leading female executives first found success in athletics. Elite women athletes now out number men. Women took home more medals (61) in the 2016 Olympics, compared to men (55). More U.S. women qualified for the Olympics (291) than men (263). The leading indicators are strong for more competitive female C-suite executives. While women are now becoming a growing, more educated part of the workforce, they hold substantially fewer leadership positions and only earn 78 percent of the salaries of their male counterparts.

If inclusion is the goal, then the path to reaching this goal is to embed diversity and inclusion into all aspects of hiring, promoting, performance management, succession planning, and learning and development while holding senior executives accountable for inclusive behaviors. This starts with identifying what is causing the inequality in the workforce. In many cases this starts with unconscious biases. Unconscious bias is defined by Catalyst, a nonprofit organization with a mission to expand opportunities for women and business, as "an implicit association or attitude about the characteristics of an individual—such as an individual's race or gender—that operates out of our control, and can influence decision making and behavior—even without us realizing it is happening." Google, PwC, and Barclays were among the first companies to call out unconscious bias for contributing to the systemic lack of diversity in the workplace. Over the next decade companies can accelerate the journey toward gender equality by offering unconscious bias training as well as embedding inclusion into all aspects of talent management. But the job of creating an inclusive workplace goes beyond what companies can do alone.

Companies must examine what can be done on the individual, team, and organizational level to create the type of workplace that mirrors the world we live in.

Rule # 9: Plan for More Gig Economy Workers

Nonemployee talent is becoming as vital to an organization's success as full-time workers. A 2016 study by Future Workplace and Field Nation found that "gig economy," workers are no longer just adjunct staff but are part of a new "blended workforce" where gig economy workers work side by side with full-time workers. With nearly 35 percent of the total workforce composed of gig economy workers—including temp workers, freelancers, statement-of-work–based labor, and independent contractors—the impact of the gig economy can be felt across all businesses regardless of size, region, or industry.

With this growth comes a new set of issues. First, according to a study by Ardent Partners, only half of all gig economy workers are formally accounted for in corporate planning, budgeting, and forecasting. While the majority of businesses expect gig economy work to grow, the bulk of their workforce planning does not account for the development and oversight of this segment of the workforce. Second, this new blended workforce of gig economy workers and full-time employees is often not managed holistically. What is missing is the creation of a total talent management approach, from onboarding to training and development, so all segments of workers are captured in total talent visibility. Finally, companies need to identify the specific training needs of gig economy workers to seamlessly contribute to their future, more blended workforces.

This rise of the gig economy worker is forcing organizations, and HR departments in particular, to *rethink* how they source and develop talent. For employers, the gig economy allows organizations to hire on demand, lower their employment costs, and have access to a flexible global talent pool. As a survey conducted by Randstad, entitled "2015 Talent Trends," found, only 47 percent of HR leaders are factoring in independent contractors as part of their talent-acquisition strategy. Organizations increasing their gig economy workforce need to rethink how to engage these workers and consider how their employer brand is perceived across the entire employee population from full-timers to gig economy workers.

As companies increase their dependence on gig economy workers, we may see a new C-suite job created: the chief gig economy officer, a role designed to maintain and grow an organization's partnerships and reputation within the independent worker community. Anyone interested in being groomed for this new role?

Rule #10: Be a Workplace Activist

As Darwin famously noted, "It is not the strongest of the species that survive, nor the most intelligent, but the one most responsive to change." Being a workplace activist is about knowing your company's business and industry and anticipating future changes. But it does not stop there. Companies can see the future unfolding, yet still not take action, as Kodak tragically illustrated. As Andrew Salzman, former head of marketing for Kodak, says, "Kodak recognized as early as 1987 that digital was going to be the next big thing. It had volumes of research on how digital would develop. But from a go-to-market point of view, from an organizational prioritization vantage point, it was tethered to the 95 percent of revenue coming from paper and chemicals."[14]

Avoid having your own "Kodak moment" and consider becoming a workplace activist. Put into place the changes you see to better prepare for and navigate the future workplace! *The Future Workplace Experience* will challenge you to examine everything you take for granted about work, the workplace, what a job is, and who is a worker. Work is becoming more about what employees do and less about where they do it.

We expand upon each rule in depth and propose an action plan for you, your team, and your organization to initiate discussion and action on reimagining your organization's future workplace experience. We introduce you to the frameworks used by leading businesses to better prepare for the future. In our final chapter, we provide you with you a powerful framework to look forward and learn how to expect the unexpected.

Ten Rules to to Navigate the Future Workplace

1. Make the workplace an experience.
2. Use space to promote culture.
3. Be an agile leader.
4. Consider technology an enabler and disruptor.
5. Build a data-driven recruiting ecosystem.
6. Embrace on-demand learning.
7. Tap the power of multiple generations.
8. Build gender equality.
9. Plan for more gig economy workers.
10. Be a workplace activist.

How Might the Future Workplace Be?

How different might the future workplace experience be for our employees? Imagine this:

Buzz. Buzz. Buzz.

Emma's smartbracelet buzzes softly. It's 6:14 a.m., and the bracelet knows Emma so well, it can determine the optimal time for Emma to wake up, given her sleep cycle and her scheduled 8 a.m. meeting, when she needs to be at peak alertness. It's a big week for Emma—her first week as a full-time employee working for Pixel Institute,[15] a leader in the wearable computing industry. Emma discovered Pixel Institute from one of the apps she signed up for while still in college. The app alerted her to internships and full-time employment at companies she followed online. At every turn, Emma is using the latest technologies to be as productive as possible at work. She regularly communicates with team members on the company's internal collaboration portal, as Pixel Institute has a zero internal email policy. Emma also uses bots powered by machine learning to organize meetings, follow up after meetings, staying in touch with her professional network, and assisting with research projects.

Emma joined the software team's BugBusting division of three full-time employees, two independent workers, and an AI (artificial intelligence) powered coach that continually learns from past interactions with Emma and makes suggestions to her.

Emma already experienced Pixel Institute before joining the company. She explored the corporate campus on Pixel Institute's app, met the avatars of her leadership team, listened to the team members each describe what they are working on, and learned about the company's culture, values, and strategic priorities by reading recent posts and viewing videos from top leaders on the company orientation app.

Emma is now ready to head over to an onsite meeting with her team members. After checking in on the retina scanner to confirm her identity and scanning her smart badge to register her location at work, Emma queries her virtual benefits assistant on her student loan balance. Thankfully, the company offers student loan debt repayment as a benefit, so she is making headway in repaying her loans. All her updated balances are instantly downloaded to her smart bracelet. This team meeting is one of the few times Emma comes to the office. She works at different locations depending on the work she is doing at the time, either from home, a client location or one of the company' local co-working spaces. Emma is thrilled to see the company headquarters, as it was named one of the top 10 "trophy workplaces" by the Association of Future Workplaces.

Next, Emma accepts the company's offer to start using iGoals, an app to help her prioritize her work and fitness goals for the first month on the job. iGoals includes a complete list of her objectives for the first month, and she can also view all objectives and key results for her colleagues—including the CEO. iGoals also identifies Emma's health, fitness, and learning goals. It is easy to check frequently to see what engaging new micro-learning opportunities she can begin, now that she knows the scope of her software project.

It's nearly 4 p.m., and Emma is ending her work day. Her usual work schedule is a four-day workweek starting at 8 a.m. and ending at 4 p.m. and then remotely collaborating with her global team from 8 p.m. to 10 p.m. This gives Emma plenty of time for meeting her health and fitness goals as well as spending time with her friends and family.

The final objective during Emma's first week is to select her manager. She does this by participating in a series of presentations delivered via HoloPresence from five possible managers, each selected by the people analytics team as being particularly compatible with Emma's work style, communication needs, career development, training goals, and requirements for purposeful work. She scans each profile, which includes a description of the projects the manager is leading, plus she views the mix of internal ratings each manager has received on the company's Rate My Manager and the external ratings from former team members and job candidates found on public employer rating sites.

Voilà! Emma makes her choice and is ready to start her new and exciting assignment at Pixel Institute.

Sound far-fetched? Think again. Much of what Emma experiences is already happening at forward-thinking organizations today.

Are you, your team, and your organization prepared for this new future workplace experience? Our book will help you create a road map to master the disruption in recruiting and engaging employees.

Now you're ready to explore each rule in depth to learn how to create a compelling workplace experience for your organization. Please also visit us at www.TheFutureWorkplaceExperience.com to learn more on how organizations are preparing for the future workplace.

THE
FUTURE
WORKPLACE
EXPERIENCE

PART I

WHAT WORKERS
EXPECT FROM WORK

MAKE THE WORKPLACE AN EXPERIENCE

1

The Focus on Employee Experience

We want work that is more than just challenging, we want meaning, purpose and an emotional connection to our work and one that gives us opportunities to learn and grow.

—Barry Schwartz
Dorwin Cartwright Professor of Social Theory and Social Action
Swarthmore College

Engaged employees are a rare breed. Gallup reports only 32 percent of U.S. employees are engaged in their jobs—meaning only one in three workers is psychologically committed to their work and likely to make a positive contribution to their employer.[1]

Organizations have been focusing on increasing engagement levels because they see the link between employee engagement and productivity. Engaged employees come to work each day with a sense of purpose, leave with a feeling of accomplishment, are more productive, and achieve higher levels of customer satisfaction. Gallup reports that highly engaged employees have higher well-being, healthier lifestyles, and lower absenteeism than their less-engaged or actively disengaged counterparts.[2]

Disengaged employees cost U.S. companies over $450 billion in lost productivity per year, while organizations with higher levels of employee engagement report 22 percent higher productivity. According to Jim Harter, Gallup's chief scientist, Workplace Management and Wellbeing, "The general consciousness about the importance of employee engagement seems to have increased in the past decade. But there is a gap between knowing about engagement and doing something about it in most American workplaces."[3]

However, forward-looking companies from Airbnb to IBM are moving beyond a singular focus on increasing employee engagement to purposefully designing compelling employee experiences, which fuel increased levels of engagement.

Diane Gherson, chief human resource officer of IBM, sees this movement to employee experience as part of the evolution of the HR function. As Gherson says, "Over the years, the HR function has moved from developing programs to match the competencies IBM needs, to creating a shared service model for optimizing efficiencies and now to designing personalized employee experiences."

There are several key drivers to intentionally designing employee experiences, including the fact that all generations of employees (not just millennials, born between 1982 and 1993) are approaching the workplace with a consumer mindset. With the rise of mobile technology and a rapidly expanding on-demand economy, employees now expect a similar experience at work to the one they have in their personal life. At the same time, organizations are recognizing the need to create one seamless experience for both employees and customers.

Gherson explains how HR systems and programs currently stack up against these increasing expectations: "For much of the last decade, HR has been about outsourcing, standardization, globalization, and self service, all at the expense of the individual employee experience. Regrettably, when an employee interacts with HR, the experience is often a lot more like an experience with the Internal Revenue Service than Zappos."[4]

HR needs to focus more on creating one seamless experience that is memorable and compelling and connects to the individual employee on an emotional level. How are organizations doing this? According to Eric Lesser, research director, IBM Institute for Business Value, "The key to designing compelling employee experiences rests with leveraging analytics to gauge the current employee experience in a similar manner as your company measures and evaluates the customer experience." Lesser goes on to say, "Analytics will move a company from just reporting data to developing insights about what is important to employees and creating a value proposition based upon this."

One interesting example of this is the IBM HR team's award of a patent to predict retention risk for employees in key job roles. Anshul Sheopuri, People Analytics director, is the point person, leading a team in using analytics and machine learning to calculate employee retention risks. He does this by analyzing the relative importance of several employee risk factors, such as location, compensation, employee engagement sentiment, and even manager engagement, at the aggregate level for specific countries and job roles. Then it's the job of the People Analytics team to identify employee groups in key job roles at risk of finding opportunities outside of IBM and to propose a program of manager intervention to prevent departures. This initiative has been reported to save IBM over $130 million, as measured by the avoidance of the inevitable costs of hiring and training replacements. The key to the program has been not only the calculation of employee retention risk but the creation of a playbook for managers to use with potential high-risk employees for engaging them in mentoring sessions or continuing learning and development opportunities.

At the heart of the increased interest in designing compelling employee experiences is the recognition that creating an emotional connection is what will ultimately drive the greatest levels of engagement. A study by Adam Grant, a management professor at the University of Pennsylvania's Wharton School of Business, reinforces this.[5] Grant studied a group of students who were raising scholarship money by calling alumni and asking for contributions. He asked a former student who had benefited from a scholarship made possible by fund-raising to talk to the group of students. Grant found that after the talk, the group raised 171 percent more money as a result of this explicit emotional connection.

Communicating a sense of purpose is at the forefront of the minds of business leaders today. In fact, it's become central to the public dialogue. A recent study conducted by Oxford University's Saïd Business School found that public conversation about purpose increased five times over since 1995.

This is reinforced by PwC Next Gen research, a global study of over 40,000 millennials and non millennials that found the emotional connection to work and its purpose drives retention in the workplace.[6] Millennials in this study reported that working at a company with a strong, cohesive, and team-oriented culture was important to their workplace happiness, even more so than non millennials.[7]

Employer Rating Sites Put the Spotlight on Employee Experience

Millennials expect employers to think about how their company provides an emotional connection to work. But isn't that what we all want out of work? A growing number of employer rating sites promote themselves as making it easier to find the match between what we want as an employee and what the company offers. Employer rating sites have become a global phenomenon, as shown in Table 1.1.

Table 1.1   Samples of Global Employer Rating Sites

Employer Rating Site	Country	Focus	Website Tag Line
JobAdvisor.com.au	Australia	Cultural match	"Find your dream employer"
RateMyEmployer.ca	Canada	Employer ratings and rankings	"Who said background checks and Pre-Employment Screenings should be reserved for employers only?"
Kununu.com	Germany	Employer rating and job listing platform	"Complete transparency in the job market"
TheJobCrowd.com	United Kingdom	Focused on recent graduates	"Graduate Employers. Reviewed by their Graduate Employees"
Glassdoor.com	USA	Employer and CEO ratings and reviews	"To help people everywhere find jobs and companies they love"

The global rise of employer rating sites such as Glassdoor, JobAdvisor, RateMyEmployer, and others has increased the importance of how a company communicates its purpose, vision, values, and culture. These websites allow employees to rate organizations based on such factors as culture, engagement, employee training, and management. Interestingly, 61 percent of job seekers seek company reviews and ratings before making decision to apply for a job.[8]

Just as TripAdvisor popularized for travel and Amazon.com for books and other products, now everyone, including current, former, and prospective employees, can publicly rate organizations, share their engagement level, and provide specific feedback. On Glassdoor, anonymous feedback is provided by a simple three-point rubric of Pros, Cons, and Advice and a summary rating of one to five stars. For Pros, raters are prompted to "Share some of the best reasons to work at the organization." For Cons, raters are asked to "Share some of the downsides of working at the organization" and then are prompted to offer "Advice to management."[9]

With job candidates and employees now empowered to provide instant feedback on employers, we are seeing the "yelpification" of the workplace, where, at any time, employees can rate a company's culture and management just as they rate a hotel, restaurant, or movie. In much the same way that marketing departments have become customer-centric, human resource departments are now equally focused on understanding their employees' needs and wants. This means applying a relentless focus on transparency and responsiveness in the workplace.

As more employees use an expanding set of these employer rating sites, power is shifting from the employer to the employee. The question then becomes what should companies do about this?

Research firm Monitor 360 took a close look at the Glassdoor.com feedback for Starbucks and found some interesting insights. In the world of retail, Starbucks is regarded as a champion of employee engagement, recruitment, and retention. CEO Howard Schultz claims that Starbucks's relationship with its people and its culture constitutes a sustainable competitive advantage. At the time of this writing, Starbucks had a 3.8 out of 5.0 rating on Glassdoor, compared with 3.3 for Peets Coffee and 3.0 for Dunkin' Donuts. How did Starbucks garner better relative ratings about its employee experience? Certainly, Starbucks increased its perks, such as full health benefits for part-timers and tuition reimbursement for Arizona State University's online courses. But are these the real reasons? Monitor 360's analysis of over 5,500 employee reviews of Starbucks on the Glassdoor site revealed a number of distinct narratives that employees shared about Starbucks. Many of the narratives focused on the pride employees feel in working at Starbucks more than the discrete set of benefits offered employees. Of course, they favored the healthcare and tuition benefits, but just as importantly, they were emotionally connected to Starbucks's mission to "inspire and nurture the human spirit—one person, one cup and one neighborhood at a time." One of the strongest narratives was stated by a Starbucks employee: "Working here is more than a job—I'm proud to come to work and to serve excellent coffee to my community. My team is fun, the company gives me health and dental, free coffee, and parking, and I have flexibility to pick my own hours." On the day we checked, another reviewer posted, "The culture of Starbucks is far superior than any other place I've worked."[10] What Starbucks learned from this analysis was that purpose-driven narratives tied to the company mission and values should be consistently communicated across the entire employee life cycle from recruitment to development and engagement.[11]

In an article for the *Huffington Post*, Sophie Sakellariadis explains how companies can process the information from employer rating sites and build proper responses, stating, "Companies should consciously design their communication and engagement initiatives around the unique narratives their employees hold to and be responsive in addressing their unique concerns."[12]

What can other companies learn from the Starbucks experience?

1. Carefully listen to employees to better understand what motivates employee engagement.
2. Build reviews of your main employer rating sites into your people process. Reach out to employees who were just promoted or have just completed a new-hire onboarding program and invite them to provide their feedback.
3. Assign a team to analyze the data and provide insights to the organization on actions to take in responding to employee feedback.

4. Use the data from analyzing employer rating sites to inform your HR strategy.

5. Capture content from employer rating sites to audit and authenticate your employer brand so it is real and speaks to prospective and current employees.

The Future Workplace Experience: Five Principles to Live By

While companies are reimagining the "place of work" by providing access to a host of amenities such as gym facilities, subsidized massages, and gourmet food, some are moving beyond just creating "trophy workplaces," to focus more expansively on creating what we call the Future Workplace Experience. The essence of this is to integrate all the elements of work—the emotional, the intellectual, the physical, the technological, and the cultural—into one seamless experience for the employee. This is shown in Figure 1.1.

Figure 1.1   The Future Workplace Experience

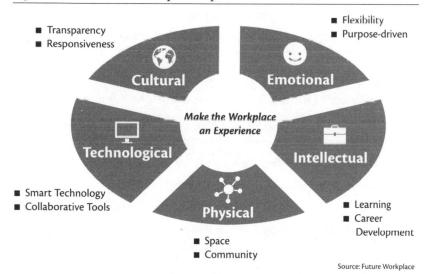

Source: Future Workplace

What Does Make the Future Workplace an Experience Mean?

What goes into creating compelling employee experiences? Mark Levy, chief human resource officer (CHRO) and global head of Employee Experience at Airbnb, explains: "At Airbnb we bring our vision of belonging anywhere to life. This vision creates a total experience for employees, spanning the food they eat together family style, to our award winning workspace, to the care with which we recruit and train them. For example, our Airbnb space has moved from open space floor plan to a 'belong anywhere working environment' where an employee can work from any number of workspaces: what we call the kitchen counter, the dining room table, or the living room, to work alone or congregate with the folks they're working with to create this sense of belonging." The engagement scores from a recent Airbnb employee pulse survey show the impact of the Airbnb focus on employee experience:

- 90 percent of Airbnb employees recommend Airbnb to a friend or colleague as a great place to work.
- 86 percent of employees state they are proud of the culture at Airbnb.
- 83 percent of employees state they feel a sense of belonging at Airbnb.[13]

These internal engagement scores are consistent with the public ratings received by Airbnb on Glassdoor.com. According to the Glassdoor ratings, 93 percent recommend the company to a friend, 95 percent approve of the CEO, and the company has a 4.4 overall rating on the 5-star scale.[14] What's interesting here is that Levy is not bearing the sole responsibility for enhancing the employee experience. His scope of responsibilities reflects his expanded vision, and his role as CHRO and global head of Employee Experience at Airbnb blurs the lines between the functions of marketing, communications, real estate, social responsibility, and human resources.

Levy is responsible not only for typical HR functions such as recruiting, talent management and development, HR operations, and total rewards, but also for "facilities, food, global citizenship, and a secret sauce of community managers called 'ground control,' which is the network of community managers who engage with Airbnb employees daily." The goodwill that these ground control employees generate is the key to improving employee satisfaction and connection to work. As Joe Gebbia, cofounder of Airbnb, says, "Everything at Airbnb is a continuation of what it's like to be a guest in somebody's house."

Taken together, our five characteristics of the Future Workplace Experience tap the full engagement potential of a company's global workforce.

Emotional Experience: How Companies Provide Flexibility, Purpose, and Meaning in the Workplace

Workplace flexibility, together with being a purpose-driven organization, taps into the core values of what motivates employees to feel connected to their job. Clearly, flexible workplace policies allowing employees to work when and where they want are fast becoming employer criteria that cut across all generations of employees. According to a survey by online job site Career Builder, the typical nine-to-five job will soon be dead. Career Builder asked 1,000 U.S. employees in fields that typically have traditional work schedules (such as IT and financial services) about their work habits. The survey found that 63 percent of survey respondents thought a fixed nine-to-five workday would soon be obsolete. Additionally, Career Builder's chief human resource officer, Rosemary Haefner, says that "about half of the research sample said that they check or respond to work e-mails outside of the office, and nearly two in five said they continue working when they leave the office."[15] All of this demonstrates how work is becoming more of a mindset than a fixed place, time of day, or location.

Phyllis Moen, a professor at the University of Minnesota, and Erin Kelly, a professor at MIT, ran an NIH-funded study to examine the interplay among work, family, and health. In an experiment with a technology company that preferred to remain anonymous, which the researchers called TOMO, they divided workers into two groups. The first group was randomly assigned to be the control group where the workplace flexibility policy was simply "at the discretion of the manager." The other group, the experimental one, participated in a new workplace flexibility initiative where employees could work wherever and whenever they chose as long as projects were completed on time and business goals were met. Not only were managers trained to be supportive of the new workplace flexibility policy, but they were also provided with a special iPod that buzzed twice a day to remind them to think about the various ways they could support their employees as they managed both their work lives and their home lives. (The special iPods highlights a creative use of technology-driven prompts in the workplace!)

The results of the Moen and Kelly experiment supported the view that workplace flexibility is much more than creating a new policy; rather it is about changing an entire culture. The study found that employees in the experimental group met their goals as reliably as those in the control group. However, what's most interesting is that employees in the experimental group reported being happier, sleeping better, and experiencing less stress. This reduced stress level also cascaded to their families and children, who also reported less stress in their own daily lives. And a year following the experiment, the employees who experienced the new workplace flexibility reported less interest in looking for a new job and leaving the company than the control group.[16]

The importance of workplace flexibility cannot be overstated. As companies expand into emerging markets and across time zones, the nine-to-five office will be slowly replaced with a work-from-anywhere mindset. But workplace flexibility has to be embedded in the culture rather than be considered the exception or seen as a perk for doing a good job. For companies that want to be magnets for top talent, workplace flexibility is smart business, as well as an important recruiting and retention tool.

Workplace flexibility is a benefit desired across the generations. According to the Future Workplace "Multiple Generations at Work" study of 1,800 multigenerational employees, almost one-half of each generation responded that a flexible working environment is very important to them.[17] In its "Connected World Technology Report," Cisco found that workers value flexibility over almost anything else.[18] Those surveyed selected flexibility as the second most important factor, after salary, when considering a job offer. In fact, 66 percent of American millennials said they felt that an organization that adopts a flexible, mobile, and remote work model has a competitive advantage over one that requires employees to be in the office from 9 a.m. to 5 p.m. every weekday.[19]

While multiple generations of employees expect and want workplace flexibility, employers are seeing the benefits of workplace flexibility as a strategic lever to deliver business results. American Express's Blue Work program marries work-style preference with workspace. The Blue Work program has identified four types of workspaces: hub, club, roam, and home:

- Hub-based employees have jobs that require face-to-face time in one of the company's office locations.
- Club employees go into a hub office no more than three times a week, because they either work part time or work some days from another location, such as home, a client's office, or another American Express campus. Club employees check into a hub office and are given space to use that day.
- Roam employees are almost always on the road or at customer sites and seldom work from an American Express office.
- Home employees are based in home offices—set up with assistance from the company—on three or more days per week.

As reported in *Forbes*, American Express's Blue Work program is not just a real estate program but also embeds training on how employees can be successful as remote workers. Reflecting this, the Blue Work program includes a series of training programs to guide both employees and managers through the productivity hurdles that can accompany the transition to virtual work. Some of the topics included in the training are "How to Use New Technology Tools," "Tips/Tricks to Be a Mobile Employee," and "How to Lead in a Mobile Environment."

The results include a savings of $10 million to $15 million annually in real estate costs and a realization that workplace flexibility is not just an employee perk but a strategic initiative.[20]

Providing Purpose at Work

Beyond providing choice and flexibility, forward-looking companies are also intent on providing purpose at work. At SunTrust Banks, Inc., where over 26,000 employees work across the southern United States, the company has moved from being mission driven to purpose driven, where the purpose is promoting financial well-being for SunTrust's employees and clients. A survey conducted for SunTrust by a Nielsen/Harris poll among 2,049 adults found that 40 percent do not have $2,000 saved for an emergency, a third have no retirement savings, and 70 percent feel a moderate to high level of financial stress.

This lack of financial confidence led to the creation of a campaign known as "Lighting the Way to Financial Well-Being." For the bank, success goes beyond financial performance to also include the impact the bank has on the lives of clients, communities, and teammates. SunTrust chairman and CEO William H. Rogers, Jr., eloquently sums this move to a purpose-driven company when he says, "People respond well to a company that's bigger than itself."[21]

Many companies that have traditionally been mission driven are now moving to being purpose driven. Tom's Shoes became one of the best known brands to millennials through its purpose-driven call to action, where for each pair of shoes sold to a customer, Tom's Shoes buys a pair of shoes for a child living in poverty. At SunTrust, "Lighting the Way to Financial Well-Being" positions the bank to be a leader in purpose-driven organizations by building financial confidence into its employer value proposition and creating an offering for both its customers and employees.

According to SunTrust's chief human resources officer Ken Carrig, "SunTrust believes so strongly in the importance of financial well-being that the company sparked a movement, called OnUp, to help people one step at a time build their financial confidence." OnUp had its debut with a commercial during the 2016 Super Bowl. Before sparking this movement, SunTrust began to fulfill its purpose with its employees first by offering a comprehensive, behavior-changing learning program. "The financial fitness program features eight learning modules that help teammates and their families set and achieve goals aligned to their values," adds Carrig. The curriculum starts with assessing one's financial goals, and then each pillar focuses on a different aspect of building financial confidence such as establishing a savings account, creating a budget, improving one's credit score, or creating a will.

"The incentive," continues Carrig, "is for all teammates, no matter what level, to receive $250 when they complete the first phase of the financial fitness program. When teammates complete the second phase of the program, they receive another $250 and that can be placed into either a savings account, a 401K, or health savings account. In addition to financial incentives, teammates are allowed to take a Day of Purpose, a paid day off each year for them to take care of their personal financial well-being." According to Scott Katz, group vice president of Learning Solutions, "Offering this type of curriculum to our teammates, coupled with their job-specific training, equips them to perform even better with our clients."

Clearly, this movement is also created to give SunTrust an advantage in the marketplace, as so many Americans admit to having little savings for either emergencies or retirement. As part of the bank's strategy, SunTrust is diligently measuring the impact on customer and employee engagement and retention levels. So far, Carrig reports employees who have completed the financial fitness program are nearly 15 percentage points more engaged than those who did not complete the program. And those who complete the program are also demonstrating higher performance levels on the job. SunTrust is just one example of how the power of creating purpose and meaning for employees and customers can produce an emotional connection and deliver business impact.

Intellectual Experience: How Companies Are Rethinking Employee Development

If you care about increasing employee engagement levels, then you should be focusing on how to reimagine and rethink your company's learning and development. Research by Aon Hewitt, published in the "Trends in Global

Employee Engagement" report, reveals a consistent, statistically significant relationship between higher levels of employee engagement and financial performance. Specifically, a 5 percent increase in employee engagement is linked to a 3 percent increase in revenue growth in the subsequent year.[22]

Some forward-thinking organizations are making the connection between engaged employees and business results. At the heart of this connection, is rethinking how they develop their employees. The Aon Hewitt research reports several ways to increase employee engagement including: building inspiring leaders, creating and communicating a compelling value proposition, and tying learning to overall career development.

However, according to a study conducted by the Association for Talent Development, only 38 percent of learning and development professionals think their organizations are ready for learners of the future. Companies now recognize that engaged employees take charge of their development and learn every day, not just when they are in an instructor-led or online program. How do they do this? Often by informally searching the web with their smartphone and finding what they need, when they need it. Marketing officers realize smartphones are ubiquitous in our lives, with mobile devices currently outnumbering people.[23] Most consumer brands have a "mobile-first" strategy, meaning that innovations often appear first on a mobile device.[24]

Now consider what would happen if HR departments pursued a similar strategy. We are seeing the "consumerization" of HR, a term we coined to refer to the need that organizations have to create a social, mobile, and consumer-type experience for employees inside the company. As MIT research finds, the expectation of social and collaborative tools in the workplace is no longer just a millennial request: 57 percent of individuals across the ages of 22 to 52 bring digital expectations to the workplace.[25]

So what are companies doing to put learning at the fingertips of learners?

At Qualcomm, the company has created the Qualcomm Employee App Store for employees to access a number of apps selected by the company. The Employee App Store numbers more than 80 apps for learning, communication, health and wellness, news, and virtual meeting facilitation. In order to make the app store successful, the learning team at Qualcomm uses what it refers to as guerilla marketing techniques. This means they will have a limited release of an app, perhaps only 500 licenses, and this is released to one internal group. Often this creates an internal buzz within the company with employees asking, "What's coming next?" The goal here is to mirror what works in consumer marketing and use this in HR to build excitement and usage among Qualcomm employees.

Other companies are joining Qualcomm to provide learning at the moment of an employee's need. Janice Burns, the chief learning officer of MasterCard, sees more and more of her department's time and resources going to facilitating and motivating employees to access curated, publicly available learning, rather than designing and delivering company-sponsored training programs. Burns shares this, "We are seeing our employees search the web to find a MOOC (massive open online course) a TED Talk, podcast, or blog, to fulfill their personal development needs. So we are now doing this for them by curating publicly available content to align with their career development needs." This is a huge shift in thinking about the role of learning. It's now about bringing learning to the learner, and this is increasingly happening on their mobile devices!

Physical Experience: How Companies Rethink Workspace

Today, top talent with in-demand skills can choose to work anywhere, anytime—which may mean working at home, working in a client's office, or going to the workplace. We are seeing companies spending more resources on creating trophy workspaces, which function as a reward for coming to the office. Workspaces are becoming healthier, incorporate better lighting, are more comfortable, and are more fun! The office cubicle is increasingly a relic of the past, as a growing number of employees instead carry their laptops, tablets, smartphones, and wearables with them, making the desk and cubicle obsolete. Instead, the office of the future will be what Steve Gale, London head of

Workplace Strategy at M Moser Associates, an architecture firm, calls "convivial workplaces," where workers socialize, swap ideas, and develop a greater sense of shared purpose.[26]

Clearly the design of the workplace impacts employee performance, engagement, and innovation. Gensler, an American design and architectural firm, surveyed 2,035 knowledge workers across the United States to examine the design factors that influence the organizational culture of the workplace.[27] Currently only one in four workers reports working in an optimal workplace environment.[28] The rest struggle to work effectively, resulting in lost productivity, engagement, and opportunities to innovate.

While the workplace is connected like never before with e-mail, enterprise social networks, instant messaging, and mobile messaging, these connections can also translate into distractions and a compromised ability to focus on one's work. According to Gensler, knowledge workers are yearning for a workplace that is designed to enable collaboration without sacrificing the ability to do focused work. Gensler finds that effectively balancing focus and collaboration leads to a more creative and innovative workplace, as highlighted in Figure 1.2.

Figure 1.2   *Benefits of balanced workspaces*

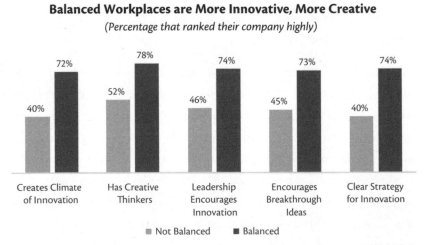

Balanced Workplaces are More Innovative, More Creative
(Percentage that ranked their company highly)

Source: Gensler

Airbnb's workspace blurs the line between work and home. It includes a kitchen; a library; a nerd cave; the demo den; a place to meditate, practice yoga, or write on the walls; and a green atrium with 1,226 square feet of beautiful greenery that stretches up to three floors high. Workspace design amenities are quickly becoming recruiting tools, recognizing the value of using elements of the outdoors, including incorporating plants and murals of bucolic scenes, to create more productive workspaces. In fact, Airbnb has pushed the limits in designing its customer call center operation in Portland, Oregon. "Rather than windowless work stations where employees read off teleprompter screens, the open-space call center is appointed with shared desks, long couches, light wood, and exposed brick," according to Wired's Margaret Rhodes.[29]

The staffers of the Airbnb customer call center do not have a traditional desk. Instead, they are provided with "landing spots," similar to the cubbies given to children in elementary school, where employees can charge all their devices. This leaves space for custom-designed conference rooms, couches for reclining, big communal tables, and small nooks for chats with colleagues.

Research is proving the importance of giving workers control over selecting the workspace that suits them. Steelcase conducted a global study among 12,480 participants in 17 countries to examine key workplace behaviors around the topic of workspace.[30] Interestingly, workers who have a greater degree of control over where and how they work, who are free to concentrate and physically move during the day, and who can work in teams without being interrupted were more engaged at work. Figure 1.3 shows that 88 percent of employees report being highly engaged if they are able to select a place within the office based on the task they are doing. Choice over where one works and the amount of privacy one feels in the workplace are emerging as critical factors to employee engagement.

In addition to workspace, another important factor that will differentiate the workplace of the future is the creation of community managers charged with providing a memorable workplace experience through meet-ups, education programs, social networking, frequent communications, and public recognition.

Figure 1.3   Engaged employees have more control over their experiences at work

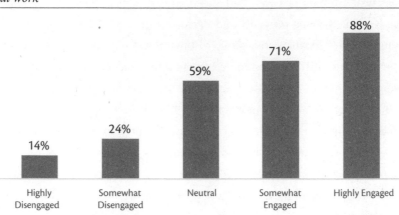

Can you choose where to work within the office based on the task?

Source: Steelcase, *Engagement and the Workplace*

Technological Experience: How Companies Leverage Smart Technologies

Today the convergence of mobile, cloud, and social technology—or the *Internet of everything* (IoE)—has driven us toward a more connected and collaborative work environment.

Consider the large number of today's professionals who use two or three mobile devices for work and personal use. Added to that, Cisco's "Connected World Technology Report" finds 60 percent of respondents would abandon their laptops in favor of a mobile device for their work and professional use.[31] With the growing demand to work from anywhere, the future workplace will depend on organizations harnessing the power of smart technologies to drive employee engagement and satisfaction. IBM is one company that is leveraging its suite of analytics technologies and social engagement platforms to reimagine the performance management process. But the story of this reinvention is not only which smart tools are deployed to reinvent performance management but how IBM embarked upon the process. IBM's use of design thinking was critical to the reinvention process. IBM's

CHRO Diane Gherson engaged employees with an initial blog post on IBM Connections, IBM's social platform, inviting IBMers to join her in reimagining performance management. This post garnered over 200,000 page views from the 380,000 global employees and led to a spirited online discussion looking at the future of performance from several angles, such as "Should one's goals be private or public?" "How can we apply design thinking to this process of reinvention?" and "How closely should performance be connected to talent decisions like stretch assignments and compensation?" The initial blog moved to a series of online discussions producing volumes of employee comments, which were analyzed to mine insights. The results were reported in more online discussions, each step playing back what Gherson and her team had heard, occasionally asking employees for clarification ("We heard this—is that what you meant?"). Says Gherson, "Our process was iterative and relied on design thinking to incorporate the needs and expectations from our global employee population. We even invited our employees to help us name the new performance management process and some took this so seriously some asked if there was an absentee ballot as the deadline was during a time when they would be away from the office and email." Further, Gherson and her team used a common vehicle of design thinking, creating empathy maps, to ensure the new design would resonate with managers and nonmanagers across all IBMers.

Employees were so involved in reinventing the performance management process, they suggested designing it as a mobile app and even coined the name "ACE," which stands for *appreciation, coaching,* and *evaluation.* The idea was met with enthusiasm. The new vision for performance management encompassed these three important areas: appreciation, to feel motivated and continue to do your best; coaching, to accelerate your learning and energy where it really matters; and evaluation, to know where you stand, set expectations, and feel reassured. About 90,000 employees are now active users of ACE—not only seeking feedback but also giving feedback . . . to both their managers and colleagues. ACE is designed to deliver *constructive* feedback, asking employees to share "What's the one thing I could have done better" rather than "Tell me what you think of Jane's performance." And instead of relying on anonymous feedback, ACE feedback is signed by a colleague and, in doing so, provides the employee receiving the feedback with the context for this.

Using smart technologies also applies to what happens inside the workplace. Sam Dunn, CEO and cofounder of Robin Powered, created an app for the process of booking a conference room inside a company. Robin Powered has created a room-booking tool that runs on mobile devices, web browsers, and tablets. Essentially employees book a room from the app, and then the app automatically detects room occupancy. Plus there's a twist for mobile users—running in the background is an iBeacon that detects when you're in a room and allows for accurate real-time check-ins on your calendar. So what happens to the role of the receptionist? According to Dunn, "This role has either been downsized at some companies or morphed into a series of higher value roles either as a Community Manager or Technical Support Manager."

Finally, the same apps used in our personal lives are being brought inside the workplace. For example at Airbnb, employees use WhatsApp to create a constant flow of communications. As Mark Levy explains, "I created a staff immersion week where everyone in the Employee Experience group travels to a different office in the same week sharing photos, learnings, and insights on WhatsApp, rather than having a traditional 'All Hands Meeting.' I believe our use of the latest smart technologies is a powerful way to both communicate with and understand the nuances of local Airbnb offices around the world."

Smart technologies are also being used in the workplace to predict optimal environmental conditions based on personal preferences. In IBM's blog *Designing Employee Experience*, IBM reports the company is experimenting with sensor-based systems that can recommend and even modify temperature and noise levels to best suit an individual employee's needs. It's a brave new world of work when employees are empowered to create their own workplace environments! The workplace of the future is about creating and enhancing the experience at work. As Paul Papas, global leader of IBM Interactive Experiences, says, "The last best experience that anyone has anywhere becomes the minimum expectation for the experiences they want everywhere."[32]

Cultural Experience: Incorporating Transparency and Responsiveness into the Workplace

Transparency in the workplace is becoming the currency of leadership. Just as individuals want to know how and where the scarf they bought online was made, they also want to know the inner workings of their employer. And it is getting easier to discover details about an employer from any number of social media sites. Increasingly, employees are approaching the workplace as consumers, and they want the same consumer type of experience at work.

What does corporate culture look like when transparency is put into practice? At Airbnb, employees freely share why the company is a great place to work. Scan the Airbnb Glassdoor.com page (where CEO Brian Chesky has a 97 percent approval rating), and you will see comments like "This company is mission driven with an incredible culture and one where you are encouraged to be yourself."[33] Or "Airbnb creates meaningful experiences, whether it is the candidate experience, travel experience, or website experience."[34] However, the comment that sticks out most is "I am in my 50s and I work for Airbnb. And this is by far the best job I have ever had. Airbnb is creating something that touches people: experience, memories, relationships, who else does that?"[35]

Transparency is also practiced by traditional firms such as Telstra, the largest telecommunications company in Australia, where David Thodey, former CEO of the company, was a visible, digitally engaged, and transparent leader.

What exactly does a leader like Thodey do to be dubbed a transparent leader? At one point after the Telstra internal social network was launched, Thodey asked the entire company, "What processes and technologies should we eliminate?" According to Charlene Li in her book *The Engaged Leader*, this question received more than 830 responses and gave Thodey an intimate look into what was not working at Telstra.[36]

In addition to practicing transparency in the workplace, companies are also becoming much more responsive to employees and incorporating responsiveness into the recognition process. At Panasonic Avionics, a company of more than 5,000 employees spread across 46 countries, David Heath, the chief human resource officer, explained how he recently moved his company's recognition system conducted manually to an instant online platform the company branded "High Five." In doing research Heath discovered that one-third of the employees who had worked for the company for more than 10 years had never had anyone say thank you. His solution was the High Five platform where employees and their managers contribute instant performance feedback. Interestingly, what Heath uncovered was a pent-up demand for this type of responsive feedback. Says Heath, "In fact, our employees in Asia Pacific region have had the highest engagement rate versus other parts of the world, 93 percent engagement rate, as compared to 83 percent in US locations. I suspect our employees in Asia see the High Five platform as a safe way to provide their feedback."

It's not easy to achieve all of the above. But some companies come admirably close, and others are to be applauded for trying. As the philosopher Thomas Hobbes points out, life can be solitary, brutish, nasty, and short. If we spend about a third of our lives sleeping and about another third working, doesn't it make sense for a company to provide a workplace experience that allows us to fulfill our personal and professional goals?

Enter the Chief Employee Experience Officer

Creating a compelling employee experience assumes a deep understanding of the needs and expectations of employees. It is truly employee-centric. This requires a senior executive to work across key functional disciplines as diverse as human resources, real estate, marketing, IT, and internal communications. In response to this vision, some companies are creating a new role in HR, *chief employee experience officer*. Forrester has designed this new role that reports to the chief people officer, Lucia Quinn.

The new role is focused on creating an extraordinary employee experience, one where new hires stay at the firm and are engaged during their first few years. Often research shows that employees with tenure of less than two years leave because of frustration with unproductive and poorly optimized work processes.

Jon Symons at Forrester is filling this role, and he comes with a background in corporate communications, outside of HR. Symons is charged with forging an emotional connection between Forrester employees and the Forrester brand, and he is doing this by strengthening the Forrester employer brand on Glassdoor and other employer rating sites and identifying Forrester employees who can become ambassadors for the employer brand.

We will see many other companies creating the role of chief employee experience officer with the goal of identifying one person responsible for all aspects of employee well-being that impact employee engagement. A workplace must meet employees' emotional, intellectual, physical, technological, and cultural needs, and this can lead to creating a deeper bond with employees and in the process and creating a more compelling employee experience. The vision of the Future Workplace Experience is one where key C-level executives in HR, global citizenship, IT, real estate, marketing, and internal communications come together to design an employee experience that is both a holistic and compelling one. This is already happening at IBM, Airbnb, SunTrust, and Forrester—to name a few companies where the CHRO either has oversight for expanded functions beyond HR, as is the case of Airbnb, or where the CHRO values the importance of creating a seamless and impactful employee experience.

Designing a future workplace experience requires a multifunctional perspective. This is not simply an HR initiative; rather it is one that is woven into the fabric of the business. When this happens, the future workplace experience can positively impact employee engagement.

MY ACTION PLAN

Myself

- What can I do to learn more about providing a compelling experience in the workplace?
- How can I use design thinking to reimagine the employee experience?
- What are our competitors doing in this area?

- What opportunities and barriers do I see in partnering with other functional areas, such as marketing, internal communications, IT, real estate, and global citizenship, to provide an extraordinary employee experience?

My Team

- How does our current employee experience impact the attraction and retention of new employees?
- What new skills does my team need to partner with other functions, such as marketing, IT, internal communications, real estate, and global citizenship?
- What track record does my team have in partnering with these functions?

My Organization

- Are we doing enough to capture insights about the employee experience?
- How could improving the employee experience at our company impact employee engagement?
- What can we learn from the customer experience and use internally with employees?
- Who has primary responsibility for designing employee experience at my company? What functions are involved today in doing this, and what functions can be recruited to join this effort?

USE SPACE TO
PROMOTE CULTURE

2

Continuing to understand where, how and in what type of space your current and prospective employees want to work, and should be working in,
will be a lasting form of competitive advantage.

—Bernice Boucher, managing director,
Workplace Strategy, Americas, Jones Lang LaSalle

Workplace is where culture happens. Workplaces manifest culture by design
or default. Forward-looking businesses recognize that their workspaces have
a huge impact on company culture, employee productivity, and financial performance. "Workplace is now a term of art" says Daniel Anderson, a partner with AndersonPorterDesign. "We talk about workplace now rather than
office. HR needs to stay abreast of the different ways in which space affects
interactions between employees." Traditionally, workspace-related decisions
have rested with real estate personnel who strive for economic efficiency by
minimizing costs and maximizing the number of employees per square foot
or square meter. Business and HR leaders need to work in partnership with
real estate, facilities, IT and Legal to steer the conversation . . . coordinating all
the infrastructure decisions to reinforce company culture.

Top organizations recognize that their workspace is an expanding part
of what sets them apart. A well-designed workspace has the capacity to help
recruit and retain top talent and foster culture-affirming work behaviors.
Increasingly, organizations are strategically redesigning their workplaces to
better align with their core values, attract the right talent, and achieve superior results.

Five Drivers for Workspace

The workspaces where people work are changing because the nature of work is evolving to be distributed, mobile, and collaborative. We see five drivers influencing how companies align their workspace and culture (see Figure 2.1). Taken together these drivers provide business and HR leaders with a framework to rethink how space can drive culture, choice, wellness, engagement, and community

1. **Drive culture.** Workspace is a physical manifestation of an organization's values and mission. How could we use workspace to drive our values and mission?
2. **Enable choice.** Employees want to choose how, when, and where to work. How could we enable more employee preferences for where to work?
3. **Promote wellness.** Workspace influences the health and well-being of employees. How could we ensure our workspace enables and facilitates wellness, instead of proliferating health issues?

Figure 2.1   Five drivers for workspace

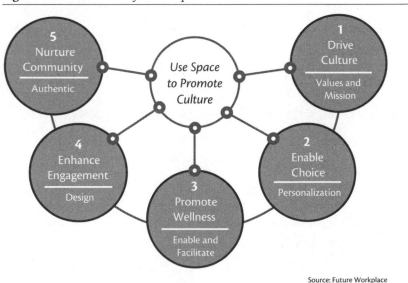

Source: Future Workplace

4. **Enhance engagement.** Employee engagement is influenced by workspace. How could we design our workspace to improve employee engagement?

5. **Nurture community.** Coworking spaces and community managers' roles are being inspired by the gig economy and adopted by established organizations. How could we apply coworking practices to nurture an authentic sense of community?

The connection between space and corporate culture is not new. Tom Peters, in his 1992 book *Liberation Management*, states, "Space management may be the most ignored—and most powerful—tool for inducing cultural change, speeding up innovative projects, and enhancing the learning process in far-flung organizations."[1]

Having a better appreciation of how workspace drives culture, choice, wellness, engagement, and community will inspire us to create a workspace that becomes a competitive advantage for our organization.

Drive Culture Through Workspace Design

Workplaces are physical manifestations of a company's culture. Kurt L. Darrow, chairman, president, and CEO of La-Z-Boy Incorporated, a furniture manufacturer based in Monroe, Michigan, says, "Space matters. Facilities matter when people are choosing where to work, where to go to school, how they can work, how they feel good." A company promoting a culture of high-paced innovation, creativity, and a sense of fun at work will find it hard to promote these values in a bland, gray, cubicle-filled workspace that likely saps employees' energy rather than inspires employees to achieve creative breakthroughs. Similarly, an organization that has critical deadlines, highly technical work, and ultrafocused workers may not benefit from a workspace filled with video game consoles, ball pits, and office table tennis tournaments. These are perhaps extreme examples, and yet they illustrate very clearly the importance of recognizing the physical role that workspaces play in curating a company's culture.

Leading organizations recognize this fact. Business and HR leaders increasingly want to use workspace to foster their culture and attract the right type of employees. These business and HR leaders are thinking critically and acting intentionally on the work environment they want to cultivate.

La-Z-Boy recognizes the power of workspace and completed a new corporate headquarters in 2015, designed to use space to attract the next generation employees. Darrow sees workspace as a way to articulate and signal a new way of working to the 8,300 employees of the company. During his 13-year tenure as chairman, president, and CEO, he transformed all facets of the company, increasing its competitiveness in the dynamic home furnishing marketplace, while repositioning the well-known La-Z-Boy brand among consumers.

Darrow summarizes his responsibilities into three categories: "Strategy, Capital, and Talent." He explains, "If I get those three things right, the rest of my job is pretty easy. If I find myself doing something that is not related to those three principles, I am probably getting in the way of my team."[2]

Building an employee-centric workspace is a long-term planning project. The space needs to be organic and flexible enough to facilitate future generational changes and shifts in working-style preferences. The workspace design should promote engagement and collaboration among employees. Darrow recognizes the critical role culture plays in the overall design. With its investment in a new corporate headquarters, La-Z-Boy sought to revolutionize its corporate culture. According to Lea Ann Knapp, the lead internal designer at the La-Z-Boy HQ project, the aim was to "bring a little bit of the past with us, but direct people to the present and the future."[3]

Darrow continues, "We design our headquarters for current and future employees who we hope will want to work here for the next 15 or more years. We talked to them all, they felt included and we listened." He jokes, "After all, we only build a new corporate headquarters once every 90 years!"

The company's new Michigan-based headquarters houses up to 500 staff, the majority of La-Z-Boy's corporate employees. It features an open-space design, large windows, and immense glass frontage, along with landscaped grounds with walking trails and backlit fountains. The campus environment is reminiscent of many high-tech companies in Silicon Valley; however, the headquarters is located in Monroe, the town in Michigan where the company was founded 90 years ago.

The design of the company's new headquarters recognizes that employees expect different ways of working. In response, the space incorporates "niche places" where employees can do their work. There's an explicit lack of seating or office assignment to combat territorial thinking and silo departments. The open-seating philosophy encourages employees to get out, be seen, and collaborate with coworkers. La-Z-Boy also provides employees with the choice to work at a desk that can convert to a standing desk at the push of a button.[4] In some rooms there are even desks with walking treadmills underneath, for those who wish to talk on a conference call or type while they walk.

La-Z-Boy created conference rooms and workrooms that employees can book to do the work they need. There are multiple room formats, ranging from one-person rooms—where people can focus on their individual work—to larger meeting rooms designed for group collaboration about new furniture designs and innovative business models. This innovative approach allows the company to break away from the unwritten rule of conference rooms only being used for meetings. The company complex also features coffee bars, a genius bar–style IT support area called Tech Deck, and outdoor seating patios, complete with Wi-Fi and piped music for ambience.

La-Z-Boy's executives recognized that reframing the culture of a 90-year-old home furniture business was a change management process beyond their experience and competencies. La-Z-Boy partnered with Steelcase, a fellow Michigan based firm, to help transition to its new headquarters.

Deep-rooted behaviors and everyday barriers are hard to revamp, but for La-Z-Boy, the challenges were worth overcoming. "I am positive . . . that if we did not have the new facility [the people we recently hired] would have passed on us," says Darrow. "Do not ever underestimate the influence physical structures have on culture."

Similarly, Rackspace, a $1.8 billion managed cloud computing company based in San Antonio, Texas, saw its new site in Blacksburg, Virginia, as the company's opportunity to strategically design space to drive company culture.

Robert McAden, director of Business Operations and Blacksburg site leader at Rackspace, believes workspace design can be an important driver to reinforce a company's core values. As he says, "Our space is really a package for our culture. You can have the brown box or you can have a package that adds value to the product."

The challenge for McAden was to design a space to be compelling enough to attract and retain critical talent to a town with a population of 43,000. The starting point was determining "how to translate our core values of giving fanatical support to employees and customers, delivering results, treating employees like friends and family, being passionate about our work, exhibiting full disclosure and transparency, and being committed to greatness into the design for a space."

For example, "one of the Rackspace core values is transparency," says McAden. "How do you manifest this into a space? Well we do this by creating a workspace where what people do is transparent to others." He continues, "To me, culture is not things like foosball tables, haircuts in the office, or free snacks and sodas—these are all perks that have very little to do with culture. Culture comes back to the core values of our company and how we create tribalism around these core values and really instill those values in each and every person that is an employee here."

As a result, Rackspace established three core design principles for its new workspace: the new design had to be connective, collaborative, and fun.

When it came to connectivity, Rackspace determined that it wanted employees to have a visual line of sight to others but not be disrupted by others. A unique interior atrium housing two stories of conference rooms was designed to create visual connectivity; multiple break areas were deemed important to enable chance encounters; and a larger, flexible-use space was needed for meetings and events. Large, flat-screen monitors were distributed around the office to foster both intrateam and interteam communication. Employees walk with laptops in hand, further reinforcing the paradigm of moving to collaborate and coordinate work in different spaces during the workday.

In terms of collaboration, Rackspace decided that an open office design would provide the foundational work areas. These spaces are supported by flexible work areas ranging from open seating to enclosed conference rooms. The office space is a very open flow environment, with bright colors on the walls, open staircases between floors, and transparent doors to enhance visibility and openness. Gone are the six-foot-tall walled-in box cubicles of the past. Instead, employees now work side by side at desks with small, two-foot-tall partitions separating them from coworkers opposite to them and often with no partition separating the employee sitting beside them.

To make the workspace fun, Rackspace looked to its cocreative culture and determined it was important to design explicit areas where employees could come together to play, recharge, and interact together. Anyone who walks through Rackspace's Blacksburg office can see the large number of employees wearing immersive headphones, listening to their favorite music. The office is a pet-friendly environment, replete with several dogs.[5] It's also hard to miss the large-scale climbing wall. Coders dressed in jeans, Rackspace-branded T-shirts, and sweatshirts fill the space, the more relaxed dress code encouraging employees to express their best, most productive selves.

By explicitly aligning workspace design principles to cultural values, Rackspace created a physical embodiment of its culture, not only in the core work areas, but in every section of the office space, including often overlooked areas like walls and passageways. Rackspace's core values are emblazoned in two-foot-tall white print on a red wall in a central location. Other inspiring slogans in foot-tall fonts adorn transition passages, transforming these dead spaces into canvases showcasing Rackspace values.

La-Z-Boy and Rackspace share a common belief that workspace drives enhanced employee engagement. It's the combination of key workspace attributes—connectivity, collaboration, and fun—that together drive greater engagement and satisfaction.

Enable Choice on Where to Work

Susan Cain's 2012 TED Talk, "The Power of Introverts," raised attention to introverts as a distinct class of employee.[6] In her talk, she asserted, "one third to one half of the population are introverts," and passionately advocated how introverts need more privacy, freedom, and autonomy at work. Cain made the case that workplaces were "designed mostly for extroverts and their need for lots of stimulation." She highlighted how introverts are highly talented individuals with a very different set of characteristics, which need to be encouraged by moving away from the prevailing norms of workplace design. Introverted employees need to find a place to concentrate on their work and also collaborate in the workplace.

So companies need to ask, "How can we accommodate both our introverts and our extroverts in our workspaces?" We propose leaders ask four simple questions to reveal where employees choose to work and why:[7]

- Where do you go to do your best work? *(Engagement spaces)*
- Where do you go to get the job done? *(Production spaces)*
- Where do you avoid meeting or working? *(Toleration spaces)*
- Where do you go to recharge? *(Restoration spaces)*

Engagement Spaces: Where Employees Go to Do Their Best Work

Leaders can empower employees to do their best work by providing them with broader choices in workspaces: open space, collaboration space, huddle rooms, quiet rooms,[8] and smaller phone booths for private chats. The space where employees choose to do their best work often depends on what the employees are working on at the moment. Thus, employees need to think about what sort of space works best for them at different stages of a project. Additionally, employees can be encouraged to leverage a number of quanti-fied self apps, such as *RescueTime*, a tool to track how you spend your time during the workday.[9]

In a similar vein, choice can also be provided by encouraging workplace flexibility, understanding that some employees may be more productive on their own time (early birds or night owls), rather than working a traditional nine-to-five day.[10] Similarly some employees may be more productive in private areas wearing noise-canceling headphones, while others may thrive in large, shared spaces with constant stimulation.

Production Spaces: Where Employees Go to Get the Job Done

Too often open-plan offices are designed with more attention paid to facilitating collaboration than completion. The noise level, distractions, and constant interruptions can cause high amounts of stress in the workplace—in fact 61 percent say they go home to get work done.[11] Planning a workspace that provides areas for focused work and privacy as well as collaboration is crucial to support innovation. People need time and space to recharge and digest the new ideas generated through collaboration.[12]

This also means people gravitate to different spaces for different activities they are engaged in. This is known as *activity-based working* and acknowledges that some spaces are distinctly suited to spending private, concentrated "think time," some to collaborating with others, and still others to engaging with staff, visitors, and other stakeholders. A workspace built around activity-based working is designed to facilitate the different types of work and increasing productivity across a broader spectrum of the organization.

Toleration Spaces: Where Employees Avoid Meeting or Working

It is also important to pay attention to spaces that are not used. Unused spaces are early warning signs for other issues. Simply "tolerating" a space is the enemy of positive engagement, a drain on finances, and will deplete the energy of employees in any department or building. Tolerating wasted space is an indication of a leadership vacuum in the workplace. We can look around and see examples of dead hallways, unused "noisy" rooms, badly situated rooms where direct sunlight makes it difficult to see computer screens, bean bags or high-end recliner chairs that are never used, TV screens that are never turned on, windowless rooms that people avoid . . . the list goes on. Laura DelaFuente, former VP, Workplace Strategy lead at JLL, calls such spaces "crimes against productivity."

"Toleration spaces" represent a number of opportunities for companies to revitalize unused spaces by bringing in a local coffee vendor or offering a department the chance to showcase new initiatives. "Toleration spaces" should be identified and eliminated on a regular basis.

Restoration Spaces: Where Employees Go to Recharge

Finally, it is important to recognize the value of space to recharge one's mind and soul. The Quality of Life @ Work study reports that employees who take at least a brief break every 90 minutes report a 28 percent higher level of focus than those who take just one break, or no breaks at all.[13] Employees need and want time to refresh their energy and employers need to provide for this.

Promote Wellness in the Workplace

The evidence that sedentary behavior at work is associated with poorer health has been building for some time. A 2015 University of Toronto led study shows the connection between being sedentary and adverse health outcomes. Put another way: sitting is the new smoking![14] Many organizations now seek to create office environments and work practices to promote standing and movement at work.

Bridget Sullivan, director of Wellness at Glassdoor.com, says "We see a trend among employers to modify how and when people move, from supporting wearable technologies, offering standing desks, to encouraging walking meetings."

Sullivan oversees a range of work programs designed to get employees to "involve themselves in a yoga, meditation, or fitness class, where they are releasing endorphins, releasing stress, helping their body to either strengthen or relax." A growing number of workspaces encourage movement, including providing employees with wearable fitness trackers that track the number of steps employees take each day and engage in walking meetings and company-wide Fitbit challenges.

Different movements have emerged internationally to promote the benefits of wellness. Public Health England and a U.K. community interest company, Active Working CIC, collaborated to create guidelines, published in an insight-packed "Consensus Statement" document (and available on www.GetBritainStanding.org), for employers to discourage prolonged periods of sedentary work.[15] The guide provides information for employers and staff who want to create more active work environments. The report concludes that along with other health-promotion goals (such as improving nutrition and reducing alcohol consumption, smoking, and stress), employers should promote the benefits of movement and the potential ills of being sedentary.

While some companies are providing the choice of standing desks to employees, other companies, like Boston Interactive, are introducing office layouts to encourage people to move. Boston Interactive CEO Chuck Murphy eliminated personal desk printers to encourage regular movement and serendipitous interactions at a centralized printing area. He also introduced whiteboards on wheels, standing desks, an open office floor plan with an array of designated informal meeting areas, and long communal dining tables to promote interactions during the day. Many organizations share similar deliberate approaches to encourage movement at work.

Why are companies interested in promoting wellness? Workplace wellness initiatives have the potential to keep insurance, healthcare, and sick-day costs down, contribute to lower absenteeism and employee turnover rates, and drive employee health, engagement, and productivity.

With the majority of our waking hours now spent working and often in an office, the demand for healthy workplaces is on the rise. This has led to the creation of the WELL Building Standard (WELL). The WELL Building Standard measures, certifies, and monitors the performance of building features that impact the health and well-being of employees. WELL provides companies with a framework to create a healthy workplace by focusing on seven concepts, including:

1. **Air.** Creating optimal indoor air quality
2. **Water.** Promoting safe and clean water
3. **Nourishment.** Promoting healthier foods, eating habits, and food culture
4. **Light.** Incorporating lighting that enhances productivity and minimizes disruption to the body's circadian system
5. **Fitness.** Fostering an active lifestyle
6. **Comfort.** Enabling a distraction-free, productive, and comfortable indoor environment
7. **Mind.** Supporting cognitive and emotional health

WELL is administered by the International WELL Building Institute (IWBI), established in 2013 to improve the way people live by developing spaces that enhance occupant health and quality of life.[16] According to IWBI founder Paul Scialla, "WELL Certification aims to do for human health what LEED (Leadership in Energy and Environmental Design), certification does for the environment. WELL marries science, technology, and architecture to improve the health and well-being of employees, students, and apartment dwellers."

Scialla sees the science of light in the workplace as a growing area that can address future workplace productivity. He stated, "The idea of circadian appropriate lighting is going to change many things for all of us." To illustrate the rate of change, he explained, "If you went to Light Fair (the largest international annual architectural and commercial lighting trade show and conference) three years ago and discussed circadian lighting, few would have known what you were talking about. This year at Light Fair, it was the one topic everyone wanted to talk about." Regulated light levels through innovations in LED lighting and controls will improve the employee experience in the future workplace. Regulated lighting has the potential to keep employees more energized, more mentally acute, and more productive.

Commercial real estate services firm CBRE's headquarters in Los Angeles, Macquarie Bank in Sydney, and TD Ameritrade Bank in Toronto were three early adopters of the WELL Building Standard. As of May 2016, there were over 150 registered and certified WELL projects across 16 countries and 5 continents.[17]

Scialla's key insight was to recognize that the work environment could be used as a vehicle to optimize health and wellness: "If real estate can be used to improve the health of employees, then this can have a positive impact on society."

We expect organizations such as Active Working CIC of the United Kingdom and WELL in the United States to be just the start of a renewed movement to leverage real estate to proactively impact the health and well-being of employees globally. They are leading the way in public-private partnerships to establish higher standards for air, water, nourishment, light, and comfort, including physical, emotional, and cognitive health.

Enhance Engagement

Company workspaces are moving beyond densification strategies (less space per person) to rethinking how to better plan and use communal workspaces. After all, there is only so much space to be cut! In 2010, the average employee had 225 square feet of space; this has now been whittled down to approximately 100 square feet entering 2017, according to Corenet, an association for corporate real estate and workplace professionals. Seventy percent of U.S. employees now work in open floor plans according to the International Facility Management Association, a professional network for the facility management industry.[18]

The new thinking about workspace focuses on creating space where employees want to be and giving them choice over the type of space and the tools they use so they can best collaborate, concentrate, and network with colleagues.

Ann Bamesberger,[19] head of Workplace Effectiveness at Genentech, says, "It's not about space, it's not about open space vs. the office or the cube; that's an old argument. It's about the way we work." When Bamesberger joined Genentech in 2013, she was told that the company was out of space and needed to build a new office building at Genentech's South San Francisco headquarters to house 900 people. Bamesberger used this opportunity to shift the focus of the new building to a shared-office approach. The new approach is based on the work practices of the intended occupants of the building rather than the traditional cubicle office formula.[20] Company studies confirmed that offices and cubicle utilization rate was 35 percent.[21] Bamesberger and her Workplace Effectiveness Team clearly needed to reinvent how to engage employees with the space. Over several months, through focus group discussions as well as prototyping different aspects of the work environment, the Workplace Effectiveness Team came up with the specifics for their new Neighborhood Work Environment model.

The Workplace Effectiveness Team identified different types of places where people can work, a series of social practices, and a common technology infrastructure to provide employees with choice on where and how to work.

This new building is Genentech's first entire building of "neighborhoods," informed by the learnings of their workplace research. Maron Demissie, of the Neighborhood Work Environments research and engagement team, describes the new approach as getting rid of the old model of an "assigned office or cube" and replacing this with teams assigned to a "neighborhood." She says, "Within that neighborhood, you've got access to a mix of spaces to use . . . and it really gives employees that sense of choice and ability, in order to make the decision of where to work based on what suits them."

Genentech's facility offers studio and enclosed spaces (including both one- and two-person rooms, team rooms, and conference rooms). Along with a little more than a thousand actual work desks, there are over 500 "collaborative seats" in the building. "This feels more like home, with sofas where people gather and take a break or work as if they are at home," says Demissie.

This new 225,000-square-foot building opened in May 2015. If it were built to the original office configuration, it would have housed about 900 people. Instead it's a shared-neighborhood work environment that currently accommodates 1,500 employees.

This reinvention of workspace is also happening at the U.S. headquarters of Credit Suisse in New York, where their activity-based work program, which is internally branded *Smart Working*, has delivered a greater sense of community and pride in the workplace. Michelle Lindgren, Americas lead, Workplace

Strategy, Planning, and Innovation for Credit Suisse, summarizes the objectives of the Smart Working initiative this way: "We want to encourage collaboration among our employees and provide them with an environment to help increase productivity and create an atmosphere for staff to become more engaged with each other. We see this as a competitive advantage as it can impact employee retention, improve our standing as an employer of choice, and create more efficient and effective workspaces which will ultimately reduce our occupancy costs." Beginning with one location in Switzerland, Smart Working is now a rapidly growing global program with locations in Switzerland, the United Kingdom, Poland, Luxembourg, Singapore, Pune (India), and New York. The program emphasizes how and where people work best and is focused on the three primary types of work conducted by the employees of Credit Suisse, also known as the three Cs: *collaborative*, *concentrated*, and *confidential*. Their insight was that often a traditional work environment was not conducive, or equipped, to fully support the three Cs. So Credit Suisse used this information, in combination with its core Smart Working principles, to guide the design and renovation of its New York space.

Like Genentech, Credit Suisse learned that employees value a work neighborhood. Lindgren says, "We created neighborhoods as an alternative to fixed desks. By assigning departments to different neighborhoods, we created a 'Home Zone' concept where staff knew where to go if they wanted to sit with or find someone from their team. Since all of the workstations are free-address, or a first come, first served basis for seating, Credit Suisse is able to oversubscribe the space based on research showing approximately 20 percent of staff are not in on any given day. So they allocate 8 desks to 10 people in their NYC Smart Working floor." Lindgren concludes, "Overall, the most important thing to us is that someone is able to work productively during their day, wherever it may be."

Nurture Community Values Through Space

For those who have never entered a coworking space, it's a worthwhile experience. A coworking space is more than just renting out desk space; it is a chance to engage with workers who hail from many different industries and kinds of expertise. It is a chance to share an identity, work within a community, and participate in networking events with other members.

In the past decade, the phenomenon of coworking has grown to such an extent that it is now recognized as a discrete "fourth place"[22] for working (after offices, homes, and coffee shops).

"This is a movement that we're building to change the way people work forever," declared Tony Bacigalupo to the audience of the Global Coworking Unconference Conference (GCUC) in May 2015.[23] Bacigalupo is a cofounder of New Work City and was one of the coauthors of the book *I'm Outta Here! How Coworking Is Making the Office Obsolete*, one of the earliest books on work culture to describe the then-nascent phenomenon of the global coworking space expansion.[24]

Coworking community leaders such as Bacigalupo see the emergence of these communities as supporting a new type of workforce that will create a sustainable ecosystem for connection, collaboration, and networked value creation. Bacigalupo's book proudly highlights over 70 unique identifiable coworking spaces in existence at the end of 2008. By the end of 2010, the number had grown to 600.[25] By the end of 2013, the figure was over 2,500 coworking spaces, supporting over 110,000 members across 81 countries.[26] By mid-2015, more than 3,000 coworking spaces were available worldwide, and the phenomenon continues to grow.[27]

Coworking has come far in the decade since Bernard DeKoven and Brad Neuberg opened the first physical coworking space in San Francisco in mid-2005.[28] The original posting by Neuberg advertising the space back in 2005 touted the "office of a traditional corporate job, but in a very unique way."[29] The *Atlantic* magazine described early coworking organizations as finding themselves "at the vanguard of a movement of people who are finding meaningful work, building community, and challenging conventional business practices."[30] The human need for community, according to Jacob Sayles of Office Nomads, is what lures people to coworking spaces. "They find communities and see the possibility of having their emotional needs met via social connections and opportunities to learn. These communities provide a place where a sense of belonging can happen."[31]

The 2015 GCUC conducted a survey among members of coworking space to highlight the special ingredients that community members see in their coworking environment.[32] When asked for the words that best describe coworking, the top responses were *community, collaboration, fun, social,* and *productivity.* Isn't that what all companies want to create in order to drive engagement and innovation in the workplace?

In the coming years we expect to see more companies becoming community members at one of the global coworking spaces. McKinsey is a case in point. When the company created McKinsey Academy, an online learning portal for both McKinsey employees and customers, rather than house the academy team in McKinsey headquarters in New York City, the company rented space at WeWork in New York City to provide the right mix of community, collaboration, and fun.

Next, we see a growing impact of space on worker satisfaction. Both Steelcase and the GCUC confirm that community influences worker satisfaction. In the GCUC survey, 79 percent of the community members reported being highly satisfied with their coworking space. This data is collected from many workers who pay to work in their own space. Imagine a level of satisfaction this high from employees who *are paid* to work in their space.

Finally, the GCUC survey documented the importance of a community manager to curate and engage community members. A total of 83 percent of respondents said the community manager was very important or important. We recommend it is time to consider the role of a community manager in all workspaces. Think of coworking spaces as being the early adopters in having a dedicated resource to focus on building community. These community managers curate content but also drive and engage members to attend various community-oriented programming, such as lunch meetings, networking meetings, and a variety of after-hours parties sponsored by companies selling snacks, eyeglasses, fitness classes, and other services.

Natalie Grasso, author of *What to Look for in Your Next Community Manager*, defines a community manager in the workplace as someone who:

1. Helps to shape the culture and norms of the space through member orientations, ongoing communication, and daily interactions
2. Facilitates connections whenever possible, growing and strengthening the community
3. Embodies the values and core culture
4. Sets the tone of the day for others
5. Draws energy from spending most of the day interacting with others
6. Empowers workers to connect directly to one another and use available resources to self-organize wherever possible
7. Is less of a provider and more of a facilitator, and approaches every interaction with a member as an opportunity to give power and permission[33]

Look for more community managers in the coming decade, and consider adding one to your workforce if you don't already have one.

Workspace Within the Future Workplace

The challenge for human resource and real estate leaders is how to realize the best opportunities to leverage space in order to reinforce culture, choice, wellness, engagement, and community. Forward-looking companies like Credit Suisse, Genentech, Glassdoor, La-Z-Boy, McKinsey, and Rackspace illustrate the range of new thinking regarding the power of workspace to increase collaboration, engagement, and satisfaction at work and lead to better business outcomes.

Increasingly, space is becoming part of the discussion in how and where we want to work. Workspace can support and embody company values and culture, cater to diverse worker preferences, enable improvements in well-being, and drive greater productivity, engagement, and community in the workplace.

We are all looking to be part of something bigger than our jobs. But how companies do this is critical. Don't be fooled into creating an array of workplace perks and think your job is done! Instead focus on how your workspace is an extension of your company culture. As Peter Drucker said, "Culture eats strategy for breakfast."[34] We all need to recognize that our workspace is where our culture happens. And we must ask ourselves how we can create a workspace where employees are engaged, motivated, learning, and benefiting from a positive community that cares about their well-being. How would you view your workspace differently if you saw it as less to do with a piece of brick than with "a piece of soul?"[35]

MY ACTION PLAN

Myself

- Take an observation walk for 30 minutes. What do I notice about how people are using our space? What does my choice of where I work say about me?
- Who do I partner with in my organization to redefine our workspace so it empowers employees?
- How do I use space personally?
  - Where are my engagement spaces, where I go to do my best work?
  - Where are my production spaces, where I go to get the job done?
  - Where are my toleration spaces, where I avoid going to meet or work?
  - Where are my restoration spaces to recharge?

My Team

- Do we explicitly discuss the role of space enough as a team? Why or why not? "It's not our job" is no longer the right answer.
- What could we learn from asking our employees for the three words that best describe their current work space and their desired workspace?
- What are the implications of their answers? How are they different from coworkers' answers of community, collaboration, fun, social, and productivity?

My Organization

- What does our workspace say about our culture?
- What are the key elements of our company culture that could be better translated into design elements within our workspace? How are we connecting our culture to our space?
- What are the coworking spaces in our community? What coworking spaces are near the communities where our employees live? Should we consider experimenting with using coworking space to cluster employees differently in a professional space while offering them greater work and travel flexibility?
- What metrics are we using as a company to measure space? Are these the most appropriate metrics for our cultural and performance goals?

RULE #3

BE AN AGILE LEADER

3

In the future workplace, a new generation of managers will need to learn to lead differently in order to be effective. Leaders who are agile and adapt to the rapidly shifting business landscape will be able to recruit the best and most productive workers of tomorrow, and leverage their talent to achieve lasting business success.

We identified seven leadership traits that are required for the agile leader of the future (illustrated in Figure 3.1).[1]

When we think about the agile leader of the future, this capability is defined along two macro dimensions.[2]

One dimension focused on the *ability to produce results*, meaning:

- **Be transparent.** Communicate and share on a regular basis.
- **Be accountable.** Acknowledge both your losses and your wins and learn from them.
- **Be intrapreneurial.** Seek out new opportunities and motivate others to think, imagine, and act in bold, enterprising ways.
- **Be future focused.** Anticipate the growing complexity of your business environment.

And the other dimension focused on the *ability to engage people*, meaning:

- **Be team intelligent.** Instill practices to make teams great in your organization.
- **Be inclusive.** Build diversity and inclusion as a value within your organization.
- **Be a people developer.** Enable on-demand individual and peer learning.

Figure 3.1   The agile leader of the future

Source: Future Workplace

Collectively, these traits promote more effective management decisions, raise awareness and understanding of the power of teams, and generate sustainable business results. Managing these two dimensions of results-oriented and people-engaged leadership is what will drive the greatest change inside organizations and set agile leaders apart from the rest.

The Ability to Produce Results: Be Transparent

There is consistently one corporate principle that correlates with happy, loyal, and more engaged staff: transparency in the workplace. Modern employees want a culture of straight talk, along with clear expectations for how to excel. These elements build trust, which is the foundation of great teamwork and the key to attracting and retaining the best talent.

One of the most obvious ways to create an open and transparent workplace is through communicating and sharing on a regular basis. While this may have been achieved in the past through a highly scripted companywide memo or a stage-managed town hall meeting, the digital age requires a more radical and open approach.

Executives are expected to be fluent in internal and external media platforms so that they can "humanize" their organization and better publicize the firm's innovations and accomplishments. They are also expected to more widely share management's thinking and strategy, in order to better establish a connection with employees and clients.

This is more easily said than done. In our Future Workplace Forecast survey, when we asked managers how important transparency is to their organization's future success, 85 percent said it was extremely or very important. But when we asked this same group of managers how transparent their organization is today, only 46 percent of managers said it was very or extremely transparent.

More interestingly, when we broke down the responses by company performance, we found that companies practicing transparency significantly outperformed their competitors. Only 21 percent of companies that were underperforming financially rated themselves as transparent, while 59 percent of outperformers did.

So what exactly does a transparent leader look like?

Many technology companies are in the vanguard of transparent approaches. Percolate, a marketing technology company with five offices in the United States and the United Kingdom, holds weekly meetings where every team member publicly judges his or her previous week's performance and sets goals for the current one. Sharing insights and objectives with the whole team lets coworkers know how they can help each other and enables each member to learn from the others' experiences.

Consider David Thodey, the former CEO of Telstra, the largest telecommunications company in Australia. Before stepping down in 2015, he was a highly visible, digitally engaged, and transparent leader, regularly communicating with employees and customers. Crucially, he also backed up his outreach with action, following up on requests for suggested process changes with real reforms. Thodey also personally engaged with employees on the company's internal social network and with customers on Twitter.

Transparency has become critical to communicating goals and creating a sense of team cohesion. John Donovan, who oversees 140,000 employees as chief strategy officer and president of Technology and Operations at AT&T, wanted to stress to his workforce just how important it was to adapt to a rapidly changing work environment. He needed employees to learn faster, which he understood was a difficult and risky request.

So he shared a personal story. At a global corporate gathering, with thousands of employees watching remotely, he showed a video in which he talked about growing up poor in a family of 11 children in Pittsburgh. He included his mother in the talk and they spoke movingly about how critical it is in life to imagine yourself in different circumstances and to work hard to get there.

"It was harder than you can possibly imagine," Donovan told the *New York Times*, to open up about his personal history in front of staff. But he believes the point hit home and inspired many people. "I get a lot of people asking how my mother is doing," he said.[3]

Transparency requires us to bring our "authentic self" to work, to model honesty and trust in our interactions, and to use emotional intelligence to understand the needs and concerns of our fellow employees and ourselves. The result will be: problems are solved faster, teams are more effective, and employees are more committed to the company's mission.

Model Behaviors to Be Transparent

1. **When in doubt, share.** Employees who understand a company's goals and processes are more apt to feel committed to that company's mission. Whether it's information on strategy, quarterly results, salaries, or your own personal motivations and aims, sharing information goes a long way toward fostering trust and engagement.

2. **Walk the walk.** Don't simply make engagement a weekly exercise. Integrate it into your daily approach, and follow up on suggestions and concerns you encounter so that employees and clients understand that your presence isn't just for show.

3. **Admit mistakes.** Transparent leaders are willing to admit mistakes and learn from them. If your goal is to have a team that genuinely wants to fol-

low you, you must acknowledge the reality of each situation. To create an environment of trust and personal transparency, provide a model of clear expectations. Outline exactly how you would like to receive feedback, and then—importantly—be ready to accept it and act on it, whether it be positive or negative.

The Ability to Produce Results: Be Accountable

Many corporate cultures encourage people to run away from outcomes that are unexpected, without regard to the fact that surprising results often lead to breakthroughs and opportunity. Being accountable means recognizing both your losses *and* your wins. Such leaders not only own their mistakes; they learn from them and feel empowered to take responsibility for the good results they produce. Our Future Workplace Forecast survey found that 35 percent of the highest-performing organizations always or very often enable peer-to-peer recognition to acknowledge employee accomplishments compared with 25 percent for all respondents.

Accountability starts with clear expectations. For decades, those expectations were communicated largely during annual performance reviews—an inefficient once-a-year process that often left employees and managers alike unsatisfied.

When Donna Morris, now Adobe's executive vice president of customer and employee experience, asked the people on her team several years ago to calculate the time eaten up by annual reviews, they found the review process required an incredible 80,000 hours of time from the 2,000 managers at Adobe each year—the equivalent of 40 full-time employees.[4]

Those results told Morris and her colleagues that it was time for disruptive change. Morris was one of the first Chief Human Resource Officers to scrap the annual performance review. In 2012. She replaced it with a series of regular check-ins that put accountability at the heart of conversations between managers and employees. These check-ins convey what is expected of employees, allow managers and employees alike to give and get feedback, and help employees with their growth and development plans. The reinvention of performance management was a key component in the ability of Adobe to transform its business. According to Morris, the move from an annual performance review process to the ongoing check-ins coincided with a major transformation of Adobe's business model. During the subsequent four years, the Adobe employee base increased 40 percent, stock price tripled, and the percentage of recurring revenue went from zero to 81 percent. Morris believes the check-in process of frequent ongoing feedback was crucial to Adobe's transformation to a more agile organization able to quickly take advantage of new business opportunities.

This transformation and reinvention of performance management and "safe" accountability is happening across a range of companies. Adobe, IBM, General Electric, Microsoft, Accenture, and Cisco, among others, are encouraging managers to be more explicit with their expectations to employees. Kee Meng Yeo, VP of Global Talent Development at Amway, reinforces the connection between accountability and mistakes: "Accountability is most often attached to failure, that's where I always take a step back when people hit me with accountability. My reply has always been, do you really want accountability or do you really want a witch hunt?" Yeo advocates framing the organization's accountability question as "Have you built an organization's culture where it's safe to be accountable?" and the individual employee accountability question as "Am I really open to taking accountability by learning from the mistakes I make?" Yeo also advocates "being honest about what you really value versus just promoting what's written down for the sake of promoting what's written down. Let's have the courage to say what we actually want to encourage and reward and what we don't. Let's be direct about these expectations and not spin them at all."

Our research highlighted how leaders exhibiting a strong sense of accountability, who give feedback often and communicate both positive and negative feedback, also reap the benefit of having higher employer net promoter scores. Quite simply, employees will be highly likely to refer friends and family to their employer if the organization practices transparent accountability from the top down.

Model Behaviors to Be Accountable

1. **Set a good example.** Denounce blame and shame tactics in favor of learning from mistakes. If you want members of your team to accept responsibility for setbacks as well as successes, you must do so as well.

2. **Offer constant and immediate feedback.** Provide frequent feedback, both positive and negative, and in both public and private forums. Emphasize what can be learned from negative outcomes, and empower teams to acknowledge their accomplishments.

3. **Think beyond finding a technology solution.** Solve for something larger than a new performance management tool, to rethink the entire employee experience and how this is impacted by "just-in-time accountability." Fine-tuning the accountability process requires going deeper than just setting goals for *what* you want done; you also need to outline the behaviors related to *how* you want results accomplished.

The Ability to Produce Results: Be Intrapreneurial

There have always been go-getters inside companies that take risks, test new ideas, and push boundaries. But never have so many companies actively encouraged employees to act like entrepreneurs on the job—to be *intrapreneurs inside their organizations.* Rather than constraining workers who have ideas, effective leaders push workers to dream big. Intrapreneurial leaders motivate others to think, imagine, and act in bold, enterprising ways, to take ownership of ideas, and to innovate within the organization.

The track record for such efforts is startlingly impressive: Google's Gmail, 3M's Post-it notes, Facebook's "like" button, and Sony's PlayStation are all products of internal intrapreneurship projects. But intrapreneurship doesn't just fuel bestselling products, innovation, and growth. It helps companies attract and retain the best employees, who increasingly want autonomy, meaningful work, and creative outlets on the job.

A significant shift in the mindset around intrapreneurship has taken place in companies across the world. In our Future Workplace study entitled

"Gen Y Workplace Expectations," 40 percent of millennials surveyed indicated interest in the opportunities that intrapreneurial workplaces provide. In that same study, 58 percent of seasoned managers reported being willing or extremely willing to support employees who want to capitalize on a new business opportunity within their company.[5] As millennials are already the largest generational cohort in the United States—and along with generation Z, they will be well over 60 percent of the workforce by 2025—businesses are exploring how to build intrapreneurial thinking inside their organizations, by incentivizing talent to stay in-house, rather than striking out on their own to develop new products and services.

Brad Smith, Chairman and CEO of Intuit, the maker of TurboTax, QuickBooks, and QuickBase, has for years championed efforts to help employees innovate from within. The company's noted Innovation Catalyst program trains employees to become innovation coaches and mentors, who then assist workers from across the company with thinking outside the box, experimenting with new products and processes, and uncovering important, overlooked opportunities.

"Regardless of whether you are leading a large enterprise or a small team, you need to remove barriers to innovation and get out of the way," said Smith.[6] Even though Intuit employs thousands of people, Smith continually stresses the importance of maintaining a start-up mindset, with the courage to take risks and stay nimble. The company's Idea Jams and unstructured time also give employees opportunities to collaborate on new ideas. Its customer-focused "follow me home" program allows workers and managers to better understand customers' needs by watching how Intuit's products are used in the real world.

"At the end of the day, it's about empowering individuals to contribute ideas and make an impact," Smith says, "as well as setting goals that challenge employees to step outside their comfort zone."

Model Behaviors to Be Intrapreneurial

1. **Create a culture of innovation.** Intrapreneurs benefit from a corporate culture in which new ideas can be shared and shaped. You need to connect the internal intrapreneurs and experimenters with each other. There are ample

communities for entrepreneurs to connect with outside organizations. The need is just as high internally, yet lacking inside most organizations. Building this kind of community requires consistent encouragement from the top to allow employees to connect with each other and try out new ideas.

2. **Believe in experimentation.** Too often, the corporate language used to describe experimentation focuses on failure: setbacks, false starts, wrong turns, and mistakes. Agile leaders flip this mindset on its head, celebrating experimentation as a catalyst for success rather than an opportunity for failure. That requires encouraging prototyping, testing, and refining, as well as finding the value and lessons in even the smallest opportunities. Remove the fear of failure and release employees from the organization's history of what has been tried or has not worked before. Only then will employees feel free to look at old problems differently and find the courage to take risks. When framed as intentional iteration and experimentation, a new mindset is created and ready for multiple learning moments.

3. **Give credit where credit is due.** People want to be recognized for the creative work they do in moving the organization's mission forward. Agile leaders consistently acknowledge innovation if they hope to keep the company's intrapreneurial culture strong. Incentives and recognition for experimenting and learning can compensate for the risks of failure. That might be realized through innovation awards, showcases, bonuses, and movement within the firm. Sometimes, a simple thank you will go a long way.

The Ability to Produce Results: Be Future Focused

As leaders, one of our primary jobs is to constantly revisit our company's strategy and mission. We must take the time to focus on where our business and industry are heading—now, 5, or even 20 years in the future—and how best to position our business to achieve results. That requires staying abreast of trends so we can make informed speculations about how to stay ahead of the curve.

Organizations that "let go at the top"—avoiding hierarchy, incrementalism, and the safety of resting on past successes—will be the ones that are agile enough to leapfrog from opportunity to opportunity in the future. Those are the businesses that will enjoy long-term prosperity in our rapidly changing business environment.

But how do you develop a more future-focused mindset? How do you develop managers who can anticipate the growing complexity of their business environment? Who can think digitally and deliver solutions with the agility of a start-up?

For the past several years, the financial sector has watched the emergence of FinTech—technology-driven financial services companies—with growing wariness. FinTech offers mobile apps for an array of financial services, from managing investments to making group payments that were once the exclusive domain of banks.

In 2014, Singapore-based DBS Bank, one of the largest banks in Asia, felt an acute pressure to remain agile in a rapidly changing business environment. So the bank's leadership decided to undertake an ambitious, innovative effort—a hackathon to help the bank come to grips with just how fast the digital world was changing and how survival depended on the ability to think and act creatively. Over 500 DBS employees and 50 start-up ventures across the Southeast Asia region were involved.

The participants were given 72 hours to create a working app to solve a specific business challenge. "You could see from the looks on their faces that they were nervous," says Laurence Smith, former managing director and group head of Learning and Talent Development for DBS. "I mean, we had non-technical people who had no programming experience partnered with startups. But in the end, they did it."[7] The three days had the teams rapidly ideating, prototyping, hitting the streets to do experiments with real customers, returning to digest their learning, and deciding whether to "persevere or pivot" based on the learnings from their experiments.

In the very first hackathon—which was an experiment in itself—six prototypes were created, one of which is an app launched as part of the digital banking strategy in India. But the organizers say the most important shift was from a traditional banking mindset to a digital one. "Our moment of being truly future focused was when we started to think like the startups, focusing on how enabling technologies can make us smarter, faster, and how we can use big data to innovate and create useful products and services for our customers," says Smith.

Several noticeable mindset and culture shifts became evident from before to after the hackathon:

Before	After
"Let's discuss this more."	"Let's do it!"
"Can this be done?"	"We will create a way to get this done!"
"72 hours is not enough time!"	"Let's get started now!"
"How will we roll this out?"	"Let's focus on one area first!"

Smith says, "What was amazing was when you see teams pitch their ideas to a panel of judges, exactly as real startups do to VCs—they were so proud of their creations, so excited about the revenue and market share opportunities, one team even said '72 hours ago we had no idea how to do this!' and then they paused, looked again at the smart phone they were holding up, and you could see their face change to that 'oh my gosh' moment, when they realized that those kids in a garage really were a threat to big banks! But then you saw them pause, look at the phone again, stand a little straighter and say to themselves 'We can do this too' and in that moment they went from fearing the unknown to being confident in their ability to invent the future of banking." DBS is the first organization in Singapore to build hackathons into its talent development program, with employees creating prototypes alongside start-ups.[8]

As Smith sees it, the key benefit of using the hackathon approach is to change the culture. DBS CEO Piyush Gupta agrees and has been lauded by local media as being one of the five most influential people shaping the future of banking. Gupta acknowledges the importance of the hackathons, saying, "How do you change [your people] so that they think like employees in Apple and Facebook? You can't do that in a room, presenting on a whiteboard. You have to create a platform so people have a chance to engage, dirty their hands, and work with different kinds of people."[9]

Hackathons have now been incorporated into the operating rhythm of DBS with a queue of business leaders wishing to sponsor hackathons as a part of a powerful problem-solving and ideation process. To date, hackathons have produced more than 50 prototypes of new DBS products, with 12 that have become real products for DBS.

But now the question is, how do you scale the success of the hackathons to the remaining 21,500 DBS employees? While asking this question, DBS discovered SmartUp (#BeMoreStartup), a mobile app for businesses providing users with insights, case studies, and lessons learned from some of the world's top leaders, including those from Airbnb, Udacity, Squirrel, and many more tech gurus—people that an ordinary person could only ever dream of meeting.

SmartUp is primarily used as part of a reverse mentoring relationship between a banker who has gone through the hackathon and his or her team members to build digital literacy skills. Hearing about this, one DBS executive, Olivier Crespin, the head of Digital Bank, downloaded SmartUp over a weekend and then sent an e-mail to his entire team of over 300 people on Monday morning saying, "I encourage all of you to download the SmartUp app. It is very well done, it has case studies, quizzes, and book extracts on anything you need to know about digital and start up. I learned a lot; it's the best training tool I have ever used. Should be mandatory to all, but do it at your own pace and leisure. In fact it's pretty entertaining; there are simulations and challenges difficult to crack but really stimulating and refreshing."

Smith ends with this: "How do I know our journey is working? One DBS executive came to me recently and shared that in three meetings he attended that week, key strategic decisions were changed as a result of insights or lessons learned just an hour before or the day before from SmartUp. Our journey in the digital world is starting to have impact inside DBS."

Model Behaviors to Be Future Focused

1. **Embrace disruption.** In the digital era, breathless audacity has become the business model for many companies, transforming how they make financial transactions, book overnight stays, or power their cars. It's an era that demands digital literacy from all leaders, especially those who work in HR. Be willing to welcome ideas that challenge current business models.

2. **Step outside your comfort zone.** Untether yourself from your desk to see the innovations that are powering change in your industry. Make a point to connect with people inside and outside your networks, attend conferences, and seek out change agents whenever possible.

3. **Watch for change.** Pay attention to understanding the causes of any results that were different from what was expected. Agile leaders have an obligation to make sure their ship is sailing smoothly, and focused on the horizon ahead and skillfully navigate unexpected situations on the journey.

The Ability to Engage People: Be Team Intelligent

While HR departments have traditionally focused on individual employees—recruiting them, developing them, and assessing their performance—we are beginning the see the advent of a new capability, one of developing team intelligence, the practice of making team performance great. According to Ashley Goodall, senior vice president of Leadership and Team Intelligence at Cisco, "One of the big misses in the HR function has been our nearly exclusive focus on individual development and performance. At Cisco we have noticed that great accomplishments are delivered through teams, not just through individuals working alone. This realization has guided our commitment to re-thinking performance management. We are solving for something bigger than just a new system for performance management. We are solving for how to find and make the best teams possible at Cisco."

Goodall goes on to say, "At Cisco we believe there are three things that form the foundation of great teams. First is enabling all team members to assess their strengths and bring their best self to work each day; second is giving teams an opportunity to understand what the team stands for and how to openly support each other in the collective efforts. Third is having leaders engage frequently in future-focused conversations so team members know where they are going, why they are making the choices they make, and how they are doing against their goals. Our insight here is that an individual employee's experience is really their team experience and this is different for everyone. So our goal as leaders is to understand team dynamics and to put the lens of the team on the entire HR process." Goodall believes it is this maniacal focus on creating the right team environment that leads to improved productivity, innovation, and engagement.

There are many economic benefits of being team intelligent. Cisco is now piloting a new team platform it has branded Team Space to help people understand and reveal their strength in working together. Goodall continues, "Once we were clear on the big picture of understanding team dynamics and making more of the best teams, then we were able to select a technology solution, Team Space, to scale team excellence across Cisco."

In the long term, Cisco wants to create an environment that provides customized tips for team leaders about what the best teams are doing. But more than that, Cisco wants to allow leaders to measure team engagement against the best teams and against their own engagement over time. But it's important not to think about this as just a technology solution. For team intelligence to thrive, the whole team has to be on board, and this demands capturing team data and metrics. And when you start to examine the entire HR function through a team lens, you can see opportunities for hiring intact teams, developing intact teams, and coaching intact teams.

But this vision is easier said than done. There are significant barriers to making this vision a reality. Perhaps the biggest barrier is being uncomfortable with not having all the answers. This is a big change for some who may have grown up in the HR function. Goodall sees one solution: use design thinking in HR to examine the entire employee experience from the point of view of the employee. Becoming employee-centric provides leaders with the opportunity to create a truly compelling employee and team experience.

Model Behaviors to Be Team Intelligent

1. **Find out who are the great team leaders in your organization.** Identify the key attributes of these leaders. Determine what they do and how they do it so this capability can be developed for key executives.

2. **Accelerate team performance.** Understand individually and collectively what makes great teams for your organization and develop this across the enterprise. Move beyond thinking of this as a technology solution; it is really about developing a team-intelligent mindset.

3. **Examine how to impact key HR processes through the team lens.** Examine all aspects of the employee experience—including hiring, training, and compensation—through the lens of team performance. When you unlock the power of teams in your organization, you are better poised for breakthroughs.

The Ability to Engage People: Be Inclusive

Inclusivity is very different from diversity. Diversity is typically a question of *whom* you recruit, while inclusivity is about *how* you include them. It is about creating and—crucially—listening to individuals or teams that represent many different voices. It is a way to foster diversity of thought, encourage more creative problem solving, and integrate the input of all stakeholders. It is about building diversity and inclusiveness as cultural values within the organization.

Our Future Workplace Forecast asked HR and hiring managers to identify the business benefits of an inclusive workplace. The top result was to add diversity of thought, and the second was to attract top talent. The third reason varied by function. HR leaders saw a more inclusive workplace as improving employee engagement, while hiring managers believed more inclusiveness impacted business performance. The good news? Inclusion promotes both.

Inclusivity is about creating teams and project groups from the ground up that represent and include many divergent voices. That process begins with possessing cultural intelligence. This means understanding how people of different genders, races, and nationalities solve problems and propose solutions and leveraging this to your company's competitive advantage.

At Cisco, Chief People Officer Fran Katsoudas has been leading an initiative to reimagine the way employees work. "The goal," says Katsoudas, "is to create a nimbler, more responsive HR department where silos, time zones, and cultural barriers are broken down so we can create innovative new HR solutions."

When one thinks of HR solutions, the list spans traditional functions, such as compliance training, career development, risk management, and performance management. This is exactly what Fran Katsoudas and her HR team wanted to change. In 2016, they used design thinking to "break" and then reimagine HR solutions for 71,000 global Cisco employees. Cisco actually closed all of HR for 24 hours and announced to employees that the company was using the time to engage the HR team and key stakeholders to create innovative HR solutions to deliver new and memorable employee experiences. To communicate the importance of inclusiveness, Fran traveled from Cisco headquarters in San Jose, California, to the Cisco office in Bangalore, India, to kick off this initiative.

Over that period of 24 hours, Cisco HR employees joined with colleagues in the services and engineering organizations in nine locations—including Tokyo, Shanghai, Singapore, Bangalore, Jerusalem, Krakow, London, Raleigh, and San Jose—to come together virtually using a mix of Cisco collaboration technologies. This initiative was called the Cisco HR Breakathon, and it gave birth to 105 new HR solutions. Two of the winning HR solutions proposed improving new-hire onboarding through a mobile app.

Cisco's HR Breakathon was inclusive not only in reaching people globally but also in reaching out to key business units to involve them in the experience. "We created a global and cross-functional event dedicated to hacking all the 'little and big things' that hinder HR from providing an extraordinary employee experience," says Katsoudas. She believes the power of the Cisco HR Breakathon was in its ability to empower the HR organization to let go of process thinking, engage globally, and put the Cisco employee experience at the center of it all.

Model Behaviors to Be Inclusive

1. **Talk inclusiveness up.** Have leaders and management continually promote the importance of diversity to the organization. Be clear on the business

rationale surrounding the benefits of increased diversity. Create a flow of applications from candidates with diverse backgrounds and then make the extra effort to hear what they have to share.

2. **Encourage diverse opinions to be shared.** Monitor your own behavior to make sure you are hearing and including opinions and contributions from a wide set of advisors, clients, stakeholders, and team members. Actively ask for views on your inclusiveness style and on the inclusiveness of company initiatives, in settings both large and small. Use the latest technologies to promote and harness inclusive thinking.

3. **Host events that put new perspectives on display.** Create formal opportunities that encourage employees from various departments and diverse geographies to offer their unique approaches and opinions. Encourage employees to participate in community and civic diversity projects and cross-cultural organizational initiatives from community days to hack-athons. Promote formal peer support groups or committees to develop programs to support diversity groups.

The Ability to Engage People: Be a People Developer

The business world pays a lot of lip service to the importance of people development. We know that it's critical to an organization's—and leader's—success. But some research paints a different story. In McKinsey's widely read article, "Why Leadership Development Programs Fail," the evidence is daunting. While U.S. companies spend $14 billion on leadership development programs, nearly 30 percent of American managers admit they have failed to exploit their international business opportunities fully because they lack enough leaders with the right capabilities.[10] The gap between the importance of leadership development and its ability to deliver results rests with the lack of context for leadership programs, an inability to tie to real business issues, the difficulty of changing the mindsets of leaders, and the failure to measure results. In the relentless push to adopt new leadership programs, often there is not enough time, resources, or know-how to apply the same business metrics to development that are applied to making other investments in the business.

In the future workplace, being a people developer requires enabling on-demand individual and peer learning. When forward-looking companies provide easy ways for employees to update skills and capabilities, they will be rewarded with a more engaged, longer-lasting workforce.

This is happening in select companies from established firms like Phillip Morris International (PMI) and Verizon Wireless to start-ups like Basecamp. At PMI, Filipe Dahlin heads Global Learning & Development. Dahlin's first task was to develop a comprehensive strategy for Global L&D. Dahlin believes, "Developing talent to our fullest extent will enable the company's future. While learning has always mattered, today it is essential and it is one of the strategic goals of our global human resource function."

The heart of his plan revolves around building an advanced global learning platform accessible on both desktop and mobile devices, as well as a state-of-the-art executive development suite for leaders assuming new roles, and, importantly, a recognition that leadership development as a function cannot change without upskilling the entire HR function at PMI.

The focus on upskilling HR includes building HR analytics as a core competency for the function. And for content Dahlin and his team are turning not only to MOOCs at select university providers but also to syndication from consumer sites such as TED, Vice, and YouTube. What is impressive about the new focus at PMI Global Learning & Development is the recognition that learning is a survival competence for the organization, and as such, the traditional approach of tapping established training partners will no longer suffice. In this brave new world of people development, the learner will be able to access on-demand development on any device, at any time, and in any location. Learning comes to the employees rather than employees "going to learning."

Innovation in people development is also happening at Basecamp, a company of under 100 employees, where CEO Jason Fried believes his employees should control both when and what they learn. Basecamp offers all employees a $1,000 allowance each year for continuing education. Some people take classes directly related to their careers, while others take photography lessons, learn an instrument, or try their hand with cooking lessons. The goal is to nurture lifelong learning, and the point is that as employees learn new skills—both related to their job and unrelated—this will enrich them as individuals and engage them as employees.

We expect to see more companies offering learning allowances where learning will not just be limited to the narrow confines of one's job, but instead employees will have the freedom, autonomy, and resources to engage in continual learning. Shouldn't this be the ultimate goal of people development: building lots of ways to learn and grow into one's daily routine?

In addition to funding employees in what they want to learn, companies are also focusing on more peer-to-peer teaching as a way to build smarter, more knowledgeable employees. This style of learning is beneficial because as employees explain their ideas to one another, they strengthen skills that facilitate collaborative working. They may learn how a fellow employee likes to receive feedback, or they may better understand the processes of other teams in the company.

Lou Tedrick, VP of Learning and Development at Verizon Wireless, agrees. Tedrick incorporates "reps talking to reps" into the company's mobile-enabled training. Frontline sales and service representatives make explanation videos of new products, promotions, and devices to share with colleagues as part of a structured learning program where learning is both fun and highly engaging.

Often in the rush of business, we think only of the formal ways to train employees and forget to create opportunities tapping unconventional modalities for sharing knowledge and growing on the job.

Think of people development is a survival skill in the next generation of work.

Model Behaviors to Be a People Developer

1. **Be comfortable going beyond traditional learning providers to integrate consumer learning.** Explore where your employees are learning today outside of your learning management system. These sites likely will include TED, YouTube, Vice, and Buzzfeed. Now reach out and craft syndica-

tion deals to bring this content in-house. Be innovative in curating popular MOOCs and integrating them into your learning offerings. Consider developing your own in-house MOOC or curating MOOCs aligned to your key capabilities.

2. **Seek opportunities to enable peer-to-peer teaching.** Peer-to-peer teaching enables employees to develop social capital resulting in enhanced reputation, the creation of trust, the development of currency, and the ability to leverage networks within. As a result, employees will contribute to each other's development and be more engaged with each other.

3. **Share your own learning journey.** Make sure your employees see you adding to your own skills repertoire. Offer details of your progress (and challenges) openly and often. Be someone others want to learn from.

Role-Modeling the Culture: An Enabler to Being an Agile Leader

If agile leadership is about the ability to produce results and engage people to get those results, then how does a company's culture play into this? It can either enable or present a barrier to putting agile leadership into practice.

Culture often gets described as the tribal behaviors of a group, the shared values, the "way that we do things around here." We all talk about it; we think, "Oh, culture, of course!" Organizations tend to have a well-documented and visible sets of values. When we hear leaders talk about the culture of an organization, the primary focus is on the aspirational. These values tend to be reflected by the written and spoken words of senior management. The values found on a company website or annual report and should be the behaviors consistent with the cultural aspirations of the firm: "These are our values, this is our culture, and this is what we expect of you."

Then there's the culture gap, a barrier to agile leadership. This is the gap between the behaviors we promote and those we tolerate. Figure 3.2 shows this culture gap.

Our Future Workplace Forecast survey asked three important questions regarding culture. First we asked, "How important is it to you that your lead-

Figure 3.2 *The culture gap*

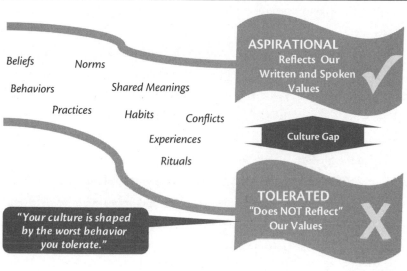

Beliefs   Norms

Behaviors   Shared Meanings

Practices   Habits   Conflicts

Experiences

Rituals

ASPIRATIONAL
Reflects Our
Written and Spoken
Values

Culture Gap

TOLERATED
"Does NOT Reflect"
Our Values

*"Your culture is shaped
by the worst behavior
you tolerate."*

Source: Future Workplace

ers model the company culture?"[11] In total, 92 percent answered very or extremely important across industries, cultures, and ages. It matters to everybody, everywhere, every function, every industry, and every age group. That's the good news.

The second question we asked was "Are your leaders role-modeling the culture?" At 66 percent, a majority of our respondents rated their senior leaders highly for their management style, actions, and behaviors as role models for organizational culture. Essentially, they were living the values and walking the walk.

Our third question was on tolerance of behaviors. We asked "How often do you see examples of your organization tolerating behaviors that do not reflect the stated company culture?" Only 37 percent of winning organizations see these poor behaviors tolerated,[12] while 47 percent of all respondents do. Winning organizations are consistently less tolerant of behaviors that do not reflect the stated company culture. It doesn't matter what's written on our wall; it's what we tolerate that matters, meaning "The culture of any organization is shaped by the worst behavior the leader is willing to tolerate."[13] If we aspire to agile leadership, where leaders are people developers, transparent, and team intelligent, and our leaders do not behave this way, that's our true culture.

Companies that practice agile leadership do so starting with the hiring process. Both Airbnb and Glassdoor shared a similar response to how important culture is in the hiring process. We asked, "How do you protect your culture when you will have more employees two years from now than you've hired cumulatively over the last six years?" Bottom line: they screen for cultural fit in the hiring process. Once hiring managers establish that a candidate is qualified, then this person is interviewed by someone else to assess the cultural fit. No matter how well qualified someone might be, the candidate must fit the culture to be offered the job. Culture is the glue that binds the seven traits of agile leadership together in winning organizations.

Implementing the Seven Traits of Agile Leadership

It might seem daunting to juggle the seven traits of the agile leader. But it's critical to note how interwoven many of the core characteristics are to produce results and engage people. None is necessarily more important than another; the traits work together as part of an organic whole, complementing and reinforcing the importance of the other. Leaders who role-model the traits of agile leadership enable this for the entire organization. An intrapreneurial employee is only able to function at full capacity within a future-focused organization. A more transparent leader strengthens trust between employees, their wider teams, and the organization at large. With greater transparency, more inclusive teams can create an environment ripe for more intrapreneurial collaboration. Greater inclusiveness often fosters a space of mutual teaching and learning where team members are more likely to hold each other accountable for group learning initiatives. With increased trust come happier, longer-tenured employees who are more likely to share expertise, strengths, weaknesses, duties, and unique experiences, leading to a stronger foundation for team intelligence. Agile leadership is about the ability to produce results.

It is also about the ability to engage people. Finally, it is about role-modeling the values of the organization and demonstrating an intolerance of culturally inappropriate behaviors not tolerating bad behaviors to get results.

MY ACTION PLAN

Myself

- Of the four traits that shape my ability to produce results (be transparent, be accountable, be intrapreneurial, be future focused):
  - Which is my strength?
  - What one model behavior do I most want to work on improving?
- Of the three traits that shape my ability to engage people (be team intelligent, be inclusive, be a people developer):
  - Which is my strength?
  - What one model behavior do I most want to work on improving?
- How do I believe I show up to others on each of the traits of agile leadership?
- What one trait does a trusted colleague think I should work on improving?
- How am I going to role-model the cultural values of the organization?

My Team

- What traits of agile leadership are most important to our team?
- Are there traits that we could pay more attention to as a team?
- What model behaviors are most important for our team?
- What model behaviors do we want to hold each other more accountable for practicing?
- How are we going to hold each other accountable for the cultural values of the organization?

My Organization

- How do our company values connect to the model behaviors of what we expect of our leaders and managers?

- Is there enough emphasis within our current training of linking development to model behaviors?
- Do our leadership training programs incorporate the seven traits of being an agile leader?
- What else could our organization do to further develop the seven traits of an agile leader among our emerging leaders?

PART II

HOW TECHNOLOGY TRANSFORMS THE WORKPLACE

RULE #4

CONSIDER TECHNOLOGY AN ENABLER AND DISRUPTOR

4

I think that novels that leave out technology misrepresent life as badly as Victorians misrepresented life by leaving out sex.

—*Kurt Vonnegut*[1]

A New Age of Technological Disruption

The term *consumerization of IT* is now fully entrenched in the workplace. It was coined back in 2007 by Intel's CEO to describe how IT technology adoption was being driven by consumers, not by enterprises. For many workers, especially those who work remotely, being able to work on your own device became a game-changing remote productivity tool. This has in turn spawned the "consumerization of the workplace experience" where employees are bringing into the workplace not merely one but a host of technologies such as smartphones, tablets, fitness trackers, smart glasses, smart watches, and, most recently, augmented reality applications.

As consumer technologies move inside the workplace, they significantly impact the employees' overall workplace experience. Technology enables companies to deliver a transformational employee experience, one that enables employees' communication and collaboration, enhances their productivity, advises their data-driven decision making, and even disrupts their individual job descriptions.

Staying ahead of the technology curve has never been more difficult for corporations. Figure 4.1 highlights the transformative impact of technology

Figure 4.1   Technology is radically transforming our workplace experience

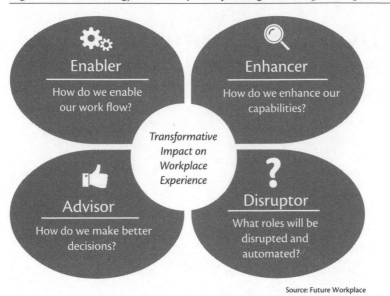

Source: Future Workplace

to enable, enhance, advise, and disrupt our workplace experience. We raise four questions to highlight the key technology drivers converging to create an unprecedented opportunity to transform the workplace experience for both employers and employees:

- **Enabler.** How do we enable our work flow?
- **Enhancer.** How do we enhance our capabilities?
- **Advisor.** How do we make better decisions?
- **Disruptor.** What roles will be disrupted and automated?

Enabler of Our Work Flow

Communication Is More Interactive and Visual

Communications at work have become "omnichannel." New forms of communication are being deployed to better suit evolving work habits. Polycom, the videoconferencing company that for years created videoconferencing technology aimed at organizations with large formal conference rooms, now recognizes the need to adapt to very different work patterns. Michael Frendo, Polycom's executive vice president of Worldwide Engineering, shares this about the evolution of his company's products: "We have now assumed usage is in small huddle rooms so we are building new videoconferencing technology with background noise cancellation and increased mobility to ensure that they are useful for those working in huddles. In addition, we are seeing a huge trend toward video communications, especially among Millennials, as active users of FaceTime, Skype, and Google Hangouts, they are bypassing audio communications and going right to video for all types of needs from group collaboration to coaching and mentoring."

Communication Is Morphing into Collaboration

One company that has explored how to best use technology for both communications and collaboration is Atos, a French IT services firm. In February 2011, CEO Thierry Breton announced a company vision of zero e-mail. Jean Corbel, the global chief change officer at Atos, and his team set out to make this a reality. Corbel says that Atos first looked at what its employees used e-mail for, and then the company identified how it could replace e-mail with other collaboration tools such as Skype for Business, knowledge management tools, or the firm's internal collaboration portal to share content, ask questions, and search for answers to business issues.

"Collaboration is not an end. It's a means for something," says Corbel. "For us, it's a means for more innovation, closer contact and bringing more value to the client. My value, and my pride in working for Atos, is to collaborate with our employees and our clients. If we work together as a team, we win in the marketplace. So when we launched a new collaboration platform as a substitute for email we invited employees to set up a collaboration space on this platform, populate it and start using it with their team members."

The company's experience has shown the benefits of shaking up a traditional technology. Atos has reduced e-mail usage by more than 80 percent. As Corbel says, "We found many benefits of decreasing email, especially in making institutional knowledge sharable so it no longer sits in private email inboxes."

The number of collaboration and video tools available to workplaces today reinforces this need to rethink how we work differently today and to consider integrating consumer technologies into our new work flows. Gartner predicts that by 2018 over 50 percent of team communication will be done through the use of tools and apps.[2] The sidebar lists the top collaboration tools being used by businesses today that you should be familiar with and explore for your organization.

10 Top Collaborative Workplace Tools

1. **Salesforce Chatter.** Social collaboration and file-sharing service
2. **Cisco Spark.** Online rooms with group messaging, content sharing, video calling, and desktop sharing
3. **Google Hangout.** Communications platform including video chat, instant messaging, and VoIP
4. **IBM Connections**. Social software, real-time social communications, content management, and file sharing
5. **Jive.** Collaboration tool with a user-friendly interface
6. **Microsoft Lync.** Instant messaging and audio conferencing designed to integrate with Office 365
7. **Slack.** Real-time team messaging, archiving, and search
8. **VMWare Socialcast.** Collaboration platform with social networking and video and content management
9. **Cisco WebEx.** Online videoconferencing, meetings, presentations, and webinars
10. **Microsoft Yammer.** Private social network for employee collaboration

Digital Motivation Is Fostering Engagement

As communication in the workplace morphs into team collaboration, we are seeing a new way to motivate employees, called digital motivation. The term *digital motivation* (also called *gamification*) refers to using technology to digitally engage and motivate an audience. Digital motivation takes the essence of game attributes—such as fun, play, transparency, design, competition, and, yes, addiction—and applies these to a range of real-world processes inside a company from recruiting to learning to career development. As Brian Burke, vice president of Gartner, says, "Digital motivation today is being used by mass audiences but is gaining traction for internal usage in an organization."[3]

Digital motivation inside companies can be a powerful way to motivate employees to learn new skills. Digital motivation can also help engage and source new employees. PwC wanted to see if it could use digital motivation to more fully engage job candidates at the firm's Hungarian location. It turns out that job candidates were passing through the PwC website quickly, often spending only 10 minutes or less. PwC believed a more engaged candidate pool would yield better candidates, resulting in workers who would stay on with the company longer after they had been hired.

PwC turned to a serious game called Multipoly.[4] The game allows job candidates to see just how ready they are to work at PwC by placing them on teams and presenting them with business problems similar to those they would encounter on the job. After a simulated job interview, candidates can try out roles such as consultant, senior consultant, and manager. Job candidates tap into their business acumen and digital skills to play the game. Noemi Biro, PwC Hungary's regional recruitment manager, shared that candidates who played Multipoly were better prepared for live face-to-face interviews because the game "pre-educated them about PwC and its vision, services and the skills they will need to succeed on-the-job." Biro reported that job candidates with Multipoly experience found onboarding at PwC easier, as they had already experienced PwC culture through the game. As a recruitment tool, Multipoly proved to be a huge improvement over the PwC career page. Rather than just skimming the PwC career site for 10 minutes or less, job candidates spent as much as 90 minutes playing Multipoly. Since introducing the game, PwC reports that the job candidate pool has grown 190 percent, with users reporting interest in learning more about working at PwC having increased by 78 percent. Finally, job candidates who were hired after playing Multipoly made the transition to a full-time employee more easily because they had a taste of PwC's culture from playing the game.[5]

Digital motivation is also being used to train current employees. At Verizon Wireless, Lou Tedrick, vice president of Learning & Development, and Pete Beck, director of Learning Technology, identified a sizable business challenge where digital motivation can be applied: reduce the training time and gamify the learning experience for Verizon Wireless retail store representatives. Tedrick and Beck saw that retail store representatives faced an average of 12 new phone launches (e.g., new smartphones or tablets, pricing, promotions, systems enhancements) each month. The amount of knowledge they needed to retain was huge. This is compounded by the Ebbinghaus forgetting curve, a neuroscience phenomenon where information is exponentially forgotten from the time it is consumed if there is no attempt to retain it.[6]

Armed with a business plan for addressing the high volume of phone launches, Tedrick and Beck's team—working with an internal lean six sigma group and external consultants—created a gamified learning experiment called Burst and Boost. First they split one store's retail representatives into three groups: a control group, a Burst group, and a Burst and Boost group. The control group was trained on a tablet launch using standard paper-based training and performance support tools for a total learning time of 20 minutes. The Burst group received similar training but in the form of video bursts on a smartphone for a total of 6 minutes. The Burst and Boost group also received training in 6-minute video bursts as well as boosts—a mix of learning reinforcements that included multiple-choice questions, open questions, and polls asking, "What is your favorite aspect of the phone?" "What is your favorite video?" and "What is your favorite feature on the new smartphone?"

When the researchers compared knowledge retention among all three groups, they found the Burst and Boost group retained 50 percent more information than the control group and Burst-only group, in considerably less time, resulting in more time selling and an estimated savings of $5 million across Verizon Wireless retail stores. Tedrick and Beck felt the key here was the gamified "boosts" over a period of two days, two weeks, and two months where retail store representatives were asked to continually think about the new phone and share personal stories about the phone. Tedrick recaps with this: "We found the key to knowledge retention is to have the retail store representatives make a personal connection with new knowledge over a 60-day period, thereby leading to increased knowledge retention, shorter time in training and overall savings."

Finally, digital motivation can be used to drive innovation by embedding it into a company's training program. Booz Allen Hamilton embedded digital motivation into its training program targeted to firm data scientists. Rebecca Allegar, digital strategist, shares the rationale for developing this: "What we know about online learning is that it is often a lonely experience and leads to low retention and engagement among learners. Also we observed that learning to be a data scientist often came from multiple learning vendors and this was often designed as a mix of online and in person experiences, done on an employee's own time" in addition to juggling multiple client engagements.

The solution was Tech Tank Stadium, an online learning experience that included several components, such as change management (why the Tech Tank Stadium was important to an employee's career development), incentives (tangible and intangible rewards for participation and accomplishment of goals), and design thinking (understanding the psyche and need to form a network among other learners). The Tech Tank Stadium has proven successful in two ways. First, data scientists enrolled in and completed the learning program. But more importantly, because the digital motivation promoted teaming, the participants developed relationships that continue to this day. The new data scientists continued to engage with each other following the completion of the program to share insights, questions, and challenges they are having at work each day. For those in learning and development, this is a pinnacle of achievement: creating the serial learner, who completes learning and continues learning and networking with like-minded employees to help increase their performance on the job each day![7]

While the audiences vary, digital motivation is a proven engagement methodology that is reshaping many workplace experiences for the mutual benefit of both worker and employer.

The Appification of Work is Intensifying

We now live in an app economy. Apps have become the primary way we interact with each other, work, learn, and play. More companies are creating proprietary apps and opening up their own corporate app stores. Enhanced security, greater productivity, and ongoing access to learning and development are the primary motivators.

After realizing the influence that consumer apps were having on its largely millennial, mobile workforce, Cognizant Technologies decided to "appify" many of its work processes and create its own corporate app store. "There was this huge disconnect we were seeing in the workforce," says Shanthy Ghosh Roy, head of Learning & Development for North America at Cognizant. "Our employees could easily access what they needed on social channels but at work people were spending needless hours updating timesheets, looking for learning & development programs, and updating their performance goals."

After Cognizant understood how wide the gap was between the personal lives of Cognizant's employees and their work lives, the executive team devised a plan to appify many of the Cognizant work processes. The key was to have each app do a few actions well, from simply booking a conference room to being part of a series of apps to complete complicated work flows such as coordinating an employee's move to an overseas office.[8]

"We suddenly realized that even if we had all of the requirements to build an app store this would be a long term project. So we decided to solve this problem through crowdsourcing," explains Ghosh Roy. She continues: "Essentially our HR department aligned with our marketing messaging which is focused on leveraging social, mobile, analytics, and cloud to solve business problems. We asked ourselves: If we are looking to provide instant, intuitive and easy access to our work processes, what will it take to do this in Human Resources?"

The solution was to create a corporate app store. Other tech companies such as Apple, Intel, Qualcomm, IBM, and GE all have their own enterprise app stores. One of the biggest benefits to having an enterprise app store is the enhanced security it provides. By keeping all the apps used in the workplace in one manageable place, a company can secure not just its own files and data but also those of its employees.

Ghosh Roy further explains: "Next we asked ourselves, 'Why does one single team have to be responsible for deciding which apps the company should create?' So we decided to crowd source with our associates the development of new apps. We started with active involvement from our CIO who presented us with a challenge: *Can we create 1,000 apps in a year*? We had such an overwhelming response from all of our associates across all functions of the company that we exceeded this goal and crowd sourced 1,000 apps within 8 months. The apps range from expense account reporting, time sheet reporting, accessing our Learning Management System as well as coaching and mentoring, all available to be accessed by all Cognizant associates."

Ghosh Roy concludes, "Thinking about the future of HR, I can see using apps for a range of associate engagement functions such as accessing training programs, coaching and mentoring."

App usage will get a further boost in coming years. Newer platforms such as smart watches and other wearables, connected TVs, virtual and augmented reality, home Internet of things, automotive and global smartphone growth will more than double the installed base of app-capable devices by 2020.[9] What will you appify?

Enhancer of Our Skills

Wearable technologies are transforming the workplace experience. Wearable technology is changing what we know about workers, how work gets done, and how skills are built. The spectrum of wearable technology at work has rapidly expanded to now include:

- Quantification and measurement
- Implantable and ingestible
- Strength and endurance
- Augmented reality
- Virtual reality

Quantification and Measurement Is Leading to the Quantified Employee

Technology is becoming ever more personal, smaller, and more powerful. We've evolved from computers that filled entire rooms to desktop computers, laptops, smartphones, tablets, and now wearable and ingestible devices to track health, wellness, and productivity. Just as mobile phones did over the past five years, wearable devices are now entering the workplace en masse and in multiple formats.

One early approach that has emerged at the forefront of adoption is integrating fitness trackers into the workplace, as employers and employees use them to motivate healthier habits at work. Amy McDonough, vice president and general manager of Fitbit, says, "The CEO of one of our clients, Houston Methodist, actually published his step count, and asked everyone who worked for the hospital to try to beat it." The hospital also learned through employee surveys that Fitbit users who have at least one friend with a Fitbit get 27 percent more steps than those who don't, so the hospital subsidized the cost for not only its employees but also their spouses or partners. "In the end, 90 percent of employees participated in the corporate wellness program and averaged 16,000 steps per day," says McDonough.[10]

Fitbits go beyond encouraging healthy behaviors. They can improve office culture by getting teams to meet their fitness goals together. And as reported in *Fast Company*, Fitbits are also reducing healthcare costs.[11] Appirio used data on an opt-in basis from employees and was able to shave 6 percent off its annual healthcare bill. Beyond the wellness outcomes, employee engagement has also increased. Workforce health is not widely recognized to be among the top drivers of productivity or performance, but most leaders believe health is a significant contributory factor.[12]

Improving safety and data collection are further drivers for deploying wearables in the workplace. Healthcare, military, and industrial employers stand to benefit the earliest. Wearable devices now track the position of employees or soldiers, providing real-time data about their location to remote data centers. Wearable devices are also used to track biometrics such as heart rate, blood pressure, and hydration of workers. To improve safety, Rio Tinto truck drivers in coal mines in Australia have been wearing a SmartCap, a baseball cap with sensors to detect how alert the drivers are, and provides a warning when drivers become too tired to drive.

Future wearables will integrate so closely with fashion, you will not be able to tell the difference. Companies like Hexoskin, OMsignal, and AiQ Smart Clothing are creating biometric garments that measure our bodies' vital signs. Adidas has embedded sensors into the jerseys of sports teams to provide coaches with data on location, heart rate, and movement of the individual players. In the not too distant future, technologists anticipate wearables hidden in contact lens, , maybe even inside the rings or pendants we wear around our neck, to measure our biometric data and our activity levels and proactively prompt us to seek a qualified medical diagnosis.[13]

Implantable and Ingestible for Convenience and Diagnosis

Finally, while it may seem futuristic and concerning to some, implantable chips and ingestible sensors are also being piloted today. Epicenter, a coworking space in Stockholm, has introduced implantables.[14] Workers at the facility are able to get a communications chip implanted into their hands by a piercing specialist. The chip then allows them to swipe into offices, register loyalty points at retailers nearby, and access the work gym.[15]

Technology is now legally ingestible. Moving beyond wearables and implantables, the U.S. Food and Drug Administration has already approved the first use of an ingestible sensor as an aid to measure medication adherence.[16] Researchers from MIT discovered a way to create an ingestible sensor that can monitor vital signs from inside the gastrointestinal tract. [17] While ingestible sensors are being designed primarily for clinical monitoring and diagnosis, they also have the potential to first show up in the workplaces of military personnel or professional athletes.

Strength and Endurance are Enhanced by Mechanical Wearables

According to the 2016 Liberty Mutual Workplace Safety Index,[18] *"Overexertion involving outside sources* ranked first among the leading causes of disabling injury" in the workplace. This "event category" includes musculoskeletal injuries and disorders that result from carrying heavy loads and costs U.S. businesses $15 billion in direct outlays annually. Companies are now deploying robotic exoskeleton suits, boots,[19] powered gloves, and other hardware formats, all designed to allow people to lift heavy loads safely and provide enhanced lower-exertion mobility.[20] Exoskeleton wearables change who can be hired for manual work (especially in industries expected to experience labor shortages such as construction and agriculture). These wearables reduce work injuries, and provide enhanced on-the-job aids to make repetitive assembly-line work easier.[21]

Augmented Reality Is a New Reality

Augmented reality (AR) augments workers' senses. AR devices project a visual digital overlay onto a real physical scene through some form of display capability, usually hand held or head mounted.[22] The most widely covered AR device was the commercial deployment of Google Glass, which, while released to developers and early adopters, was not given wide release. AR technology is still in its early stages, and the possibilities for the application of augmented reality in the workplace are vast. Significant early successes are taking place in warehouses where stock pickers use augmented reality technology to process shipments and products faster and with fewer errors. Many companies are developing AR devices for enterprise use, efforts hastened by the greater availability of higher wireless broadband speeds. Greater awareness of AR has been further fueled by mobile AR games that blend digital and real-world play. Recall how Pokémon Go, became a viral global phenomenon with 30 million downloads within two weeks of its July 2016 release date with high levels of average daily engagement time (over 48 minutes per day) by its players.[23] Now imagine if you could replicate this level of engagement and excitement over a new hire onboarding or a leadership development program? This will be the next frontier of AR in the workplace as organizations proactively integrate this new form of user interface into training and development and importantly, provide prospective new hires with a glimpse into the workplace experience their brand is known for in the market.

More elaborate augmented reality devices, such as the DAQRI smart helmet, use ultra-accurate sensors, photography, video capture, and augmented reality to precisely inform workers of their surroundings, providing a truly augmented contextual awareness experience.[24] A newer version of the DAQRI helmet includes an x-ray function that allows the wearer to look into the workings of objects using a real-time overlay of information. This enables maintenance workers to see exactly where an object is broken, and how they can fix it, without even opening it up. These types of AR-enabled devices will change the way jobs are carried out in many different industries and significantly lower the number of years of experience required by technicians to be fully productive in the field, opening up a wider pool of technical job candidates who can be trained in real time to perform their jobs.

Virtual Reality Enhances Job Skills

Prepare for workers wearing immersive headsets. Virtual reality (VR) is a fully immersive digital experience. The goal of VR is "to engage a user to interact with a simulated auditory, visual and kinesthetic environment as if it were real."[25] Virtual reality enables users to navigate different digital environments. VR headsets are rapidly becoming less expensive, more practical, and better suited to an emerging role in the workplace. VR technology is ideally suited to encourage users to experiment within the digital environment. The year 2016 was the breakout year for virtual reality, with Oculus Rift VR, HTC Vive, PlayStation VR, and Google Daydream all enabling quality virtual reality devices and apps on the market. In the workplace, Volvo was an early adopter of Microsoft's HoloLens to enhance collaboration work between its auto design team members. Tilt Brush from Google was one of the better early apps that drove consumer awareness for VR.[26] The top 10 VR platforms and headsets are listed in the sidebar.

Top VR Platform and Headsets

1. **Google Cardboard.** VR platform developed by Google[27]
2. **Microsoft HoloLens.** Developed by Microsoft Corporation
3. **Samsung Gear VR.** Developed by Samsung Electronics in collaboration with Oculus and manufactured by Samsung
4. **Oculus Rift VR.** Developed by Oculus VR, Oculus Touch
5. **HTC Vive.** Developed by HTC and Valve Corporation
6. **PlayStation VR.** Developed by Sony Interactive Entertainment and manufactured by Sony
7. **Google Daydream.** VR platform developed by Google[28]
8. **Sulon Q.** Designed by Sulon Technologies Inc.
9. **OnePlus Loop VR.** Developed by OnePlus
10. **OSVR.** Open-source virtual reality developer ecosystem with open-source headsets by Razer and Sensics

Some jobs are now literally a game. *Job Simulator* is the flagship VR game developed by creative games studio Owlchemy Labs. The Job Simulator game envisions a world in 2050 where robots have replaced humans at all jobs. Players are encouraged to "step into the Simulator to learn what a job, such as an office cubicle worker, gourmet chef, automotive repairman, or convenience store clerk was like."[29] In each game, a player operates from the enclosed space of the job (cubicle, kitchen, garage, or store counter) and interacts in a satirical and fun way with many of the objects commonly found in those workspace environments. The Job Simulator VR experience was made available for the HTC Vive, Oculus Touch, and PlayStation VR platforms and has received early accolades as a fun, immersive workplace experience environment.

Job Simulator illustrates the potential of VR to simulate serious work environments for immersive training purposes. Imagine a new-hire onboarding experience where the new hire accesses a VR experience before joining the company. She could experience the corporate campus by walking through the hallways and into various buildings, meet the avatars of her leadership team, listen to different team members interactively describe what they are working on, and learn about the company's business and culture by engaging in meetings and online training scenarios all experienced within the VR environment.

The potential to rapidly train workers to perform more complex tasks is astonishing. VR training improves retention, removes the logistical issues of organizing in-person training sessions, and lowers maintenance on actual equipment traditionally used for training purposes. The role of a trainer will be redefined as immersive tutorials tap a multidisciplinary team of video and subject matter experts to create the AR experience. New augmented virtual reality applications raise the potential levels of all employees and should be experimented with for many workplace situations. Make an effort to experience AR and VR soon and imagine the possibilities for your *immersive* future workplace experience!

Advisor: Applying Technology to Make Better Decisions

Technology is driving better business and people decisions. Recruitment, goal alignment, and operations efficiencies are among areas where organizations are applying technology to inform decision making.

With hiring, many organizations have still to apply the proven capabilities of hiring analytics. A National Bureau of Economic Research study[30] found that using analytics leads to better hiring decisions. The research highlighted how the more hiring managers disregarded the advice of the algorithms, the shorter the period of time an employee stayed at the company.

Just as performance management has gone from a closed-door, once-a-year process to being more frequent and transparent, so have goal setting and performance feedback. Goal setting and performance feedback can be accessed online through the web, a mobile device, or even a smart watch, allowing all to see overall goals and how they fit into them. John Chu, vice president of

Global People Operations at App Annie, a 450-person mobile app analytics firm, shares how his firm is starting to use OKRs (objectives and key results). According to Chu, "We realized we needed a transparent and consistent way to align the goals of our leaders to the overall company goals as we grew across 13 countries and multiple cultures. We started with sharing the overall company goals and then implemented a phased approach empowering our top 60 leaders to share their objectives and key results with the rest of the company. This not only led to greater transparency but also increased accountability as our leaders shared their goals with the department and the enterprise. While it's too early to capture hard business results, we can see how increasing transparency and accountability leads to greater cross collaboration and improvements in employee engagement." Chu is implementing OKRs in the HR department to establish a great place to work, an overall company objective. The sidebar shows how OKRs are applied to HR team members!

OKRs at a Glance

App Annie Company Objective:

- Establish a great workplace for great people

HR Goal:

- Improve employee engagement

HR Results:

- Improve employee engagement score to 7.4 (75th percentile among benchmarks)
- Implement skip level meetings across all levels, all regions
- Complete global manager training in Q1 with 100 percent participation
- Implement flexible work arrangements in the Americas

Source: App Annie

Technology is also being used to implement operational efficiencies. Using badge swipes, a financial services firm established where and how often employees were moving around the office, and by using meeting invite records the company was able to tell exactly how many meetings employees had, how many participants on average were in each meeting, and whether attendees were internal or external. With this information the company was able to prevent a 20 percent overbuild of facilities such as meeting rooms and offices, a substantial saving on real estate costs. Collecting this type of data from devices employees are comfortable with, such as swipe cards and mobile devices, has become much easier, but, and this is key, there are limits to collecting such data for optimizing workplace efficiencies without employee knowledge. We have seen data collection on employee activity done best when organizations transparently communicate a policy of what data will be collected, how, from what employee activities, and for which decisions.

Disruption and Automation— Exponential Growth Ahead

Every job will be impacted by technology. The increased usage of technology has the power to create new jobs, reshape existing jobs, and in some cases eliminate jobs entirely. Research from the World Economic Forum's "Future of Jobs" report predicts that over 5 million jobs will be lost by 2020 as a result of developments in genetics, artificial intelligence, robotics, and other technological changes. A study completed by the Martin School at Oxford suggests that 47 percent of jobs are at high risk of being replaced by technology in the next one to two decades. The study "The Future of Employment: How Susceptible Are Jobs to Computerisation?" evaluated 700 jobs based on the skills and education required for each and then weighted them according to the likelihood that they could be automated. The result: all 700 jobs were ranked from low-risk occupations (recreational therapists, emergency management directors, and healthcare social workers) to high-risk ones whose more repetitive tasks (library technicians, data entry operators, and telemarketers) make them more likely candidates for partial or complete automation.[31]

But while much media commentary has been on job elimination due to technology, not enough focus has been on how technology will disrupt and at the same time augment jobs. Chatbots are one example of how bots are "botifying" the workplace. A chatbot is an artificial intelligence computer program designed to simulate a conversation through written or spoken text. At Microsoft, Facebook, Slack, and Hipchat, workers are interfacing with chatbots to help get tasks done. Facebook's AI virtual assistant called M can make restaurant reservations and complete other tasks that combine AI with a team of "trainers" and customer service experts to ensure M is performing each task requested of it.[32] Microsoft has a chatbot for employees called ADbot that mines the corporate directory for information for answers to any number of queries. The goals for these bots are to "make internal employee communications faster, easier, more fun and in turn save money."[33]

A new breed of mobile intelligent assistants such as Google Assistant,[34] Microsoft's virtual assistant Cortana, Apple's intelligent assistant Siri, and Amazon's Alexa have also entered the workplace. As more developers build bot interfaces that respond interactively to human dialogue, the botification of the workplace will exponentially expand and allow knowledge workers to work smarter. These bots powered by machine learning have the potential to enhance our current jobs and augment how we learn, communicate, and mentor colleagues.

Now, take the example of journalism, where reporters have forever felt safe that their daily tasks couldn't be automated, given the amount of creative thinking that goes into their work. Today, journalists can tap into algorithms behind Narrative Science and Automated Insights, two firms that leverage machine learning to write an article in a matter of seconds. The first reaction from a journalist could well be one of panic—will this automated writing software take over all journalism jobs? The answer is clearly no. Journalists are still needed for tasks involving more complex stories, and robots are unable to seek out and interview people, write captivating articles, or turn a phrase in an entertaining way.

What the technology does do for journalists, however, is free them up to write more exciting and challenging pieces of journalism. If a computer program is writing the initial report on a company's end-of-year financial results, it frees the journalist covering that company to focus on analysis and follow-up articles.

The Machine Knows Best

At the top of the artificial intelligence hierarchy is IBM's Watson. Watson is an extremely advanced piece of intelligent assistant technology distinguished for being able to answer questions posed in natural language. Watson entered the public imagination in 2011, when on the quiz show *Jeopardy*, it beat two former winners to claim the first place prize of $1 million. The system's ability to take a very human question and return highly accurate and detailed answers suggests it is capable of supporting many client-facing roles. Watson is now commercially available to support AI-enabled decision making across multiple industries, with particularly noteworthy performances in medical diagnosis. When asked if Watson would soon eliminate the need for frontline call center workers, Dr. Bernard Meyerson, IBM Fellow and chief innovation officer at IBM, responds, "Think of Watson as the backup to the client facing humans. We've not yet seen as much work elimination as we are seeing client satisfaction rise." Meyerson's view is simply stated: "Human + Machine is working best at this time." However, he continues, "In the long term there is no doubt that the simplest queries will be handled by machines."[35]

Avoiding the Technology Skills Gap

For younger workers starting out in their career, how can they ensure against technologically induced unemployment? The advice from the Martin School at Oxford University is this: develop skills in creativity, social intelligence, and perception and manipulation as these will be the ones least likely to be disrupted by technology. These jobs require skills in consulting, negotiating, critical problem solving, and influencing of others. AI is not yet a match for the empathy that is so relied upon to engage and connect with our fellow workers.

Contrary to media headlines focusing on jobs that technology will eliminate, jobs are constantly being created by new technologies. Thomas Davenport, a professor at Babson College and a research fellow at the MIT Center for Digital Business, and D. J. Patil, a data scientist at Greylock Partners, declared data scientists to be one of the sexiest new job roles of the twenty-first century.[36] Separately, a World Economic Forum report on the future of jobs also identified "data analyst" as one of the two roles that stand out most, based on the frequency and consistency with which they were mentioned across industries and geographies. "The second is the specialized sales representative, as practically every industry will need to become skilled in commercializing and explaining their offerings, whether due to the innovative technical nature of the products themselves, or to their being targeted at new client types with which the company is not yet familiar, or both," the report stated.

In discussions with clients and academics, Future Workplace captured 20 job titles that now exist across multiple industries that did not exist 10 years ago (see the sidebar).

20 Jobs That Did Not Exist 10 Years Ago

Jobs Leveraging Soft Skills

1. Chief employee experience officer
2. Chief gig economy officer
3. Community manager
4. Director of corporate storytelling
5. Director of employee wellness
6. Learning experience manager
7. Manager, contingent workforce
8. Millennial generational expert
9. Social learning manager
10. Workplace strategist

Jobs Leveraging Hard Skills

1. Chief digital officer
2. Cloud computing services analyst
3. Cloud services specialist
4. Data scientist
5. IOS android developer
6. Market research data miner

7. Recruiting scrum master

8. Ruby on Rails web developer

9. Social media expert

10. User experience designer

Source: Future Workplace LLC and Digital Marketing Institute

But what does all this mean for the future workplace experience? Regardless of industry, technology is enabling, enhancing, advising, and disrupting jobs. The most important lesson for HR professionals is to stay on top of these technology shifts in order to avoid the dreaded skills gaps that leave people and technology underutilized. If employees are undertrained and unable to take full advantage of the current technologies within a company, the benefits of that technology decrease significantly, and the employee is no longer capable of achieving maximum potential at the company. If technology is underutilized, then so are employees, and this can lead to an erosion of resources, morale, jobs, and ultimately efficiency. For these reasons, it's important we keep our companies and employees on the right side of the continuous technological evolution by ensuring they are at least fully trained to work on the technologies already within our organization.

The best way to predict the future is to create one for yourself![37] We need to push ourselves to master the technologies available to us in our workplace and encourage experimentation with new technologies. To understand the impact of technology on the workplace experience for ourselves, our teams, and our organization, we must be committed to continually experiment with new technologies and ask ourselves, how can these be used to deliver a transformational workplace experience?

MY ACTION PLAN

Myself

- How could I avoid being disrupted in my job?
- Who could introduce me to new apps or technology that could I use to improve my productivity?
- What do I need to learn to be prepared for intelligent technologies in the workplace?

My Team

- What technologies and wearables should we be experimenting with next year?
- What new technologies did we pilot in our workplace in the past year and with what results?
- What intelligent technologies (apps, wearables, AI, Internet of things, machine learning) can we envision being used inside our organization and for what purpose?
- How could we push further on reshaping our work behaviors using technology?

My Organization

- How could we use technology to make better business decisions?
- What roles are prone to technological unemployment in our organization over the next two to three years?
- What roles will be enhanced or created because of the new technologies we are bringing into the organization? What new job roles will technology create in our industry?

BUILD A DATA-DRIVEN RECRUITING ECOSYSTEM **5**

> Recruiting is the canary in the coal mine; if I listen to what recruiting feels and hears in the marketplace, I will be wiser, stronger, faster, and better.
>
> —*Pat Wadors, chief human resource officer,*
> *senior vice president of*
> *Global Talent Organization, LinkedIn*

The Continuous (and Tech-Savvy) Job Seeker Emerges

Technology is rapidly eroding passive candidates. Conventional wisdom in recruiting is that a small percentage of people are active job seekers and the rest are passive candidates, defined as the pool of happily employed people who aren't looking for a new job but who might consider a new position if the right opportunity emerged. However, research from Indeed.com, the job listing site, suggests that technology has all but eliminated passive candidates. The implication is that most candidates should now be regarded as continual job searchers, always on the lookout for new gigs—whether full time or freelance. As Paul D'Arcy, senior vice president at Indeed.com, says, "The data shows that far more people are keeping their eye on jobs and applying for jobs."

The process of continual job searching has been made much easier with apps like Anthology, Jobr, and Switch, as well as proprietary apps developed by employers themselves, each designed to quickly match job seekers' skills with open positions and introduce job seekers to recruiters—all without alerting their current employers that they are considering a move.

Food and facilities services corporation Sodexo got a head start in this process four years ago, when it launched both a mobile-optimized career site and a smartphone app to pull together all the information about the company's recruiting efforts into one easy-to-access place. Since then, Sodexo's, recruiting efforts have increasingly focused on leveraging mobile devices and apps. It was one of the first companies in its industry to mobilize its online presence and offer the ability to apply for jobs directly from a mobile app, Sodexo invested in mobile recruiting as a direct response to the changing ways in which we all use mobile devices. The Sodexo careers job app has become a platform for job seekers to learn about the company's corporate culture and career opportunities, connect with recruiters, as well as search and apply at their convenience, wherever and whenever they are ready—all on the go.

The results stemming from the careers job app, as recently measured, are impressive: 35 percent of job traffic from potential new hires came from the mobile platform. In the first year, Sodexo's mobile-app downloads totaled 15,000, leading to over 2,000 new job candidates and 141 actual new hires, at the same time saving the company $300,000 in job board postings. Well over 700 new hires at Sodexo originated from mobile devices.

Recruiting is also taking a page from dating apps where swiping right has become shorthand for liking someone. Swiping right is revolutionizing the way companies find talent. As a generalized example of how these job seeking apps work, users complete a short profile in which they are asked to answer questions on topics such as "Which companies in your field do you admire?" and "What is the next job title and salary you are looking for?" Next, the app examines the answers—looking also at job seekers' more extensive profiles on LinkedIn or other websites—and they match the data with job descriptions placed by recruiters and hiring managers. The best matches are the ones most closely aligning with the individual's qualifications and salary requirements. These matches appear as text alerts on the job seeker's mobile devices as they become available.

What do apps that work like this imply for the future of recruiting? One answer is that mobile is becoming the dominant way to search for a new job. According to research conducted by Census Wide, on behalf of Indeed.com,

65 percent of people are using their mobile devices to do just that. Moreover, this trend isn't isolated to younger job seekers. While 77 percent of people aged 16 to 34 use a mobile device in their job search, 72 percent of people aged 35 to 44, 54 percent of people aged 44 to 54, and 35 percent of people aged 55 and over also use mobile devices to search for jobs.[1] Second, with the job search process now (literally) in our pocket, job seekers can expect relevant jobs to find them via outreach through the same apps. Anthology, Jobr, and Switch represent massive changes in how employers can find talent and how easily job seekers can connect to their next opportunity.

Our own Future Workplace Forecast identified the top seven recruitment methods used by HR leaders and hiring managers both in the United States and internationally. These are outlined in Figure 5.1. In the United States, the method expected to increase the most over the next three years is the use of mobile apps for recruiting. Outside the United States, social media is the top recruiting method expected in coming years. Both findings point to how mobile recruiting and social media recruiting are on the rise with employers.

What's also interesting is that our research found a decrease of 3 percent in usage of professional recruitment firms in the United States and flat usage internationally over the next three years. This contributes to yet another shift: mobile and social technologies will put a significant amount of information about employers directly into the hands of continual job seekers. For employers, this means access to vast quantities of data about prospective new hires. These signals imply employers have a better opportunity to identify the best suited candidates and employees can find a match for their skills with an employer.

Diving deeper into how companies are tapping social media for recruiting, a separate Jobvite Recruiter Nation survey of human resources leaders and hiring managers illustrates, as shown in Figure 5.2, the various ways companies are using social channels, with Linkedin, Facebook, Twitter, Glassdoor, and YouTube being the top five platforms for recruiting on social media. Interestingly, Snapchat, a photo messaging app now used by over 200 million users on a monthly basis, is making headway among employers as a tool for building a company's employer brand in the recruiting process. For employ-

Figure 5.1   Top recruitment methods

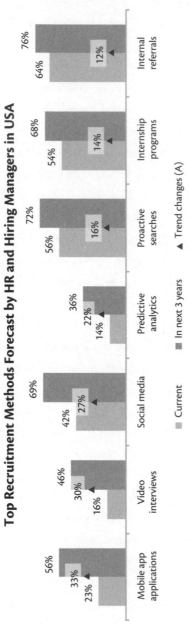

Top Recruitment Methods Forecast by HR and Hiring Managers in USA

Mobile app applications — 56%, 33%, 23%

Video interviews — 46%, 30%, 16%

Social media — 69%, 42%, 27%

Predictive analytics — 36%, 22%, 14%

Proactive searches — 72%, 56%, 16%

Internship programs — 68%, 54%, 14%

Internal referrals — 76%, 64%, 12%

■ Current   ■ In next 3 years   ▲ Trend changes (A)

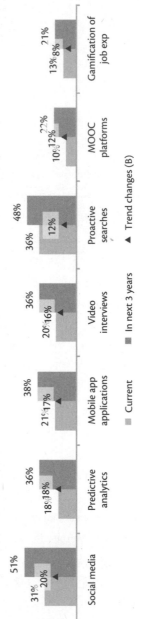

Top Recruitment Methods Forecast by HR and Hiring Managers Outside USA

Social media — 51%, 31%, 20%

Predictive analytics — 36%, 18%, 18%

Mobile app applications — 38%, 21%, 17%

Video interviews — 36%, 20%, 16%

Proactive searches — 48%, 36%, 12%

MOOC platforms — 22%, 10%, 12%

Gamification of job exp — 21%, 13%, 8%

■ Current   ■ In next 3 years   ▲ Trend changes (B)

Source: Future Workplace

Figure 5.2   Recruiting on social media

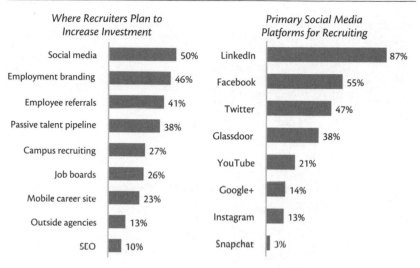

Source: The Jobvite Recruiter Nation Survey, 2015

ers, Snapchat allows a company to give candidates access to live events (like an industry expo or your company's sports day) or to post new job openings to the company's Snapchat followers first. It is simple, highly personalized, and adds value to the recruiting process. In addition, applicant tracking systems from providers like Boston-based Workable are now capable of automatically aggregating links to candidates' social media profiles, providing employers with a fuller view into all of their candidates' social media activity to help source passive candidates and pre-screen job applicants.

Now let's turn to the recruiting ecosystem, as depicted in Figure 5.3. This recruiting ecosystem intentionally builds the employer brand, uses analytics to vet candidates, leverages employees to pursue referrals and communicates in a transparent fashion every step along the candidate experience.

The Recruiting Ecosystem: Manage Your Employer Brand

As companies search social media sites for potential new hires, they must also realize job seekers are doing the same thing in search of potential new

Figure 5.3   *The recruiting ecosystem*

Manage Your Employer Brand	Intentionally build the employer brand
Train Before Hiring	Gain early insights to vet candidates
Use Smart Sourcing	Use analytics for targeted reach-outs
Tap Employees for Referrals	Leverage existing connections for high quality referrals
Be Transparent with Job Seekers	Encourage sharing on multiple touch points

Source: Future Workplace

employers. Building a strong employer brand, one that communicates the tenets of your workplace culture, is critical in this increasingly transparent job search process.

Your employer brand is essentially what your business is all about, the "what and why of the things we do at this company." Organizations that build strong employer brands and focus on culture become magnets for continual job seekers.

GE has transformed its employer brand within the last five years. In 2011, Jeff Immelt, chairman and CEO, made a big bet on the launch of GE Digital to create a cloud-based operating system for the industrial Internet and reposition GE as a digital industrial company. In 2015, GE earned $5 billion in software revenue, and GE Digital has grown from 100 people in 2011 to more than 20,000 in 2016. Hiring digital talent has become a key focus for the company. Leading this effort is Amber Grewal, global head of Talent Acquisition for GE Digital. To help build its employer branding campaign, GE unveiled a campaign called "What's the Matter with Owen" to create a new employer brand, one that goes beyond being a 124-year-old company to one that is revolutionizing how planes, trains, and hospitals operate. The campaign focuses on Owen, a programmer who has just taken a job at GE Digital and explains why to his friends and family. The videos on YouTube have generated more than 400,000 views to date and the Owen campaign has been credited with an eightfold increase in job applications to GE.

Beyond the Owen campaign, GE Digital is applying software development methods to recruitment to create a new job role known as *recruiting scrum master*. In rugby, *scrum* is short for *scrummage* and refers to a method of restarting a play, where players pack closely together with their heads down and attempt to gain possession of the ball. Similarly, scrum methods are at the heart of implementing an agile recruiting model. This model incorporates the scrum methods used in software development, infusing speed and managing unpredictability in the recruiting process.

Grewal and her team created the role of recruiting scrum master to apply many of the scrum techniques to recruiting employees by breaking down the massive hiring needs into incremental and iterative steps. Through conducting daily scrum meetings, recruiters are able to deliver talent needs within 2 to 6 weeks versus the average of 10 to 15 weeks. The recruiting scrum master also supports and coaches an entire recruiting team.

This approach helped GE Digital recruiters engage and connect with prospective employees—using technology hackathons to source candidates, then connecting with them via open-source code sites on GitHub or interacting with them through gamification. GE Digital has been able to reduce the time to hire by 70 percent for in-demand roles in software engineering and commercial software sales.

How do we know the employer brand is so important? Job seekers tell us so. Recent research conducted by the Talent Board finds 41 percent of all job seekers search for information about a company's culture and brand before they apply.[2] After all, this is where the job seeker starts, by using apps like Anthology, Jobr, and Switch, or by going to sites such as Fortune's Best Places to Work list, Glassdoor's Employee Choice Award, and LinkedIn's Most In-Demand Employers list. They also search online resources to read reviews and ratings about other job seekers' experiences with a given company. "Candidate loyalty to a brand can be a huge boost if people are willing to recommend their friends apply to the same company," writes Emily Smykal at Jibe, a company creating data-driven solutions for applicant-tracking systems, regarding Net Promoter scoring.[3] "Straightforwardly asking candidates a question like, 'Based on your experience here, how likely are you to refer others to apply?' is now recognized as the primary way to measure the performance of the candidate experience."

Another method of managing the employer brand is to create content that conveys the organization's culture, says Dan Black, the Americas director of recruiting at EY. The company pursued 13,000 new hires in 2015.

"Online video is kind of where it's at," Black says. "We have a whole platform built around being able to see and hear our employees. So that has been big. The other thing that we've experimented with is video job descriptions. We ran a pilot this past year to say, OK, when you're looking for a staff consultant position, in addition to reading the specs, the skills required, the background, you can also click a video and see the hiring manager, and hear what he or she is looking for—hear it in his or her own words. If you are looking to be a manager, you can get a video of an existing manager. You want to know what the job is? You can read about it, but also here's what I do. I am in this job."

For Black, the process is also about introducing the recruiting brand in whatever digital spaces job seekers choose to frequent. "It's not just social media," he says. "It's 'where are they?' And they are on social media a lot, but they're also in a lot of other places. Hence, we advertise on Spotify and on ESPN, because that's where students spend their time." The idea behind this content is, "Can we create a viable set of media [impressions], through which we can draw people back into the mother ship?"

These examples from GE Digital and EY further reinforce how technology is dramatically changing the ways employers and job seekers find each other. How HR recruits HR is also shifting. New roles in HR are increasingly being filled with a more diverse pool, which include those with expertise in computer science and software engineering, as well as consumer marketing and video production. As recruiting becomes data driven and uses new methods to find the best talent, the mix of professionals in HR is evolving to also include many different non-traditional HR specialties.

The Recruiting Ecosystem: Train Before Hiring

Job seekers and recruiters are incorporating training before hiring into the recruiting process. Algorithms are helping recruiters to create and refine job seeker skill sets. Data analytics also helps employers better understand what in-house skills are needed to develop their company's teams, achieve their organization's goals, and successfully fill open positions.

An interesting data-driven approach is under way at Aquent, a creative staffing agency that recently launched a MOOC program it calls Gymnasium. At Aquent, Gymnasium draws on the connotation of the gym as a place for fun, applying it to digital training via a series of "workouts." The way the program works, with its approximately 56,000 registered users, is to match the employee skill sets that employers say they need with classes offered by Gymnasium. Then Aquent matches standout students with job opportunities. In areas such as Writing for Web and Mobile and Query Building Blocks, the activity and results generated by Gymnasium's students become analyzable data that the company uses to make empirically sound referrals for both sides of the employer–job seeker equation.

"We pick the courses very specifically based on data that we can see, in terms of evaluating skills gaps, both quantitatively and qualitatively," says Andrew Miller, program director of Gymnasium at Aquent. "We can also see in our own job data what roles are being sought at different levels, salary groupings, titles, discrete skill sets, responsibilities, names of software packages, and even certain design activities."

"Our students tell us what courses we should offer, as well," Miller continues. "It's not all that surprising that the courses that they want us to offer are the courses that the clients are suggesting we should offer."

On a qualitative level, talent-acquisition teams can also count on Aquent's interviewing staff to thoroughly vet candidate students, confirming they not only have the skill sets but also demonstrate the work styles, business ethics, proclivities, and affinities to match their online-course performance.

Aquent is doing all this with real-world practitioners as instructors rather than college lecturers. Following its first year of offering a range of Gymnasium MOOCs, the company saw a 10-times return on the program's investment.

As Aquent demonstrates, training before hiring transforms employers' understanding of job seekers. It is a nuanced, empirical, and newly holistic approach. Using training to identify the best talent is the type of smart sourcing that will gain headway as more companies leverage MOOCs to source the right type of candidate for the organization's skill needs.

The Recruiting Ecosystem: Use Smart Sourcing

Smart sourcing is becoming a crucial way for companies to find talent and predict their success on the job. Identifying and amplifying skill sets among promising job seekers is one aspect of a broad and proactive data-driven approach to smart sourcing. Two companies that are using people analytics in new ways to source talent include LinkedIn and JetBlue. In both cases, smart sourcing starts with data to find optimal candidates—whether the candidate sought is a software engineer or a flight attendant.

Brendan Browne, vice president of Global Talent Acquisition at LinkedIn, works with his team to continually develop and fine-tune the company's data-driven emphasis on the value of internal employee referrals. One element of focus for LinkedIn, Browne says, is a search for job seeker signals.

"The signals I'm talking about [include the job seeker] publishing data that shows that he or she is a smart, thoughtful person around a key skill such as solving infrastructure problems," says Browne. "Then I examine the data and ask, Does the job seeker follow my company on LinkedIn, or the one that I'm recruiting for, online? Does she follow companies that would be a proxy for mine; is she smart enough to be following really great companies? And probably the most overlooked easy to find signal is, Does the job seeker know someone of influence at my company—someone I know, from whom I could get a lead on recruiting them?"

In other words, recruiting in the data-driven ecosystem is not just about grinding large quantities of data in pursuit of potential matches; it's about refining analytical efforts so they generate the best matches. For example, analytics can show not only that a job seeker has 500-plus followers on the LinkedIn platform, but also that a significant percentage of those followers are deeply connected to the kind of position that the company is looking to fill in the first place. Data analytics can next show an even more granular subset of matches that represent just the job seekers who have one-to-one connections with established employees of influence at the recruiting organization—internal referrals to whom talent acquisition can reach out.

Browne says the results of putting such strategies to work are measurable and significant. To follow up on the above example with which he started, response rates during LinkedIn's targeted search for an infrastructure engineer tripled thanks to the company's data-driven pilot program. Furthermore, although early iterations of the LinkedIn approach conducted most of this work in a manual way, now the process is increasingly automated. LinkedIn recruiters utilize a new feature in LinkedIn Recruiter, called Spotlights. With Spotlights, recruiters can surface much of the sought-after results without needing to "hand-crank" the analytics each time.

"When you run a search today for infrastructure engineers, Spotlights buckets them by a number of the signals I talked about," Browne says. "If there are 250 infrastructure engineers, our data shows what percentage are connected to your employees—meaning they know someone at the company. It also shows what percentage of those job seekers you interviewed before. These details drastically change who you go after, and why . . . and now the data is organized automatically with the click of a button."

Of course, clicking the button still requires making strategic choices. Recruiters leverage tools such as LinkedIn Recruiter, but this is the first step in the process. Recruiters must next create strategies for reaching out to candidates based on what the data tells them. Given a short list of job seekers, these can be arranged on a two-by-two axis with quality on one axis and affinity on the other as shown in Figure 5.4.

Figure 5.4   *"Smart sourcing" prospects*

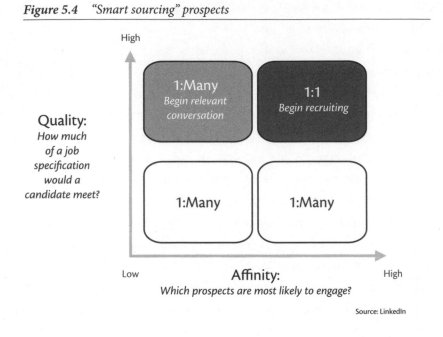

Browne suggests a clearly segmented sourcing strategy differs depending on the signal data: "High quality candidates with high affinity to the organization and [thus] most likely to engage would be targeted with focused, personalized, warm introductions—with them, the recruitment process gets fully underway.

"In contrast, candidates with low affinity to the organization and therefore less likely to initially engage would receive carefully crafted content—perhaps a white paper, with a note suggesting the material sent along is relevant and interesting to the job seeker's current work. Outreach of this second type begins an ongoing conversation, bringing the candidate into the company's talent community and keeping the prospect aware of the employer brand. This approach creates opportunities to develop the relationship into a potential hire down the road."

Whether it is LinkedIn's databases or a similar highly structured set of information, the key to data analytics in recruiting—and elsewhere, for that matter—is not simply to aggregate large quantities of job seeker data. Successful talent acquisition depends on a concentration of curated and structured data. This data is coupled, in LinkedIn's case, with the aforementioned two-prong approach: on the one hand, high-touch, one-to-one outreach and, on the other hand, consumer marketing–style strategies to other candidates in the mix until they're ready for next steps.

Recruiting leaders need to shift their mindset to one of leading with data analytics. Applying data analytics to selecting the best talent is what Andy Biga does in his role as director of Talent Acquisition at JetBlue. As Biga explains the importance of finding optimal flight attendants, he says, "You can imagine how important the role is to the company and to our brand. They are literally the face of the brand, and are able to change a regular experience with us to—hopefully—an amazing experience."

JetBlue receives approximately 25,000 applications each year for the job of a flight attendant and hires 1,000. "Initially, we thought the key characteristic of a flight attendant was 'being nice.'" Last year, using people analytics and customer data in a study conducted with Professor Adam Grant of the Wharton Business School, the airline found that "being helpful trumps being nice. Being helpful even balances out the effect of somebody who is *not* so nice."[4]

Biga goes on to say, "In addition to being helpful, our data showed us the importance of being a problem solver in this role. This is one of the critical characteristics we now look for in a prospective flight attendant." The results of applying people analytics to finding optimal talent have been impressive. According to Biga, these results include the ability of a new hire to go through a rigorous flight training program, higher employee engagement and retention after hiring, and a 12 percent decrease in total absences. Attendance is critical in the air travel industry, since a crew member's last-minute absence can mean a flight delay or cancellation.

The Recruiting Ecosystem: Tap Employees for Referrals

As Brendan Browne of LinkedIn points out in the previous section, quality referrals are key to the recruiting ecosystem. Further evidence indicates that internal referrals in particular are a significant factor in recruiting success:

- Our Future Workplace Forecast showed that 64 percent of recruiters polled plan to tap internal employees for referrals. Over the next three years, this number is expected to jump to 76 percent (as highlighted in Figure 5.1).
- When it comes to the quality of hires stemming from internal referrals, 88 percent of employers surveyed in a recent CareerBuilder study say inside recommendations rank above all other source types.[5]
- In the area of employee fit and retention, an iCIMS Hire Expectations Institute study finds 60 percent of internally referred job seekers make strong matches with company culture and 59 percent stay with the organization longer than other types of hires.[6]

With the value of internal referrals in mind, the question becomes how does a company tap internal referrals and importantly how does using this process impact the diversity of the workforce?

As a case in point, data is driving employee referrals at Red Hat. The software company's recruiting profile is highly active—approximately 8,300 people across 80 offices worldwide, 700 net new hires in 2014, and about 1,000 new hires in 2015. With such a burgeoning workforce, Red Hat incentivizes employees to participate in identifying the best new talent via its Red Hat Ambassadors program.[7] The Red Hat Ambassadors program pursues a gamified system of rewards.[8] Every referral that leads to a successful hire advances the employee ambassador in rank and confers tiered bonuses and prizes. And it works. According to L. J. Brock, vice president of the Global Talent Group and People Infrastructure at Red Hat, approximately 50 percent of the newest employees were invited to join the company because of internal referrals.

Here's where technology comes into the picture: Red Hat is using data science and predictive analytics to further amplify its ambassador referrals and recruiting. "Now our team can use multiple systems," Brock says. "They can look objectively at the data and say, here's somebody Red Hat should really target—they look relevant, they have great skills. And then they can go back to LinkedIn and cross-reference that assessment and say, 'Oh, somebody inside the company already knows them: let's have this person reach out so that we're getting that first-person benefit of a referral, and we're driving up our response rate.'"

Furthermore, a Red Hat Ambassador can proactively recommend somebody, and the organization can use data analytics to inspect that recommendation, looking for other connections among job seeker profiles. A more complete, 360-degree profile of the candidate comes into focus. Data fuels referral opportunities; referrals create starting points for new data-driven searches. It is an especially powerful scenario for Red Hat, given that the company is often seeking highly specialized talent and its job seeker population may well be moving within a concentrated network of colleagues and contacts.

"The universe we target is more networked all the time, and one overarching connection that we've found using analytics," says Brock, "is that everybody we hire is almost, without exception, connected at some degree to someone already working here."

The results of all this analysis, Brock says, are also quantifiable.

"Our data is generally showing us that people we hire from [internal] referrals are more engaged, they're staying longer, and their performance is very strong," says Brock. "Anecdotally, I think you can chalk that up to employee advocacy. It's great to have somebody in there who's giving you an insight into what life is like and helping you make sure that Red Hat is the right match for you."

As data analytics glean new insights about how pools of job seekers intersect with internal referrals, companies will need to leverage technology to also broaden their talent diversity even further.

"We are well aware at Red Hat that we don't want to just keep replicating the same employee population," Brock says. "So the next generation analytics and predictive tools need to help individuals make their referral populations more diverse than they naturally are."

Going forward, this means Red Hat's use of data analytics will need to generate recommendations for new contacts and networks that its employees can explore so they can grow their own personal and professional networks—and the potential of future internal referrals. As they do so, whether Red Hat turns to data to find the best new candidates or encounters new job seekers right from the organization, the referral pool will become larger, more diverse, and perpetually increased in data-validated ways.

Employee Alumni Networks Tap Former Employees for Referrals

It used to be that when employees left a company, managers would wish them well, and both parties would simply move on. However, the employee life cycle now includes tapping alumni and engaging them as ambassadors of the organization. To address this changing landscape, a growing number of organizations are proactive in reaching out to former employees and creating corporate alumni networks.

Many companies in the professional service and technology fields like Accenture, Deloitte, KPMG, and McKinsey, to name just a few, are creating the corporate version of a university alumni function. In fact, many university alumni functions could learn from what the corporate alumni networks are doing to nurture and build better long-term relationships. According to Katya V. Meza-Doyle, director of Global Alumni Relations at Accenture, "The benefits of the Accenture Alumni Network range from building a sense of community, networking, recruiting former employees as potential boomerang employees, engaging alumni to be brand ambassadors and of course, business development."

Clearly, employees want to stay in touch with their former employer. LinkedIn now hosts over 118,000 corporate alumni groups, including 98 percent of the Fortune 500. Yet surprisingly, most of these alumni groups have little to no relationship with their former companies.

In fact, the majority of alumni networks that do exist are run completely independently from the company. A study from the University of Twente in the Netherlands showed that while only 15 percent of the companies surveyed had formal corporate alumni networks, another 67 percent had employees who independently organized informal alumni groups. Think about that—alumni want to connect so eagerly that they are spending their own time and money to set up these networks.

This should be a wake-up call for companies to explore if there is a volunteer alumni network already in existence and to take the leadership of this and use it for the company's strategic benefit.

The Accenture Alumni Network is an example of a well-run and tightly aligned initiative. The Accenture Alumni Network, created in the late 1980s, now has over 150,000 active members in 38 countries hosting an average of 150 events, virtual and in person, annually. (Disclosure: Jeanne Meister is an Accenture alum and member of this network.) The network's vision is simply stated: "Once Accenture, Always Accenture." As the company has expanded in scope and geography, so has the alumni network, which added a number of interesting features such as allowing Accenture clients to post open positions on the network and exploring a return to Accenture by working with local recruiting teams. According to a study of 1,800 HR leaders, 600 people managers, and 600 employees entitled "Corporate Culture and Boomerang Employees" conducted by Kronos and WorkplaceTrends.com, a subsidiary of Future Workplace, 76 percent of HR leaders indicated they are more accepting of hiring boomerang employees today, while nearly 40 percent of employees would consider returning to their former employer. Research by the Society for Human Resource Management has shown that individuals who return to previous employers cost about half as much to bring on board as new hires. These boomerang employees have specialized expertise and inside knowledge of an organization's culture and values, enabling them to make an immediate contribution.[9] One of the biggest benefits we see, says Accenture's Meza-Doyle, is to build global brand ambassadors who understand our core values and culture and are viewed as objective third parties for referrals and connections to new business opportunities. We want them to have a lifelong affiliation to Accenture."

The Recruiting Ecosystem: Be Transparent with Job Seekers

There are two types of transparency that job seekers look for in the workplace: first, potential new hires want to work in a culture that is transparent; second, job seekers want a talent-acquisition process that is transparent.

Ideally, these elements of transparency should form a through line, a complete interview-to-exit experience of open communication and frankness about salary, benefits, promotions, career development, company culture, and the expectations business leaders set for employees around growth, behavior, and work style. In fact, the majority of job seekers today demand this type of transparent candidate experience: a recent 15Five survey of full-time employees found that 81 percent preferred to join companies that promoted transparency as a value in the organization.[10]

Furthermore, evidence tells us that tech-savvy organizations want much the same thing. According to the Future Workplace Forecast, organizations using the latest social, mobile, and predictive analytic tools are more likely than their counterparts to value the power of transparency.

One organization furthering transparency in the workplace is Glassdoor. Since its launch in 2008, Glassdoor has created and expanded its database of company and CEO reviews to the extent that, as of 2015, more than a third of Fortune 500 companies use the service.[11]

Glassdoor works with the help of user-generated data. Current and former employees of organizations fill out an online review template, describing in their own words the pros and cons of working for a given company, its salary structure, its interview process, interview questions, and benefits package. They can also offer written advice to senior management. Job seekers then use the Glassdoor website to search for these user-supplied details and reviews about the companies to which they want to apply. Enter an organization's name and location, and the site matches the query to its resident data. The results are organized somewhat like what users find at sites such as Yelp. In Glassdoor's case, the company's recommendation rate and CEO approval score are given as a percentage. It costs job seekers nothing to use Glassdoor; the company makes its money by charging recruiters for job postings. Some 3,000 employers sign up monthly for the opportunity.[12]

For the job seeker, Glassdoor's aggregation of data about company offerings and employee experiences is central to the concept of transparency. Says Kirsten Davidson, head of Employer Branding at Glassdoor, "Transparency allows the employer to hire people who are better positioned to come on board and do what they need to do. The more transparent a company is about what's good and what's bad, the more open the job seeker's eyes are, the more they can see what the challenges are in front of them and how willing they are to take those on."

A key result, Davidson notes, is that prospects who use Glassdoor to research a company and then apply to the organization are less likely to be surprised by information during the process—this is a powerful result, because surprise creates the risk a candidate will withdraw an application.

"A great employer brand not only articulates who you are, but it also articulates who you're not," she says. "And it helps to more clearly reach the people you want to reach without pulling in people who get three interviews in and say, 'This really is not right for me.' You want to be able to have those people self-select out at the very start."

Think of Glassdoor this way: it's Yelp for C-level executives. And while today people can rate a company's CEO on the site, services such as Glassdoor are well positioned to eventually allow employees to review all types of C-level executives. Imagine interviewing for a new job, one in which you'd report to the company's chief human resource officer. Your first step might be to see the rating and comments regarding the CHRO's willingness to be a people developer and how future focused he or she is within the company—and industry!

So what can an HR leader do to create a strategy recognizing the growing importance of Glassdoor among job seekers? First, HR should build Glassdoor into some key HR processes. For example, encourage employees just finishing their first 90 days to go on the company's Glassdoor page and share their feedback about the company. Next, be responsive to both positive and negative comments about the company. This will show current and prospective employees your company reads these comments and reflects on them. Finally, create a process to regularly share Glassdoor data with the entire HR team, business leaders, and employees. This will likely inform key processes such your employee culture survey, how your company sources new employees, develops them, and engages them. Lastly, recognize that Glassdoor and other employer rating sites are now part of a prospective new employee's research on your employer brand. You can shape what they will read about you.

In addition to analyzing data on Glassdoor, IBM is leveraging its Millennial Corps, the IBM employee affinity group for millennials and those with a millennial mindset. Deb Butters, former vice president, Human Resources IBM shares how IBM taps its Millennial Corps (the IBM Millennial Employee Affinity group highlighted in Rule #7) for advice on how to improve the recruiting process. "For example, last year, we asked this group four simple, yet powerful questions about candidate perceptions during recruiting and we took their guidance to make enhancements." The four questions are:

- If you had 30 seconds to sell your friends on why they should work for IBM, what would you say?
- What programs or support should IBM provide to help you build your career?
- What can a manager do to make you more engaged and excited about working for IBM?
- What manager actions or behaviors inspire you to perform your best?

The feedback pointed to new directions IBM could take during the recruiting process, such as focusing more on storytelling, hearing firsthand from recent IBM hires, and creating a differentiated value proposition for each employee segment. Campaigns like #IBMTechTalk and #InsideStory were the direct result of these employee listening campaigns. With this kind of information at the fingertips of the recruiting teams, IBM is able to create stronger messaging to prospective employees.

The intersection of data analytics and talent acquisition provides recruiters with the opportunity to gain deeper insights about their prospective new hires and similarly job candidates to tap into a wealth of data about a prospective employer. Ultimately this level of transparency ensures a solid match both at the point of hire and throughout the future that employees and employers build upon together.

But how do these changes in recruiting impact the role of recruiters? Jill Larson, SVP of Strategic Talent Acquisition, People Planning and Services HR at Cisco, believes "The relationship with the hiring manager is the number one driver and four times more important than any other performance driver." For Larson, she sees four new capabilities recruiters must build in their skill set, namely, be data driven, possess a deep organizational knowledge of the business and industry they operate in, understand the growing importance of employer rating sites, and importantly commit to become a brand ambassador for the company. Taken together, these new capabilities are needed to transform the role of a recruiter from filling job specs to becoming a talent advisor.

MY ACTION PLAN

Myself

- What skills do I need to develop now to be a next generation recruiter?
- How do I develop these skills?
- Which industries and companies are on a path to developing next generation recruiters?

My Team

- What components of the recruiting ecosystem does our team excel in?
- What areas do we need to develop?
- What new skills does my team need to use a data-driven approach to recruiting?
- Are we fully tapping current employees for recommendations?

My Organization

- What key business results can be realized if we improve our recruiting process?
- What are our competitors doing when it comes to sourcing top talent?
- How could we get to the top job seekers first?
- If our organization wants to train before it hires new employees, what new and innovative approaches could we implement?

EMBRACE ON-DEMAND LEARNING

6

Using Learning to Prepare Employees for the Future

AT&T, nostalgically known as "Ma Bell," goes back under a succession of names to when Alexander Graham Bell invented the telephone in 1876. Today Randall Stephenson, AT&T's chairman and chief executive, is reinventing the company to compete in the global marketplace. For the company to survive, Stephenson believes he needs to embed a culture of continual learning. He has gone on record saying that AT&T employees should be spending 5 to 10 hours a week learning online, or they "will obsolete themselves with technology."[2]

What we are seeing is the ultimate connection between learning and earning where the development of new technical skills such as machine learning and app development will lead to higher-paying jobs at AT&T.

Learning at the Speed of Business: Employees Take Charge of Their Own Learning

The future of learning requires reimagining how we help learners, learn at the speed of business (Figure 6.1). A focus on continual learning is the answer not only for companies like AT&T that are upskilling their workers but also for workers themselves who want to take a more proactive approach to career

Figure 6.1   *Learning at the speed of business*

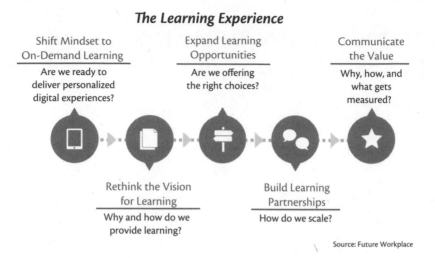

The Learning Experience

Shift Mindset to On-Demand Learning
Are we ready to deliver personalized digital experiences?

Expand Learning Opportunities
Are we offering the right choices?

Communicate the Value
Why, how, and what gets measured?

Rethink the Vision for Learning
Why and how do we provide learning?

Build Learning Partnerships
How do we scale?

Source: Future Workplace

development. What we are seeing is a movement for workers to become serial learners as one way to avert technological unemployment, defined as the loss of jobs caused by technology disruptions. Helping learners learn at the speed of business requires revisiting every aspect of the learner experience while scaling and measuring differently.

Serial learners possess some of the same qualities as serial entrepreneurs. They are intellectually curious, not satisfied with business as usual, always reaching beyond their current role to learn something new, make connections out of seemingly unrelated topics, and seek out different networks and experiences. The concept of serial learning was brought to life by Chess Grandmaster and marital artist Josh Waitzkin on the Tim Ferris podcast. Waitzkin identifies how to become a serial learner, namely to allow space in your day for the development of creative ideas, plan out your learning, think carefully about what you need to learn and when you can do this, and do small experiments with big potential payoffs that give you an opportunity to learn and test out your ideas.[3]

What does this serial learning mean for employees, organizations, and their learning leaders? Employees must "own their learning" and see the connection between learning and career advancement. Companies must embrace on-demand learning by offering employees a marketplace of learning opportunities including a mix of all types of learning, integrating TED Talks, podcasts, MOOCs, and other forms of informal learning plus the company's own customized development programs. As the pace and rate of change accelerate, companies will no longer be solely responsible for providing all the learning for their employees. Instead, employees will shift to accessing on-demand learning to expand their current skills and prepare for the next set of skills needed in the marketplace. We are finding that what Louis Ross, former vice chairman of the Ford Motor Company, said more than 20 years ago rings truer today than ever: "In your career, knowledge is like milk," says Ross. "It has a shelf life stamped right on the carton. . . . If you're not replacing everything you know by then, your career is going to turn sour fast."[4]

When futurist Buckminster Fuller created the "knowledge doubling curve," he noticed that until 1900, human knowledge doubled approximately every century. By the end of World War II knowledge was doubling every 25 years. Today various types of knowledge have exponential rates of growth—for example, nanotechnology knowledge is doubling every two years. On average, human knowledge is doubling every 13 months. But when we think about intelligent products like those built around the Internet of things, IBM is forecasting that this type of knowledge is doubling every 12 hours![5]

Knowledge doubling every 12 hours. Think about it. Are companies and their learning leaders ready for this brave new world? Despite the urgency of the need, companies are facing a digital transformation of the learning function. Research from Deloitte shows less than 25 percent of companies feel comfortable with today's digital learning environment.[6]

Shift Mindset to On-Demand Learning

The education marketplace is going through a seismic shift. The size of the education market in the United States, as estimated by GSV (Global Silicon Valley), is $1.6 trillion. This is projected to grow to $2.0 trillion in 2020. When the cumulative five-year growth of the education market between 2015 and 2020 is examined by sector, we see that:

- The lifelong learning sector is projected to grow 30 percent (composed of companies enabling MOOCs and other differentiated learning experiences such as CAEL, Degreed, Grovo, Edcast, Lynda, General Assembly, Iron Yard, NovoEd, and Pathgather.
- Postsecondary education is projected to grow 15 percent.
- Corporate learning firms are projected to grow 6 percent.

It is no surprise that greater growth is expected for the lifelong learning sector, given the rate and pace of change that companies and their workers are experiencing today.

As we move to 2020, we foresee employees selecting employers based upon the breadth, depth, and access to lifelong learning and career development. The transformation of learning from designing formal training to creating on-demand learning experiences requires leaders of corporate learning to shift their mindset, budget, and resources from developing content to identifying learning from a number of open sources. This move from training to on-demand learning is depicted in Figure 6.2.

A company's commitment to provide learning of all types is increasingly important to attracting and keeping top talent. The most telling barometer

Figure 6.2   *From training to on-demand learning*

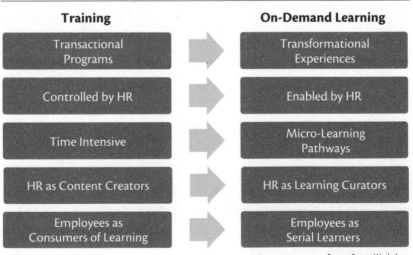

Source: Future Workplace

of this importance can be seen in the results of Universum's global survey of 49,000 generation Zers (born between 1994 and 2009) from 47 countries. This survey found 15 percent of generation Zers would consider joining the work-force instead of getting a formal education at a college or university. What's more, 60 percent say they welcome getting information on the type of learn-ing that companies offer to those with no university degree![7]

Rethink the Vision for Learning

Best-of-breed learning leaders should consider themselves intrapreneurs who run the business of learning inside their organization. They must have an understanding of where the company's business is going and what mix of skills and capabilities employees need to reach the strategic goals of the orga-nization. For HR and learning leaders, this starts with creating a compelling vision of why and how a company is providing learning to its workers.

A global research survey conducted by PwC entitled "Millennials at Work, Reshaping the Workplace," asked 4,364 millennials from 75 countries about what three benefits they would most value from an employer. Not surpris-ingly, a company's investment in training and development was ranked num-ber one, with flexible working hours and cash bonuses ranked numbers two and three, respectively.[8]

Some companies, like adidas Group, with more than 51,000 global employees with an average age under 30 years, recognize that learning must be engaging, relevant, and fun. The adidas Group vision statement for learn-ing is simple: "You Learn, We Grow." This shows the the power of a vision statement that is inspiring, memorable, and concise. As Christian Kuhna, director of HR, Strategy, and Think Tank for Innovation at adidas, says, "We are intent on going beyond designing distinct learning programs to creating consistent and compelling learning experiences." The vision of "You Learn, We Grow," requires adidas leaders to become learners and teachers and embed learning, teaching, and sharing into all their interactions with team members. The learning team at adidas recognizes that millennials, who have been raised on YouTube, Pinterest, and Instagram, require a heavy dose of video, edgy headlines, and infographics to get their attention. The adidas Group challenge to employees is quite provocative with its headline, "If You Think You're So Smart, Why Don't You Share Your Knowledge?" This headline reads less like a corporate learning brochure and more like a campaign created by Vice Media, the hip online go-to news site.

The lesson for learning leaders is this: rethink why the investment in learning is so important and develop a concise and memorable vision that resonates with your company culture. Perhaps the best word to describe all this is *exhilarating*, or that mix of terror and excitement that motivates us to action!

Create Cross-Functional Alliances and Engage Marketing as a Partner

For learning leaders, bringing a new vision to reality requires developing deep partnerships across the organization. Learning is now very much a team sport. No longer can corporate learning operate as a silo, independently designing and developing learning programs. Instead, learning leaders must realize every employee is a potential customer and every customer is a potential employee. This blurs the lines among learning, communications, employee engagement, and marketing. Lincoln Financial Group has taken the bold step of combining HR, learning and development, and marketing into one function reporting to the chief human resource officer. Lincoln Financial Group's EVP and CHRO Lisa Buckingham sees not only a blurring of the lines between HR and marketing but a mandate to combine both functions. This integrated function oversees Lincoln's brand, enterprise communications, and corporate social responsibility activities, as well as the entire suite of HR functions including compensation, benefits, talent development, diversity and inclusion, HRIS, and talent acquisition. A view of the combined functions at Lincoln Financial Group can be seen in Figure 6.3.

The rationale for this is shared by Buckingham, who says, "I believe we need to create one consistent employer brand value proposition, internally and externally." One of the key objectives for both CHRO Buckingham and the company's former chief marketing officer, Jamie DePeau,[9] is the ability to

Figure 6.3   *Combined HR and marketing functions*

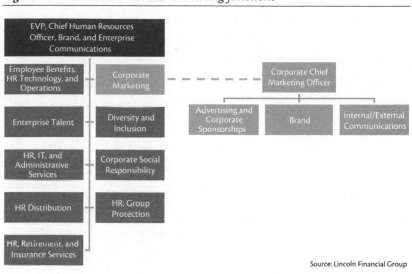

Source: Lincoln Financial Group

be both a destination employer and a top consumer brand. HR joined forces with marketing to create the Lincoln Financial Group campaign known as "Chief Life Officer," which encourages consumers to take charge of their own lives and grow and develop on the job.

Are companies ready to merge HR and marketing functions? Time will tell. More pilots are needed where marketing and HR work together on talent-acquisition campaigns and employee segmentation research studies to see how these two functions can add value to each other.

Expand Learning Opportunities

For decades, the leaders of corporate learning have been the gatekeepers of what is included in a company's corporate university. The process of identifying the skills and capabilities needed for success on the job has resulted in a fixed set of learning offerings pushed to employees. This is changing as learning leaders shift their focus to create more of a consumer experience in how, when, and where workers access learning. Why? Because employees expect an experience that parallels how they order a movie on Netflix or a book on Amazon. In both cases, they can easily select what they want, order it or add it to their wish list, and then, if ordered, choose whether to "binge" on the movie or book in one sitting. When they are finished, the entire experience can be rated and shared with others. Workers are looking for a similar experience in accessing learning, one that mirrors the consumer experiences they have in the rest of their lives. General Electric is doing just this with the development and launch of BrilliantYOU, a marketplace for learning and development.

BrilliantYOU operates much like the Apple Store for Learning. As described by Mani Gopalakrishnan, senior leader, Digital Learning & Technology at GE, "Our learning market network, dubbed BrilliantYOU, is a curated list of learning experiences organized by topic. GE employees access this at any point of time, and can download learning that best meets their personal and professional goals. Now that we have a product catalog and have employees around the world accessing, rating, and leaving a data footprint, we are exploring ways to bring in personal recommendations. Our role in L&D is now about connecting employees to the world's best learning opportunities."

The business model at the heart of BrilliantYOU allows GE employees to pay for learning each time they access it via a code funded by their department manager. Mani goes on to say, "In this new world of learning, employees are the ones selecting the learning that meets their needs rather than having GE pre-pay for an entire library of content. I think of this as employees voting with their dollars for the learning that best fits their needs." Figure 6.4 shows how BrilliantYOU is organized for ease of access by GE employees.

Mani and his team have come up with a way to add course ratings and comments much like buying a product on Amazon. Ratings are based on a five-point scale: courses with ratings of 4 and 5 are voted up, and those with a 1 or 2 are removed from the course offerings. So the marketplace determines the quality and value of learning. Lastly, if GE employees can't find what they are looking for on BrilliantYOU, there is simple form to request what they are looking for by noting, for example, "I'm looking to learn data analytics and I am a novice, and I want to learn in an on-demand online course."

While this ability to easily access learning in multiple formats "on the go" is an obvious need as proliferation of mobile devices grows exponentially, it is

Figure 6.4   BrilliantYOU—a learning market network

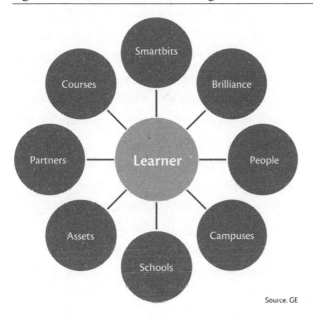

Source. GE

not the norm. According to the Institute of Corporate Productivity, only one-third of employers based in the United States have learning programs accessible on a mobile device, and less than 20 percent of learning management system shoppers make mobile a "must-have" requirement.[10]

Build Learning Partnerships

Incorporate MOOC Design Principles to Scale Corporate Learning

Thomas Friedman, op-ed columnist for the *New York Times*, wrote the forward-looking column "Come the Revolution," where he summed up the disruption of MOOCs on higher education this way: "Big breakthroughs happen when what is suddenly possible meets what is desperately necessary." This is the case with the MOOC movement inside corporations. According to data from Class Central, the total number of students who enrolled in at least one MOOC has reached 35 million, up from 18 million since inception in 2012.

More than $400 million has been invested in Coursera, edX, Khan Academy, and Udemy, and MOOC providers have emerged as learning marketplaces for on-demand learning.[11]

In 2012, the first MOOCs were on IT topics such as artificial intelligence, computer science, and programming. Today, MOOCs cover a wide range of business and management topics, with a MOOC called "Learning How to Learn" ranking as one of the most popular MOOCs offered with over 1 million students enrolled to date (see Figure 6.5).

The revolution in MOOCs has moved from higher education to corporate learning as a way to incorporate credentials, provide access in multiple languages, and, importantly, redesign e-learning using an engaging cohort model.

Corporate learning officers are now partnering with MOOC providers to offer these credentials as one way to upskill the workforce. For example, let's assume you work in marketing and graduated from a university 10 years ago. That was before you needed to know about how to design a social media amplification campaign. So what better way to keep a company's marketing

Figure 6.5   *The 10 most popular MOOCs*

1	Learning How to Learn | University of CA at San Diego
2	Mastering Data Analysis in Excel | Duke University
3	Programming for Everybody | University of Michigan
4	Machine Learning | Stanford University
5	R Programming | John Hopkins University
6	Data Scientist Tool Box | John Hopkins University
7	Tibetan Buddhist Meditation | University of Virginia
8	Introduction to Programming in Python | Rice University
9	Successful Negotiation | University of Michigan
10	Introduction to Financial Accounting | University of Pennsylvania

Source: Business Insider

employees current than by including relevant MOOCs that also offer a credential for completion to employees.

A second reason MOOCs are growing inside companies is that many MOOCs have been translated into multiple languages and are offered in places where companies are growing their operations. For example, the popular Learning How to Learn MOOC is offered in English, Russian, Chinese, Portuguese, Arabic, Dutch, Spanish, and Vietnamese. Companies are starting to pay attention to potential employees across regions who complete a MOOC and receive an accredited non degree credential. The engagement required to complete all the assignments, participate in threaded discussion groups, and become a peer reviewer of other students' assignments says volumes about a learner's dedication to the topic, and recruiters are taking note.

Finally, perhaps the biggest reason the MOOC movement has entered corporate learning departments is the power of the MOOC design to engage, inspire, and personalize the learning experience. This includes flipping the classroom, where learners engage in learning prior to the actual formal class experience, watch short engaging videos (usually no more than two to three minutes), participate in threaded online discussion groups, and have the opportunity to be both a learner, a peer reviewer, and a learning coach, all while the learning leader has access to a learning dashboard monitoring how each learner is proceeding through the course. Several companies have integrated the MOOC model into their corporate learning offerings, ranging from Microsoft to McKinsey, Tenaris, and Anthem.

Microsoft is on a mission to transform learning so the experience of learning is more like a consumer experience than a corporate training mandate. According to Chris Pirie, general manager, Field Readiness and Learning, "The relentless and accelerating pace of change now makes it impossible for our employees to learn effectively using traditional approaches. Long design cycles, weeks of classroom training and detailed roadmaps are being replaced with learning on demand. The result has been the creation of a strategy to scale learning across multiple cultures and time zones." Pirie continues, "Our journey began when Ludo Fourrage, Head of Virtual Learning at Microsoft, signed up for the Yale MOOC 'Financial Markets' on Coursera and was impressed enough with the quality of the online pedagogy that he proposed taking this inside at Microsoft."

The financial costs of producing a corporate MOOC for Microsoft were low enough to encourage Ludo to create a MOOC pilot for Microsoft's top salespeople. The MOOC Business Strategy and Financial Acumen course was created in partnership with INSEAD Business School targeting Microsoft's top sellers, nominated by their managers. Ludo shares his vision for the first MOOC created at Microsoft: "This one MOOC drew over 1,000 Microsoft sales people over a six-week period and incorporated the key aspects of the Coursera MOOC I had taken: the feeling of being a fly on the wall with unprecedented access to best-of-class learning, the reward of a certificate from a university paired with the fear of failure, the application of the learning delivered via a final assignment and an innovative peer-review mechanism. We took this formula and made it even better with small cohorts of learners working in teams, gamification of learning with the top 10 percent receiving a 'distinction' badge, threaded discussion groups, and finally a leaderboard recapping weekly engagement. The results were impressive: 85 percent completion rates and a certificate from INSEAD, which participants who finished the program could add to their LinkedIn profile. But it was the emotional connection of the learners that was impressive and something we frankly did not see in current classroom programs." An important goal for Pirie and Fourrage was to ensure the MOOC had a tangible impact on the jobs of the Microsoft salesforce. They accomplished this by creating a capstone project where the learners created an account plan using the course concepts and then had their account plan reviewed by peers and the instructional staff.

Since the start of this journey, Microsoft created four MOOCs in partnership with INSEAD, Wharton Business School, and London Business School, as well as with internal stakeholders for product training, marketing, user design, and manager training. Fourrage believes not only that Microsoft has reimagined learning to be scalable, engaging, and on demand but that the MOOCs have created a global dialogue on each topic where Microsoft employees network and share their best practices in driving sales in their accounts.

McKinsey, with more than 1,500 senior partners, has also gone on a similar journey with its partners. According to Liz Gryger, director of Functional and Diverse Profiles Learning at McKinsey, "Typically our partners learn about trends through conversations with peers. We wanted to find a way to scale that."[12]

The solution: Partner University, a set of carefully crafted learning experiences including SPOCs (small private online courses) and followed by content developed by two live experiences—one at Harvard and the other at Oxford University—where McKinsey partners convene in person to discuss and debate what they are learning and how this is being used in client engagements. Partner University started by identifying 10 critical questions a partner's client might ask, such as "How can I grow revenues while still serving customer needs?" Then Partner University set out to build content to answer those questions. "At the heart of Partner University is the active engagement of our partners who regularly reflect on what they are learning," says Ashley Williams, COO and deputy CLO (chief learning officer) of McKinsey in Atlanta. In addition to Partner University, McKinsey has gone on to create McKinsey Academy, an online learning portal targeting McKinsey mid-level professionals and customers, offering learning on such topics as business strategy, team management, problem solving, and corporate finance.

At Tenaris, MOOCs are being used as a lever for building the Tenaris employer brand globally. Rolando Lange, the global director of Tenaris University, has extended the scope of MOOCs to include current employees, university students who may become new hires, and customers. Tenaris's MOOCs range from industry-specific courses such as Introduction to Computer Numerical Control and Introduction to Steel to broader business courses such as Relationship Marketing and International Trade. Says Lange, "Our driver to launch MOOCs was to reduce the cost of corporate education while improving the quality. Our results to date show we did this. Tenaris saved $800,000 and improved the quality of the learning experience as well as winning recognition such as ATD's (Association for Talent Development) Excellence in Practice award."

Ingrid Urman, head of Learning Methods at Tenaris University, goes on to say, "Our MOOCs were first designed for internal employees to update their skills. Now we are applying MOOC design features across the corporate university, such as introducing each course with a short engaging video, creating small learning cohorts of 30 per course, and incorporating an online certificate and badge. For Tenaris, our MOOC journey has resulted in rethinking our learning model for all our employees."

Flipping the Classroom

Companies are not just creating their own MOOCs but also embedding MOOC design principles into their current learning offerings. Anthem identified individuals in three customer-facing roles: sales, clinicians, and customer service representatives, to pilot a "flipped classroom" approach pioneered by Sal Khan of Khan Academy, where learners are in charge of their own learning, receive individual coaching and mentoring along the way, and practice in the classroom what they learn online in discussion boards and in micro learning video lessons. Figure 6.6 shows various components of the flipped classroom model.

Figure 6.6   *The Anthem flipped classroom model*

Lessons (Blending self-paced with instructor led)	Performance Support (Knowledge library, SharePoint, and my learning)	Coaching (Group and individual)	Assessments (Performance-based)
Workbook-based self-paced training with LOB specific practice scenarios	Single point of access to all training materials	Office hours 1:1 coaching/ mentoring with facilitator	Skill observation through mentoring
Microlearning video lessons and simulations	LOB specific documentation Quick reference guides	Discussion boards Peer-to-peer collaboration	Badges and certifications upon completion
Instructor led training for complex processes	Interactive simulations and job aids	Floor support at Go Live Go Live Hotline 30-60-90 day follow up	Skill-based practical assessments 30-60-90 day follow up

Courtesy of Anthem

The Anthem flipped classroom model is the outgrowth of a learning strategy developed by Mike Melloh, chief learning officer, to provide scalable learning to customer-facing roles while also embedding peer-to-peer collaboration in the learning design. Melloh and Jennifer Hammond, staff vice president of Learning & Development, identified customer service representatives as a key to pilot this new learning method as there are several thousand customer service representatives at Anthem.

Anthem has already started to see results in learner feedback and satisfaction, as well as improved job performance. Anthem is on target to "flip" more than a dozen curricula to be used in over 100 classes. This will result in freeing up over 10,000 hours for the Anthem training staff to be redirected to other training needs. Of course, this just represents the beginning of where Anthem intends to apply flipped learning. By 2018, Melloh and Hammond estimate the majority of training will be in a flipped classroom format.

Design New Roles for the Learning Team

As learning shifts from a single classroom to being able to access multiple forms of learning in either a MOOC or a flipped classroom, the roles within a learning department are evolving to incorporate a focus on marketing, community building, curation, and editorial planning.

As the rate and pace of change accelerate, more companies will migrate from designing transactional learning programs to designing learning experiences. And as this happens, new roles will be created not only for the learning team members but also for the chief learning officer, who will focus more on orchestrating and facilitating learning rather than leading a team to design and deliver learning. After interviewing a number of chief learning officers and their staff, we are seeing five new roles emerge, which are outlined in the sidebar. These roles may not translate into new full time jobs but a rethinking of current roles to incorporate this new expanded focus on creating learning experiences.

Five Emerging Roles for the Learning Department

- **Community manager.** Seeds, feeds, and weeds content so employees can share, debate, and learn from each other
- **Learning experience manager.** Creates memorable experiences on par with consumer experiences to inspire and engage a learner
- **Communications manager.** Develops a communications campaign building learning investment into the employer brand
- **Editorial manager.** Designs, curates, and embeds learning into all aspects of the learning experience
- **Marketing manager.** Creates a marketing plan for the experiences, touting benefits for individuals and companies

Consider the Employee a Learner and a Teacher

American companies spent more than $130 billion on corporate learning in 2014, an increase of 15 percent over the previous year. This demonstrates the need of companies to close the skill gaps among their employees. According to research by Bersin by Deloitte, "Not only do more than 70 percent of organizations cite 'capability gaps' as one of their top five challenges, but many companies say it takes 3–5 years to transform a seasoned professional into a fully productive employee."[13]

Is the money invested in learning put to good use? Laszlo Bock, SVP of People Operations at Google and *Work Rules!* author, believes this investment is often insufficiently targeted, delivered by the wrong people, and measured incorrectly.

So how does Google design and deliver its learning? Google has reimagined the learning model altogether by having Googlers deliver most of the learning. This is known as "Googler to Googler" and places employees from across departments into teaching roles that would otherwise be filled by the HR department (or, in Google speak, the People Operations department). It is estimated that about 55 percent of the programs offered at Google are taught by Googlers.[14]

Laszlo says that telling employees that you want them to learn is different from asking them to promote that culture themselves. Giving employees teaching roles, says Google's head of People Operations, Karen May, makes learning part of the way employees work together rather than something HR is making them do.[15]

Laszlo Bock elaborates on this in *Work Rules!* He explains, "It is generally far better to learn from people who are doing the work today, who can answer the deeper questions and draw on current real life examples. They understand your context better, they are always available to provide immediate feedback, and they are mostly free."[16]

The pace of change is simply too fast to create a hard-coded curriculum. Instead, at Google the goal is to create peer-to-peer learning where Googlers become teachers and share their knowledge will grow as a key mode of delivering learning to employees.

Communicate the Value: Focus on the Why, How, and What of Measurement

Most organizations measure training success based on the learner's satisfaction. "Did the employees like the training?" This form of measurement only scratches the surface of measuring success. Satisfaction surveys immediately following a training session typically determine how happy the students were with the process and the environment; the surveys ask subjective questions focused on whether the students felt the information was helpful.

CEOs are requesting a much more strategic approach to measuring learning investment. In a survey conducted with 96 CEOs by PwC's ROI Institute, 96 percent said they want to see the business impact from learning and development investments, but only 8 percent currently see this. Meanwhile, 74 percent of respondents say they want to see the ROI in people, projects, and initiatives associated with learning. Unfortunately, only 4 percent are receiving that information.[17]

Indeed, analytics should drive an organization's decisions on recruitment, development, and engagement. By applying Simon Sinek's model of the Golden Circle in his bestselling book, *Start with Why*, we propose three simple yet powerful questions to frame a company's learning investment in the language of business. The first question is "*Why* is the investment being made?"—what is the business problem that the training is solving for? The next question is "*How* is the organization analyzing the data?" In other words, what methodology is being used to measure learning? Finally, the last question is "*What* specific business impact is being measured?" Applying these three simple questions to measurement of learning sounds simple, but most measurement is done backward. This means that companies start with the what, then move to the how, and often neglect to focus on the why. And more alarmingly, many of them don't even know why they do what they do!

If we start our analysis with defining *why* the organization is investing in learning, we can more clearly communicate the purpose of creating a learning experience rather than designing learning content. Let's return to the members of the adidas Group. Imagine if their vision for learning was simply, "We design and deliver high-impact training to meet business needs." (We have seen versions of this learning vision at many companies.)

Instead, the members of the adidas Group figured out that they had to inspire employees to join them on a learning journey. Hence their vision of "You Learn, We Grow," starts with why. People want to be emotionally connected to the why rather than being told about the what.

After firmly understanding the why of investing in learning, then identifying the how, the what falls into place. In explaining a company's investment in learning, learning leaders often become enamored with the how and what without a solid understanding of the why.

As Simon Sinek says, "Leaders don't have all the great ideas; they provide support for those who want to contribute. Leaders achieve very little by themselves: they inspire people to come together for the good of the group. Leaders never start with what needs to be done. Leaders start with 'why we need to do things.' Leaders inspire action."[18]

Let's rethink the entire learning process to better meet the needs of our employees and our strategic business priorities. Consider stepping back and asking why your organization is investing in learning, and remember that employees will more easily rally around the why rather than the what of learning.

The Future of Learning

As companies shift learning from designing transactional courses to creating transformational learning experiences, the role of the chief learning officer becomes more strategic and expands in the process. Originally hired because of their background in employee and leadership development, CLOs and learning leaders must now grow their expertise in communications, digital and consumer marketing, and learning technologies. The learning leaders of the future must understand that employees, regardless of their age, want learning to be personalized, leverage the expertise of their peers, and be available at their moment of need. Our workers take for granted they have ready access to "Siri-type learning," or instantaneous answers to their questions, whenever and wherever they are. Shouldn't learning incorporate the same type of consumer experience?

The challenge for CLOs is to navigate this new world of learning with a consumer mindset and understand the needs and expectations of learners in the same way as chief marketing officers know their customers.

The future of learning will be about developing this mindset shift inside training departments so that learning is inspiring, engaging, and on demand! It's a brave new world for learning. Are you ready?

MY ACTION PLAN

Myself

- What can I do to rethink my role as a learning leader from developing learning content to designing learning experiences? (Learn by example!)
- What opportunities and barriers do I see as my role expands?
- What new learning programs should I enroll in to develop new skills in digital marketing and communications?

My Team

- How do we move our team from creating transactional learning programs to offering transformational learning experiences?
- What roles on our team need to be reimagined, and how will we lead this effort?
- What criteria does my team need to select new learning partners?

My Organization

- As we adopt a new direction for why our organization learns, what types of new measures must we put into place?
- How could we communicate our value back to the organization?
- How could we work with and learn from our organization's chief marketing officer?

PART III

THE CHANGING COMPOSITION OF THE WORKFORCE

TAP THE POWER OF MULTIPLE GENERATIONS 7

Age is only a state of mind.

—*Lailah Gifty Akita*[1]

Navigating Multiple Generations in the Workplace

Every workplace needs age diversity. Why? When organizations encourage employees of diverse ages and cultures to work together products and processes are approached in new and innovative ways. Quite simply, age diversity drives the type of creative thinking that leads to greater engagement and innovation.

Multiple generations in the workplace is the *new normal*. Workers are staying in their jobs longer. The growth of older workers is driven in part by an increased life expectancy. According to the Social Security Administration, men who reach 65 years old today can expect to live until age 84.3 and women until age 86.6 years.[2] So if we are living until our mid 80s and want to retire on 50 percent of our income, it is likely we will want and need to continue working until our mid to late 60s and even into our 70s.

What is the implication of living and working longer? We believe we will see more employee compensation packages that include not only salary, bonus, and stock options but also generous learning allowances funding skill development for employees. A company's commitment to invest in the employability of all its workers will become an even stronger component of its recruiting message.

Figure 7.1   Key generational cohorts in the workplace

Generation	Gen Zers	Millennials	Gen Xers	Boomers and Traditionalists
Age *As of Jan 1, 2017*	8–23	24–35	36–52	53–72, 73+
Birth Years	2009–1994	1993–1982	1981–1965	1964–1945, before 1945
Key Abilities	Super tech savvy, embrace diversity, globally connected	Confidence, competitiveness, workplace flexibility advocates	Independent, pragmatic, self-reliant	Strong work ethic, equal rights generation, optimistic
Attitude on Education	Questioning value	An expense (may have large student loans)	A way to get there	A birthright
Tagline	"Seeking varied experiences"	"It's all about me"	"Help me balance"	"Not ready to leave work"

Source: Future Workplace

What generation are you? Figure 7.1 outlines key generational cohorts in the workplace.

We increasingly see multiple generations working side by side as part of their everyday experience at work. Sometimes this means five generations on a single team!

This mix of generations in the workforce, as shown in Figure 7.2, is as age diverse as it's ever been with millennials (those born between 1982 and 1993) the largest generational cohort in the U.S. workforce as of 2015. Millennials and Gen Zers are targeted to comprise over 60 percent of the U.S. workforce, with 73 percent aspiring to be leaders in the next five years.[3]

One implication of age diversity in the workplace is younger bosses managing older workers. This phenomenon is already prevalent in industries like IT, professional services, and accounting, and it will likely become the norm across all industries as companies promote millennials and Gen Xers into leadership positions while boomers remain in the workplace.

In our "Multi-Generational Leadership Study," sponsored by Future Workplace and Beyond.com, we found 83 percent of employees have seen

Figure 7.2   *The changing mix of generations in the workforce*

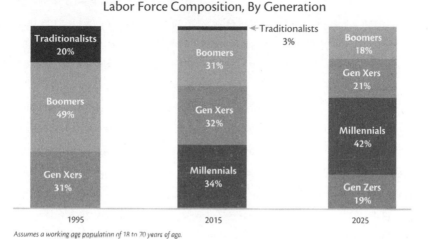

Labor Force Composition, By Generation

Assumes a working age population of 18 to 70 years of age.

Source: Bureau of Labor Statistics and the U.S. Census Bureau

millennials managing older workers in their office, and the majority (75 percent) of respondents across all age groups see this is a growing trend.[4] What's telling is that 37 percent of millennials admit that it is difficult to manage people who are older than they are.[5]

Dan Schawbel, millennial partner at Future Workplace, shares this; "the sheer size of the millennial generation means more will be in leadership roles and it's causing anxiety for them because they've never had to manage older generations before." These skills are not taught in school, so millennials are relying on their managers to coach them. Our data supports the importance of this, with 45 percent of boomer and Gen Xer respondents indicating that millennials' lack of managerial experience could have a negative impact on a company's culture.[6]

We do see pockets of success among younger manager and older employee combinations, but it takes coaching and open communications among both sides. One of our clients is a 65-year-old instructional designer who needed and wanted to continue to work after getting laid off from her prior employer. She was thrilled to find a new full-time position after one year in the job market, but to her surprise her manager was the same age as her 44-year-old son!

She handled this role reversal with humility, emphasizing her desire to focus on her job, not the age difference, and to think positively about the opportunity of sharing her years of expertise with her new manager. Her manager was sensitive to this and today she is celebrating three years working with her younger manager often traveling together to human resources and training conferences.

We will see more of these situations where a younger manager supervises an older worker, so it will be up to the manager and the employee to make this work. Our advice: leaders will need to move beyond focusing on generational differences to build generational intelligence, tapping the power of multiple generations to provide insights into launching new products, services, and markets. We define *generational intelligence* as the ability to understand the similarities, differences, and expectations of each generational cohort. Understanding multiple employee generational cohorts is important to serving multiple generations of customers. Generational intelligence requires a constant focus on the benefits an age-diverse workforce can bring to the organization.

The New Face of the Workforce

Looking across the workplace, in addition to age diversity, the Bureau of Labor Statistics reports today's workforce is composed of more women and is also more culturally diverse than ever before.[7]

According to William H. Frey, senior fellow in the Brookings Institution Metropolitan Policy Program and author of *Diversity Explosion*, "For the first time America's racial and ethnic minorities now make up about half of the under-5 age children."[8]

This trend is likely to continue: by 2020, 40 percent of the population will be racial minorities, and more than half of the population under 18 will be racial minorities. By 2023, whites will total less than half of the U.S. population under 30.[9]

What does this imply for your workplace? We expect cultural intelligence to become as important as emotional and generational intelligence. Cultural intelligence requires a combination of knowledge, experience, and social connections of and with other cultures. Author Dr. David Livermore *defines* cultural intelligence as the capability to function effectively in culturally diverse situations. In his book, *Driven by Difference*, Livermore shares how Novartis, the Swiss pharmaceutical giant, deliberately creates multicultural new-product teams to launch new brands: "Novartis uses multi-cultural employee resource groups to provide market research for launching new brands. The company estimates they've saved millions of dollars by using built-in diverse multicultural teams in the new product development process."

In addition to the workforce being more age and culturally diverse, it is also now composed of more women, making up nearly 50 percent of the U.S. workforce. They are the majority of students in American colleges and graduate schools, and they own 30 percent of small businesses. Women are increasingly becoming breadwinners in their families. Of the more than 1,400 women surveyed—40 percent of whom were single or divorced—53 percent stated they were the breadwinners in their households. Nearly a quarter of married women surveyed said they earned more money than their spouses.[10] Our Rule #8: "Build Gender Equality" explores the gender equality issue in more detail and provides recommendations to address gender inequality in the workplace

Workplace Generational Intelligence Framework

As we see multiple generations working side by side, we are also seeing attitude, rather than age, characterizing these generational cohorts. The IBM Institute for Business Value conducted a survey of 1,784 multiple-generation employees across 12 countries and found roughly the same percentage of millennials (20 percent) want to do work they are passionate about, as do Gen Xers (21 percent) and boomers (23 percent).[11] While these attitudes and desires on what to expect from work may be similar, there are some distinct preferences and goals important to each of the generations. While these key preferences are powerful influencers, ultimately they are only indicators of what's important to each generational cohort.[12] For example, millennials are expressing a desire for student loan debt repayment while generation Xer's want help with saving for college for their children. Forward-looking companies are recognizing this and adapting differentiated talent management strategies on personal, team, and organizational levels.

Let's look at each of the U.S. generations to understand the specific preferences and mindsets each brings to the workplace. After reviewing numerous research studies and working with Future Workplace clients, we created the Workplace Generational Intelligence Framework as a way to highlight the unique needs of the generations within the context of the workplace experience.

Our Workplace Generational Intelligence Framework shares what is important to each generation on three levels:

- **Personal level.** What do workers want for themselves? We highlight insights on learning and development.
- **Team level.** What do workers seek of colleagues? We highlight insights on collaboration.
- **Organizational level.** What do workers expect of the organization? We highlight work preference expectations.

An overview of the Workplace Generational Intelligence Framework is illustrated in Figure 7.3.

Understanding Generation Z

The oldest members of Gen Z are now in the workforce. By 2020, Gen Z will make up one of every eight workers, but Gen Z workers may exert disproportionate influence for their numbers.[13] Like millennials, Gen Zers are keen to learn, be mentored, and engage deeply in the workplace. Unlike millennials, they are more realistic with their career pursuits and are even more entrepreneurial, with a passion for being ambitious and high achieving.

Figure 7.3   Workplace Generational Intelligence Framework

Generation	Gen Zers	Millennials	Gen Xers	Boomers and Traditionalists
Age *As of Jan 1, 2017*	8–23	24–35	36–52	53–72, 73+
Personal Expectations (Learning and Development)	Deliberate and goal-oriented learning	Mentorship	Customization of job and benefits	Opt-in learning and development
Within Teams (Collaboration Preferences)	Experimental mindset—trial and error	Synergy of employee affinity groups	Structured development opportunities	Younger manager/older worker training
From the Organization (Support Preferences)	Early career connections	Purposeful work and financial support	Future focused career opportunities	Support to work longer

Source: Future Workplace

Personal Expectations: Deliberate and Goal-Oriented Learning

Members of generation Z want to build skills early. While other generations have regarded play as a break from learning, Gen Z views learning itself as play. Eighty-nine percent of Gen Zers state they currently spend part of their free time in activities they consider to be "productive and creative" as opposed to simply "hanging out."[14] Gen Zers are also more likely than millennials at the same age to have worked on developing a skill or craft (42 percent versus 25 percent).[15] They appreciate on-demand learning and prefer learning to be accessed when and how they wish, exhibiting a high preference for mobile learning.

Gen Zers also show an interest in developing a range of actionable how-to skills, including how to start a business (58 percent), how to use graphics for design (51 percent), how to shoot and edit videos (50 percent), and how to build or create apps (50 percent).[16] Gen Z is a visually oriented group that gravitates to learning via outlets such as YouTube, Instagram, and other social channels rather than written communications. Companies that recognize this will adapt how and where they recruit and develop Gen Zers.

Gen Zers focus on goal-oriented learning, and this has resulted in a number of new start-ups, led by Gen Zers themselves. Consider Zach Latta, who tested out of his Los Angeles public high school at 16 to work as an engineer and web developer. After receiving Peter Thiel's $100,000 fellowship to defer college, Latta, at the age of 18, started his own organization, Hack Club, a coding curriculum offered to high school students, and is honored as one of the youngest on the *Forbes* 30 Under 30 list. In just one year, Hack Club has been adopted in 62 schools across 16 states. The vision, says Latta, "is to offer a turn-key coding curriculum, using the latest coding software, and to encourage a more diverse segment of high schoolers, women and young people from multiple ethnic backgrounds, to learn coding." To capitalize on the growing global phenomenon of developing coding skill for school aged children, Latta is expanding Hack Club globally. There are currently clubs in Australia, Canada, Estonia, India, the United States, and Zimbabwe, with further countries to come.

Within Teams: An Experimental Mindset

Gen Zers exhibit more entrepreneurial interest than millennials. Their prevailing attitude is very much "Be experimental—let's try and see." In fact, Lotta points to one of the high school students in the Hack Club who is working to kill the collaboration tool Slack by building a better app for real-time messaging, quite an ambitious goal as Slack generated more than 1 million daily active users in just three years! You can read more about the experimentation mindset in the "Be Intrapreneurial" section of Rule #3: "Be an Agile Leader."

We also see Gen Z questioning the value of higher education. Lotta (whose parents are social workers with graduate degrees) never attended college, and he believes a college degree simply is not essential to ambitious 16-year-olds or even to employers. According to research by Universum, among a global sample of 49,000 Gen Zers, 55 percent say they are interested in starting their own company—a figure that is even higher in emerging markets. And when asked if they would join the workforce instead of pursuing a college degree, 15 percent in North America said yes, and 47 percent said maybe. Nearly 60 percent of global Gen Zers are open to learning about an employer's investment in continuing education in the job search process.[17]

From the Organization: Early Career Connections

Gen Zers exhibit an early interest in experiential volunteering and job shadowing as a preferred development need. Secondary schools are addressing this need by incorporating internships and job shadowing into the curriculum. While internships are understandably important during college, they are now cropping up as commonplace among 13- to 17-year-olds as well. One partnership, the Minnesota Center for Advanced Professional Studies, provides high school juniors and seniors with the option of working half time with a local employer to learn a skill, job-shadow, or be involved in a mentoring program to acquire real-world skills. Kristi Broom, the parent of a 15-year-old living in Minneapolis, enrolled in this program and is herself a mentor to students in the program. She sees huge benefits to this. "This is what more high schools should be doing, nurturing their students' entrepreneurial bent and giving them an opportunity to view various professionals firsthand." Interestingly, according to Broom, the school system came to form the partnership when it ran out of space in the local high school and had to think creatively about what to do with the student population. "In the end, this opportunity to get involved in the workplace early is a win-win for employers and students," says Broom.

Questions to Ask About Gen Z

1. What can we show Gen Z in visual form (video, infographics) to convey our employer brand?

2. What opportunities could we provide for Gen Z to learn in a self-directed way?

3. Could our organization create opportunities to recruit local Gen Zers to job-shadow key managers in our organization?

4. How could we develop partnership programs with secondary schools in our area to build career discussions with Gen Zers?

5. How is our organization touting our investment in new-hire training and development to college recruits *and* those in secondary school?

Understanding Millennials

As millennials are now the largest generational cohort of the U.S. workforce, it's the millennial mindset that business leaders need to be cognizant of. Millennials want to collaborate and cocreate with their employer, and this translates into creating a product, a new service, and even the workplace experience.

Alex Castellarnau at Dropbox, the file transfer service, says, With millennials, "a new brand, service or product is only *started* by the company; it's finished by the customers.[18]

Leaders need to recognize the importance of building cocreation into various aspects of the workplace experience and allow millennials to contribute their input and learn from each other.

Personal Expectations: Mentorship

Millennials recognize the competitive landscape for new jobs. More than 70 million boomers will be vacating the workforce over the next decade, and there is plenty of competition for the new positions from the more than 80 million millennials on top of the 50 million-plus Gen Xers. The millennial solution to this: learn from each other in stretch assignments and mentoring relationships. In fact, 53 percent of global millennials surveyed say mentoring is the most effective way for them to learn and grow on the job.[19] Companies are listening to these requests for mentoring and are launching programs such as PepsiCo's "Conn3ct," which pairs millennials with executive sponsors who mentor them. But millennials are not waiting for their company to create a mentoring program; they are finding mentors on their own and persuading them to help accelerate their career development.

Some are finding mentors only a few years older. For example, Andi Litz, a millennial who formerly worked at General Electric and is now a senior HR manager at Activision Studio, explains, "I look for mentors who are only a couple of years senior and can relate to my experiences. Their input and advice will be realistic and achievable." Additionally, as she points out, it's often "easier to develop a trusting relationship" with them, because they're more accessible than senior executives.

In Litz's case, she took a new position in Selma, Tennessee, working for GE, and she knew almost no one. "It can be quite difficult to move into a remote job in a small town, while working with a big organization like GE," she said. "I decided to reach out to the person who had been in my job, even though he was now in Georgia. Since he had just left the job, he was really helpful on things from what to do on the weekends to navigating the big picture at GE. We had lots of phone calls, text messages, and instant messaging. I'd be on a call with people from all over the place, and I could IM him to find out what an acronym was, or what significance there was to the initiative we were discussing. The funny thing is, I never even met him in person until I'd been there a year."[20]

While some millennials are taking mentoring into their own hands, others are being paired to mentor a senior executive in what is being called reverse or reciprocal mentoring. MasterCard has been an early adopter of reciprocal mentoring where senior business leaders at the firm are paired with millennials, often to build their social media expertise. Ron Garrow, formerly chief human resources officer of MasterCard, took advantage of this. Garrow's reverse mentor was Rebecca Kaufman—an avid social media user in her mid-twenties—who worked with Garrow on using Twitter and LinkedIn to drive business results. Across MasterCard, this reciprocal mentoring program now has over 300 participants. Janice Burns, chief learning officer at MasterCard, sees multiple benefits here; an important one is having senior executives develop an understanding of how millennials consume information differently and examine the implications of this on creating a more consumer-driven HR organization.

Within Teams: Synergy of Employee Affinity Groups

Employee affinity groups (also known as employee resource groups, or ERGs) started in the 1960s. The first one was at Xerox Corporation in 1964. Today, they bring employees together to discuss common issues within groups such as female leaders, veterans, people with disabilities, working parents, single parents, LGBT employees, Latino leaders, and now generational groups. Among the most innovative of the generational employee affinity groups is a group known as the Millennial Corps and led by Samantha Klein, a millennial at IBM, who, with three other IBMers, started the Millennial Corps in 2014 after presenting the idea to senior executives.

Today the Millennial Corps includes more than 4,000 IBMers in over 70 countries and is a community of millennials and millennial-minded employees who come together both in person and online (using IBM Connections, the online collaboration portal) to spark innovation and share feedback with senior leaders on key initiatives within the company. The Millennial Corps consists of both millennials born between the years 1982 and 1993 and those who describe themselves as "#MIBB!" ("Millennials in Boomer Bodies").

Says Klein, "Millennial Corps is a volunteer group and while it is not a formal ERG, we act like one, advising IBM leaders on how to better create IBM products and services appealing to those with a Millennial mindset." Klein goes on, "Millennial Corps has sparked a number of new insights for IBM in the past year. We were advisors to the IBM + Apple partnership and generated more than 500 ideas for industry-specific enterprise apps. In the last year, Millennial Corps forged a partnership with IBM's Transformation & Operations executive and advised IBM on the development of a real time app to provide instant feedback anytime, anywhere." The Millennial Corps' input ranged from identifying the need for an agile approach to giving and receiving feedback, proposing specific capabilities for the app, and then assisting in naming it. It is officially called ACE, which stands for appreciation, coaching, and evaluation, and as noted earlier in Chapter 1, it is now part of IBM's global performance management program allowing IBMers to receive real-time feedback from managers and peers.

Klein is now expanding the Millennial Corps globally with other millennial employee affinity groups that currently exist at IBM customers and partners, including PepsiCo and MetLife. These multiclient gatherings of millennials will discuss the changing needs and expectations of millennials in the global marketplace.

From the Organization:
Purposeful Work and Financial Support

What do millennials want from work? At a macrolevel, millennials want what we all want from work: purposeful work, flexibility to work where, when, and how they want, and access to continuous on-demand learning! Millennials are simply the first to so clearly voice their needs and expect them to be met.

However, some of the millennial expectations are unique to this generation. One continuing millennial request is the desire to experience global opportunities at a young age. One in ten U.S. undergraduates now studies abroad before graduating. A PwC global survey of millennials finds that 37 percent of millennials view working abroad as a desired career path and are requesting this as early as possible compared with 27 percent of nonmillennials.[21]

Dow Chemical company was one of the first organizations to combine sustainability efforts with leadership development. Dow along with IBM, Deloitte, Accenture, and EY has created a powerful alliance between global citizenship and human resources to provide future leaders with firsthand exposure and experience in the regions of the world where the company is poised to grow. At Dow Chemical, the program is called Leadership in Action. Employees work in teams of five to solve some of the challenges facing local organizations. The countries Dow has focused on include Ghana in 2013, Ethiopia in 2014, and Indonesia in 2015. Dow employees work on projects such as addressing STEM education, providing sustainable farming techniques, and ensuring access to safe high quality drinking water. While these programs are good for society and the world, they are also beneficial to Dow. "There are multiple facets of this project that are exciting," says Johanna Soderstrom, vice president, Human Resources at Dow Chemical, namely to expand our future leaders, understanding of Dow and what we are doing for society. We believe if we can make our employees' jobs more purposeful, then we can earn their engagement and loyalty. We have anecdotal stories of prospective employees who hear about the Leadership in Action program and apply for a job at Dow. That's pretty powerful in terms of talent attraction." Dow employees are nominated for participation in Leadership in Action, and this includes seven months of virtual consulting with one week on the ground consulting with a local community.[22] Programs like Leadership in Action and IBM Corporate Service Corps are building the type of globally minded leaders needed for future growth.

In addition to incorporating global citizenship into human resource programs, companies are also creating customized benefits targeted to attract and retain millennials. One of the most innovative is student debt loan repayment. According to a U.S. White House report, the total student outstanding loan debt surpassed $1.3 trillion, making it the second largest category of household debt. The national default rate on student loans made by the government is now 11.8 percent. The average student loan debt for graduates with a bachelor's degree is $37,000, up 78 percent from a decade ago.[23]

A small but growing number of companies are stepping up to address this. While the Society for Human Resource Management reports only 3 percent of businesses offer a student loan repayment benefit, forward-looking companies competing for top talent, such as PwC, Fidelity Investments, Natixis Global Asset Management, and NVIDIA, have recently announced student loan debt repayment as a new benefit to recruit and retain millennials. The loan repayment a company funds varies, from $2,000 per employee per year at Fidelity Investments to $1,200 per employee at PwC with a maximum benefit of $10,000. These funds are directly deposited into an employee's student loan account and taxed as ordinary income. "Since offering this benefit in January 2016," says Jennifer Hanson, Head of Associate Experience at Fidelity Investments, "Our employees who have taken advantage of this have collectively saved $5 million in principal and shaved off an average of eight months of loan payments."

As more companies add this benefit, the government is taking note. Representatives Rodney Davis, Republican of Illinois, and Gwen Graham,

Democrat of Florida, introduced a bill to allow workers to receive up to $5,250 in tax-free payments each year to help repay student loans. This is on par with the existing benefit for employer tuition reimbursement.[24]

Look for continued innovation in how companies assist millennials in repaying their student loans as a lever to both attract and retain talent.

Questions to Ask About Millennials

1. Does our organization have an employee resource group for millennials?
2. Does our organization link organizational purpose and global citizenship to developing future leaders?
3. What is our organization doing to develop millennials as cultural leaders?
4. What new benefits could our organization create to target the unique needs of millennials?
5. Has our organization considered a reverse mentoring program pairing millennials with more senior executives?

Understanding Generation X

The youngest of Gen Xers are 36 and the oldest 52. Generation X is often referred to as demography's long-neglected "middle child." Numbering just 46 million in the United States, Gen X is small compared with the 76 million boomers and 80 million millennials. Yet Generation X makes up the bulk of potential successors for many management jobs.

Personal Expectations: Customization of Job and Benefits

As Gen X workers move out of their thirties and into their forties and fifties, they are increasingly interested in workplace flexibility. While this is of interest to all the generations, Gen Xers are one of the first generations where both parents are working full time and juggling the demands of a growing family with the demands of a career. In regard to benefits, 40 percent of Gen

Xers report that they worry about reduction in work benefits, in contrast to 33 percent of millennials and 26 percent of boomers. As companies create customized benefits targeting millennials—such as student debt loan repayment—Gen Xers are also looking for customization of benefits, especially as many are saving for their children's college educations. As Gen Xers voice their needs for benefit customization, expect more innovation in policies customized to retain Gen Xers such as offering contributions to 529 college savings accounts. Since Gen Xers are in the prime of their careers and prone to job hopping, this could be a smart move for companies.

Within Teams: Structured Development Opportunities

Job hopping is now how we manage our careers, as we noted in Rule #5 with the advent of the continual job seeker. The Bureau of Labor Statistics reports that the average worker today stays at each job for only 4.4 years. The expected tenure of the workforce's youngest employees, millennials and Gen Zers, is about half that time.[25]

While the media focus has been on millennials job hopping, it turns out that talented Gen Xers are also prone to job hopping. A study by Deloitte Consulting reports that only 37 percent of Gen Xers plan on staying with their current employers, compared with 44 percent of millennials and 52 percent of boomers.[26]

High-performing Gen Xers are in demand as companies target employees with specific skill sets. All this points to a new focus on retaining Gen Xers and keeping them engaged with the company either through customized benefits or structured company development programs. One company exploring this is JetBlue with its JetBlue Scholars program, which acknowledges talented Gen Xers who have amassed both job experience and certifications at the company but do not have a college degree. The JetBlue Scholars program provides both mentoring and career counseling to JetBlue crew members (employees) who want to gain college credit for their work experience.

From the Organization:
Future-Focused Career Opportunities

Some forward-looking companies are creating special developmental stretch assignments and opportunities to keep talented Gen Xers who are susceptible to poaching from recruiters and former employers.

According to research from the Center for Work-Life Policy, nearly 40 percent of Gen Xers report they eventually want to become entrepreneurs.[27] One way that companies are addressing this need, is to build an intrapreneurial mindset through assignments at a company innovation center. According to research by Capgemini Consulting, 38 percent of the leading 200 companies have set up an innovation center, or a physical space in a global tech hub, to test new disruptive solutions and business models in the marketplace.[28]

These innovation centers provide high-performing Gen Xers and others with a passion for new-product development to work on disruptive business models. Examples abound: BMW is setting up an innovation center in Mountain View, California, to develop new digital product offerings to add to the BMWConnectedDrive. And Axa Lab is the insurance company's innovation outpost in Silicon Valley launched to better understand the insurance needs of the digital customer.

Questions to Ask About Gen Xers

1. Does our organization track the workforce needs of Gen Xers?
2. Is our organization tracking the retention of Gen Xers? What are we learning over time?
3. Are there opportunities to create stretch assignments for high-performing Gen Xers?
4. Could our organization offer customized benefits to help with the education of their children or the elder care of their parents?
5. What could we do to better address the specific mid-career challenges of Gen Xers through more online continuing education opportunities?

Understanding Boomers

The average age at which U.S. retirees are leaving the workplace is 62, up from 57 in 1991 when Gallup first began tracking this data.[29] Recent studies by Wells Fargo suggest that only 48 percent of Americans aged 60–75 have saved enough to live comfortably in retirement, demonstrating that many older Americans will stay employed longer out of financial necessity. Others remain working for the intellectual challenges and the sense of continuity and identity that work provides.

Boomers constitute the most experienced generational cohort in the workplace. The challenge for employers is how to best leverage their knowledge and experience while providing them ways to continue to contribute in the workplace, and when they are ready to exit, to pass along their institutional knowledge.

Personal Expectations: Opt-in Learning and Development Opportunities

While the myth is that boomers are stuck in their ways and resistant to change, a number of more recent studies suggest that boomers are highly adaptable workers and respond particularly well to opt-in learning opportunities and temporary in-house job rotations.[30]

Some companies, like MasterCard, have launched career mobility centers similar to the in-house career centers often found in universities. These career mobility centers allow employees to work on company projects that are not associated with their daily roles. The initiative, called Smart Steps, allows managers to post the details of a project in the system, and employees from all across the company register their interest. Employees do not need the approval of their managers to apply for a project, mainly because the experiences are in addition to their day job.

"When we started this," explains Janice Burns, MasterCard CLO, "we were thinking this would be ideal for our Millennial employees, but we have been surprised to see the uptick among our Boomers as a way to keep learning on the job!" She continues, "Registering for the Career Mobility Center allows employees to manage their own development. It's not quite mentoring but it does expose our employees to a range of new functions and roles inside the company."

Within Teams: Younger Manager–Older Worker Training

Younger leaders managing older workers is becoming increasingly common in the workplace. A CareerBuilder survey of 3,800 full-time workers and 2,200 hiring managers found that one-third (34 percent) of U.S. workers say they have a younger boss, and 15 percent work for someone at least 10 years younger.[31]

These new reporting relationships can take getting used to. Keith Craig, a boomer who is a public relations manager for Linode, a cloud-hosting provider, reports to Casey Smith, the company's VP of marketing, a Gen Xer who is more than a decade younger than Craig, who is in his fifties.

While this can create generational conflict, Keith sees the reporting structure as a partnership just as we profiled earlier in this chapter with the older instructional designer working for a younger manager. As a boomer parent, Craig identified a new market segment for the company: targeting high schools with computer science clubs. With his manager's approval, Craig presented new offerings for both internships as well as guest lectures by Linode employees.

Craig does admit to feeling his age. "I am a Boomer who grew up on *Captain Kangaroo*. I talk differently and dress differently than most of the people I work with," he says, adding that when his colleagues' water cooler chat crosses into unfamiliar territory, he returns to his desk and does a quick Internet search. "Google is a great cheat sheet."[32]

From the Organization: Support to Work Longer

Many boomers want and need to work longer. A 2015 study by Allianz found that 82 percent of boomers claim that a traditional retirement is a "romantic fantasy of the past." And some plan never to retire, according to a Allianz.[33]

This is reinforced by a Bankers Life study reporting 41 percent of boomers still in the workplace expect to work until age 69 or never retire! Six in ten boomers say they work for nonfinancial reasons, such as staying mentally sharp (18 percent), keeping physically active (15 percent), and maintaining a sense of purpose (15 percent). Of those already retired, 69 percent of boomers say they would have liked to have been able to work longer.[34]

Some companies are recognizing this and starting to recruit boomers for new jobs. TD Ameritrade recently launched a recruiting program called "Grey Is the New Green," inspired by a line in the film *The Intern*, profiling a boomer (played by a 71-year-old Robert De Niro) who interns for a millennial (played by a 31-year-old Anne Hathaway). TD Ameritrade's rationale was to identify boomers who want to return to the workplace and specifically work in their call center. As Catherine Manginelli, managing director of Talent Management for TD Ameritrade, reports, "I'm noticing older generations still want to work and we as a company have to do a better job of recruiting them and identifying job opportunities for them. While we focus much of our recruiting efforts on Millennials, we are now turning to Boomers who want to return to the workplace on a flexible schedule."

Questions to Ask About Boomers

1. How common is the younger manager and older worker trend at our organization and do we need to explicitly address this?
2. Is our organization creating opportunities for boomers to be mentors and coaches and be involved in employee resource groups targeted to multigenerational employees?
3. Are there opt-in learning and career development programs to allow boomers to learn new skills and job roles?
4. Are we involving boomers enough in formal and informal job rotations as part of continuing education?
5. Is our organization conducting enough workforce analytics to estimate the percentage of boomers eligible to retire in the next two to five years? What are we doing about this expected exit of boomers from the workplace?

Generations Are a Global Phenomenon

Political, socioeconomic, and cultural events in a country have a transformative impact on shaping generational cohorts. The generational cohorts commonly defined to date have been those in the United States. The defining year was 1945, the year that marked the end of World War II and the beginning of the boomer generation. But what about globally?

While distinct generational cohorts reflect a country's socioeconomic and political events, the same technology that enables millennials to post a million selfies a day also gives them a window into the lives of people around the globe. In this sense, present-day millennials have been called the first global generation. Millennials born in the United States (between 1982 and 1993) may be more similar to their generational cohorts in China, India, and South Korea than they are to people of different ages in their own country.

Consider China, where the defining year was 1949, the foundation of the People's Republic. What followed was 30 years of economic and political turmoil that had a significant impact on the attitudes, aspirations, hopes, and fears of the population. Change in China introduced cultural and economic transformation in each decade, causing four generational groupings: post 50s, post 60s, post 70s, and post 80s. However, the generations present in China mirror the broad generational cohorts of boomers, Gen Xers, and millennials found in the United States.

Take two of these Chinese generational groupings, post 70s and post 80s. The post-70s generation (including those born between 1970 and 1979, analogous to Gen Xers in the United States) are more Western in outlook than preceding generations because they include the first college graduates who choose their own careers and benefited from on-campus recruiting at college.

By comparison the post-80s generation (including those born between 1980 and 1989, analogous to millennials in the United States) is the first generation of single children following the introduction of the one-child policy (abolished in 2015). Members of that generation have a reputation for being confident and individualistic. Post-70s leaders who manage a post-80s team find these younger team members more focused on career self-development than they are, and the post-70s leaders experience similar generational tensions as their American counterparts who manage a millennial team.[35]

What this implies is the importance of leaders to understand the demographics, values, beliefs, and expectations of talent in each country and how these are both similar and different and then adjust recruitment, development, and retention strategies accordingly.

What Will the Next-Generation Workforce Look Like?

While we have examined the major generations in today's workplace, we also need to recognize the generation beyond Gen Z. This is Generation Alpha, only 7 years old in 2017 and 15 years old by 2025. Generation Alpha members will be the most diverse of all the generations. In 2011, Generation Alpha reached a demographic milestone: there were more Generation Alpha babies born to minority families than white families in the United States. By 2020, more than 50 percent of high schoolers, the foundation of the future workforce of the 2030s, will be non-white.

In addition to being ethnically diverse, Generation Alpha members are literally growing up with a connected, interactive device in their hands and with their millennial parents chronicling their every move on social platforms like Instagram and Facebook. Even more than millennials and Gen Zers who use technology extensively, many alphas will spend the bulk of their formative years completely immersed in technology, growing up in environments where their actions and movements are quantified, and will see this as part of how they experience the world around them.

If you have not already seen the popular YouTube video *A Magazine Is an IPad That Does Not Work,* it is worth the 90 seconds of your time. The video shows a one-year-old girl playing with an iPad. She is then handed several magazines. She tries to turn the print pages of a magazine by touching them. Nothing happens, and she quickly returns to the iPad as she is accustomed to making something happen by her touch. The popular YouTube video (seen nearly 5 million times) ends with this statement: "A magazine is an iPad that does not work. And it will be so for the rest of her life! Steve Jobs has coded a part of her OS (Operating System)."[36]

Members of generation alpha will likely enter the workplace as 15-year-old interns by 2025, driven by the ambitions of their millennial parents. As they have grown up with technology built into many of their toys, from customizable robots teaching engineering concepts to mobile apps accompanying toys, we can expect this generation to be the most hyperconnected of all.

Just as IBM is using the Millennial Corps to inform the company on the needs of millennials in both the workplace and the marketplace, we will see companies tapping both Gen Z and over time even Generation Alpha to inform them on the needs and expectations these next generations will have in the workplace.

The Diverse Next-Generation Workplace

The key to navigating a workplace with multiple generations and cultures along with increasing numbers of women is to recognize that all of this adds to the diversity of thought in solving today's pressing business issues. The opportunity for leaders is this: use workplace diversity to your advantage and build an inclusive work environment where diversity adds to innovative thinking.

Perhaps most importantly, leaders need to recognize that the age, gender, and cultural diversity of a company's employees mirrors the diversity of its customer base. So this is not only a human resource issue; it is a business issue and an opportunity to better serve your organization's diverse market segments.

MY ACTION PLAN

Myself

- How do I fit into the generational preferences described in the Workplace Generational Intelligence Framework?
- Which of my preferences reflect those of my generation, and which are different? Am I a millennial in a boomer body (#MIBB)?

- What biases do I hold about the different generations or cultures that I work with?

My Team

- Do we exhibit "unconscious bias" in how we treat the different generations, cultures, or genders that work for us?
- What are the various generations represented on our team? How does this affect our team dynamic?
- Do we take into account the different cultural preferences of team members in our organization?

My Organization

- What are the age demographics of our organization's global workforce today, and what do we project this to be over the next three to five years?
- Does the age and cultural makeup of our workforce resemble that of our customers? What are we doing to learn about both?
- How do we proactively plan ahead for the generational and culture shift of our future job candidates?

BUILD GENDER EQUALITY

8

> The time is long overdue to encourage more women to dream the possible dream.
>
> —*Sheryl Sandberg, COO of Facebook and cofounder of Lean In*

Despite progress in recent years, gender inequality persists. To achieve gender equality will require a commitment to change at all levels—from institutions to individuals.

In her bestselling book *Lean In*, Sandberg highlights this through a story about the importance of raising your hand. Sandberg was speaking to a group of 150 Facebook employees shortly after her book was published. At the end of her talk, Sandberg told the audience she had time for only two more questions. After she answered these two questions, hands continued to wave, and so she continued to call on people. Eventually she went back to her office and found a young woman waiting for her. Sandberg asked this woman what she had learned from the talk, to which the young women replied, "I learned to keep my hand up." Puzzled, Sandberg asked her to elaborate. The young woman explained, "After you took those two final questions, I put my hand down and I noticed all the other women also put their hands down. A bunch of men kept their hands up and you took more questions." The men ignored the limit on questions, and the women obeyed, "If we as women don't raise our hands in the workplace, we're not going to get the same opportunities men do. Because men keep their hands raised."[1]

However, the burden of change cannot rest on the shoulders of women alone. The men in the room at Facebook gained extra opportunities in part because they weren't afraid to ignore boundaries by keeping their hands raised beyond the end of the session. But they also gained those opportunities because—consciously or unconsciously—the person in power rewarded this behavior. As Sandberg says, "Even though I was giving a speech on gender issues, I had been blind to one myself. If we want a world with greater equality, we need to acknowledge that women are less likely to keep their hands up. We need institutions and individuals to notice and correct for this behavior by encouraging, promoting, and championing women. And women have to learn to keep their hands up, because when they lower them, even managers with the best intentions might not notice."[2]

Mika Brzezinski, cohost of MSNBC's *Morning Joe*, seemed to have it all, as an accomplished journalist, wife, and mother of two teenage girls. However, she admits to failing to raise her hand when it came time to ask for a raise. Mika's book *Know Your Value* tells her story of how she finally demanded a raise as an acknowledgment of her efforts in the success of *Morning Joe*. Says Mika, "It took me 25 years to understand that I played a role in my success. For too many years, I let others do the talking and made the same mistakes time and time again."[3] Mika shares the dichotomy between her daily on-air persona as the charismatic and outspoken cohost of *Morning Joe* and her passive, apologetic manner when asking for a raise by saying, "I'm sorry, I know you are super busy but . . . "

Then, after months of working nonstop to help make *Morning Joe* a success, she found out her cohost, Joe Scarborough, was being paid 14 times her salary. Initially neither Mika nor Joe could convince MSNBC to appropriately compensate Mika for her work contributing to the show's success. Finally, as Mika shares in her book, she took action, supported by Joe, her coanchor, and confidently had a discussion with her boss, Phil Griffin, telling him that she deserved to be paid more, no apologies needed!

These stories play out again and again in the workplace. Research by Prudential Financial reports that while women are 33 percent more likely to gain a college degree than men, a gender pay gap prevails.

In the United States, women make up almost 60 percent of the university graduates, 60 percent of master's degree recipients, and 52 percent of those with doctorates. Women are the more educated part of the workforce even though they only earn 78 percent of the salaries of their male counterparts.[4]

In the digital economy, where one might expect a more even playing field, women who auction products for sale on eBay still receive 80 cents for every dollar that men get on eBay.[5]

Glassdoor conducted a study entitled "Demystifying the Gender Pay Gap," analyzing male-female pay differences in five countries: The United States, the United Kingdom, Australia, Germany, and France. Overall, Glassdoor economist Andrew Chamberlin finds an undeniable gender pay gap both in the United States and around the world. Men earn more than women on average in all the five countries. In the United States, men earn on average 24.1 percent higher base pay than women in Glassdoor salaries. Amazingly even when Glassdoor compared workers with the same title, employer, and location, the United States gender pay gap is about 5.4 percent, and in the other four countries examined there was a similar pattern.[6]

According to Lean In and McKinsey's survey of 30,000 men and women at 118 North American companies, women held 45 percent of entry-level jobs at the companies surveyed, but their ranks thin out as they rise in the organization. Only 27 percent of vice presidents at those companies are women, followed by 23 percent of senior vice presidents and 17 percent of C-suite executives.[7]

These figures represent only a slight improvement from 2012. Women are underrepresented at every level of the corporate pipeline, and this disparity is greatest in senior leadership, as shown in Figure 8.1.[8]

Global Gender Workforce Participation

Across countries, despite educational gains, women lag behind men in income, new business ownership, and earnings. The "Global Gender Gap Report" issued by the World Economic Forum ranks gender-based disparities across the globe by examining four categories: economic participation, educational attainment, health and survival, and political empowerment. In the 2015 ranking of gender equality, the United States is listed as number 28 out of 145 countries.[9]

Unsurprisingly, the Nordic countries—Iceland, Norway, Finland, and Sweden—come out on top as the best countries for working women. These

Figure 8.1   *Gender representation in the corporate pipeline*

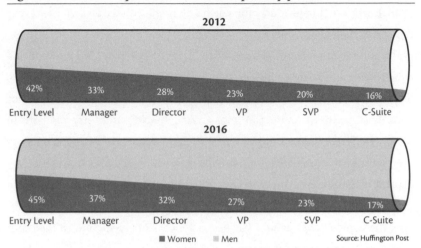

2012

Entry Level	Manager	Director	VP	SVP	C-Suite
42%	33%	28%	23%	20%	16%

2016

Entry Level	Manager	Director	VP	SVP	C-Suite
45%	37%	32%	27%	23%	17%

■ Women   ■ Men   Source: Huffington Post

countries have the largest percentage of women in parliament, as well as laws mandating a percentage of female board members. Finland and Norway have legal mandates that require at least 40 percent of state-owned or public limited company board members be female.[10]

On the other hand, Japan, a G20 country, ranks number 101 in the 2015 Global Gender Gap Index. In Japan, several issues come together to create a large gender gap, from the Japanese workplace culture of long office hours to the lack of affordable daycare centers for working moms. In fact, there is such a severe shortage of daycare centers that there is a specific Japanese word, *hokatsu*, to mean "actively searching for a childcare center." These factors, among others, create an environment where it is especially difficult for women to thrive in the workplace.

Global Gender Workforce Participation Statistics

The average woman working full time in the United States will lose more than $460,000 over a 40-year period in wages due only to the gender gap. To catch up, the average working woman would need to work for 12 additional years after the age at which the average working man retired from the workforce.

Source: Catalyst

The prime minister of Japan, Shinzo Abe, set an ambitious goal: by the year 2020, women should hold 30 percent of senior jobs, compared with just over 8 percent currently. In April 2014, the country's Labor Ministry launched a program offering financial rewards to small and midsized firms for promoting women into supervisory positions. Under the program, companies must offer 30 hours of training to educate their workforce about equal opportunity rights and the potential of hiring and training women. The Japanese government budgeted 120 million yen ($1.4 million) for the program. However, within 17 months of its inception, not a single company had applied for the incentive.[11] Clearly, setting quotas does not work without addressing the larger issue of workplace culture, lack of affordable childcare, and lack of female role models.

The lesson: the gender gap is a complex issue, and sustainable solutions require a mix of new policies, a more accepting workplace culture, and a set of support services targeting both women and their families, allowing them to thrive in the workplace.

If Gender Equality Is Good for Business, Why Have We Not Made More Progress?

Research from McKinsey and Lean In estimate closing the gender gap could drive between $12 trillion and $28 trillion in gross domestic product growth by 2025. McKinsey's latest report, titled "Diversity Matters," examined proprietary data sets for 366 public companies across a range of industries in Canada, Latin America, the United Kingdom, and the United States. The findings are clear: companies in the top quartile for racial, ethnic, and gender-based diversity are more likely to have financial performance above their respective national industry medians—by 35 percent for racial and ethnic diversity and 15 percent for gender diversity. In the United Kingdom, greater gender diversity on the senior executive team corresponded to the highest performance uplift in the data set: for every 10 percent increase in gender diversity, EBIT (earnings before interest and taxes) rose by 3.5 percent. Gender equality is smart economics; the companies that embrace an inclusive workplace statistically outperform their peers.[12]

What is holding companies back from closing the gender gap? Research by LeanIn.org and McKinsey suggests the issue is primarily one of workplace culture. "Historically, we thought women were less interested in promotions because of their concerns with family responsibilities," Rachel Thomas, the president and cofounder of Lean In, says. However, "This study points to a new reason. . . . Women say stress and pressure in the workplace is a top obstacle for them—and this includes all women, those with and without children." The stress, Thomas asserts, comes from the conscious and unconscious biases that lead women to face bigger hurdles at the office.[13]

Glassdoor research points to an additional issue, what Chamberlin calls the "sorting of men and women into jobs and industries that pay differently throughout the economy." For example, as of 2014, only 18 percent of computer science bachelor degrees were earned by women, despite the fact that it is known to be a gateway to a number of high-paying jobs. And computer science is where there has been a decrease in the number of women earning bachelor degrees since 2002, even after a recent modest increase.[14]

One key to change, according to the Anita Borg Institute, a nonprofit with a mission to equalize the number of males and females in technology, is for high schools and universities to proactively drive greater participation among women in computer science courses and clubs. One such strategy employed by Harvey Mudd College is to reconfigure the beginning computer science course into three tracks; Beginning, intermediate, and advanced, so students with no programming experience are not overwhelmed by others who may have been coding since they were 10 years old.

Managing Work and the Rest of Life

With 40 percent of the global workforce female, there is still much work to be done—and yet never before has a generation entered the workforce with such high levels of female participation.[15] PwC, as one example, recruits 20,000 millennials annually from around the globe and estimates 50 percent of their PwC workforce is female. How does this surge of female workers square with the parenting expectations of millennials? In many ways the "gender revolution" has had lopsided results: younger men are much more committed to equality at home than previous generations of men. However the division of work at home is still disproportionately falling on the shoulders of women resulting in a slow evolution rather than a revolution.[16]

Research by Sarah Thébaud, a sociologist at the University of California, Santa Barbara, finds that men and women ages 18 to 32 tend to have egalitarian attitudes about gender roles, across education and income levels. However, when faced with a lack of family-friendly policies in the workplace, many default to traditional roles rather than follow their preferences.[17]

In a study by sociologists Thébaud and David Pedulla, entitled "Can We Finish the Revolution? Gender, Work-Family Ideals, and Institutional Constraint," the authors surveyed a sample of unmarried men and women ages 18 to 34 about their desires for their future work and family arrangements. They were randomly divided into three groups, and each group was given a different scenario, with varying degrees of supportive policies.

When offered supportive policies, a majority of men and women across all educational backgrounds preferred an egalitarian relationship structure. In fact, 95 percent of college-educated women chose an egalitarian relationship and 75 percent of college-educated men did as well.

Yet in the face of constraints such as unfriendly family leave policies and inadequate childcare, their choices more often aligned with traditional gender roles. In scenarios without supportive policies, 64 percent of college-educated women opted for an arrangement where one spouse—typically male—serves as the primary breadwinner and one spouse—typically female—serves as the primary caregiver. For millennial men, the percentage choosing this arrangement increased to 87 percent.[18]

Why is this? We think the key obstacles to more egalitarian family roles may be a combination of an unsupporting family work culture and extreme schedules of working parents. Gallup reports that Americans work an average of 47 hours per week, with 4 in 10 reporting they work at least 59 hours per week. It is not surprising that in the absence of supporting workplace policies, working parents who struggle with demanding schedules are opting for traditional family structures.[19]

Millennial women start off wanting egalitarian arrangements at home, but often the reality of the workplace forces pragmatic choices. According to a survey of 25,000 graduates of the Harvard Business School conducted by Robin Ely, Pamela Stone, and Colleen Ammerman, 50 to 60 percent of men across three generations (boomers, Gen Xers, and millennials) were "extremely satisfied" or "very satisfied" with their work and professional accomplishments, opportunities for career growth, and compatibility of work and personal life, while only 40 to 50 percent of women were similarly satisfied on the same dimensions. "In the end," the Harvard study authors write, "we find not just achievement and satisfaction gaps between women and men, but a real gap between what women and working mothers expect as they look ahead to their careers and where they ultimately land."[20]

Family Friendly Policies Are Slowly Emerging

As the percentage of two-income families increases, workplace policies designed to support working parents become more important than ever before. But currently, according to the Society of Human Resources, only 21 percent of employers offer some type of paid maternity, while 17 percent offer paid paternity and/or adoption leave.[21] Figure 8.2 lists the leading companies that offer paid maternity leave, ranging from a high of 52 weeks to a low of 12.[22]

The Bill & Melinda Gates Foundation and Netflix are generous outliers, providing a year of paid maternity leave. But the United States as a whole is still woefully behind other countries. Unlike nearly every other country in the world, the United States mandates no paid leave for mothers or fathers following the birth of a child.[23] Our Family and Medical Leave Act requires employers with more than 50 employees to provide new parents with 12 weeks of leave; however, it does not require this leave to be paid. In the United States, this is starting to be dealt with on a state-by-state basis, with some states, including California, Rhode Island, and New Jersey, creating some type of paid family leave policy. In the vast majority of U.S. states, though, there is no required paid parental leave. In contrast, the average paid leave available

Figure 8.2   *Top U.S. companies offering paid maternity leave*

52 Weeks	Bill & Melinda Gates Foundation, Netflix
20 Weeks	Amazon, Microsoft, Twitter
18 Weeks	Apple, Bloomberg, Google, U.S. Navy
17 Weeks	Reddit
16 Weeks	Facebook, Goldman Sachs, Fidelity Investments
15 Weeks	Johnson & Johnson
12 Weeks	Bank of America

Source: *Time* Magazine

to mothers across all 34 OECD countries is 54 weeks, with an average of 17 of those week fully paid.[24] Interestingly Swedish parents are entitled to a combined 480 days paid parental leave, with 60 of those days reserved for fathers.

When companies are offering paid maternity leave, there are pockets of innovation. Fidelity Investments offers a customized package of maternity benefits allowing women the ability to create their own path forward following the birth of a child. Jennifer Hanson, head of Associate Experience at Fidelity Investments, stresses the importance of choice. "For mothers returning to work following the birth of a child, they have the ability to customize the last six weeks of their 16 week paid leave choice and break this up into three blocks of time, of at least one week in length, creating their own personalized path back to work."

Increasingly, some companies offer paid paternity leave for fathers. As examples, Facebook offers 16 weeks paid paternity leave, Yahoo offers 8 weeks, and showing this is not just a "Silicon Valley initiative," Bank of America offers 12 weeks, and Johnson & Johnson provides 8 weeks of paid paternity leave. While paternity leave may seem like an unexpected benefit for new fathers, in the long run, all parents—male and female—as well as the children win. One of the benefits of of paternity leave is that it creates opportunities for men to become more involved at home, not only for the duration of the paternity leave but also for years to come. In Quebec, as reported in an article entitled "The Daddy Track: The Case for Paternity Leave," there is a "use it or lose it" approach granting each family member a total amount of leave, a certain portion of which can be used only by fathers. The result: women whose husbands took paternity leave were more likely to resume full-time work themselves, with their original employers.[25]

Some companies that offer paid paternity leave recognize the cultural barriers around new fathers taking time off, and they are creating policies to address this. At State Street Bank, which offers four weeks of paid paternity leave, new fathers have the opportunity to customize their leave. This means they do not have to take the four weeks of paternity leave all at once; they can take one week, return to work, and then customize the remaining three weeks of leave across several months. State Street managers make a point of communicating this policy so new fathers who are too hesitant to ask for their leave are encouraged to have a conversation with their manager.[26]

Recent announcements to enhance maternity leave programs have added a new benefit, a Work Life Coach, for women and men returning to work after the birth of a child. So far this benefit is cropping up in firms engaged in highly competitive talent markets such as accounting, law, and investment banking by organizations that include EY, KPMG, Grant Thornton and Proskauer Rose, and K.K.R. Life Coaches provide access to parents to ensure a smooth transition to the workforce. While only a small and privileged group of employees have access to this, it is the beginning of a recognition that employers must take more action to assist families in their transition to the workforce following the birth or adoption of a child.[27]

The Breadwinner Mom and the Emergence of the Chief Household Officer

As more women take on leadership positions, we are seeing the emergence of the breadwinner mom. A Pew Research Center analysis of U.S. Census data finds a record 40 percent of all U.S. households with children under the age of 18 include breadwinner moms, who are either the sole or primary source of income for the family. The share was just 11 percent in 1960.[28] These bread-winner moms are made up of two very different groups: 5.1 million are married mothers who have a higher income than their spouses, and 8.6 million are single mothers.[29] Despite the different profiles of these two groups, the recent growth of breadwinner moms is connected in part to women's slowly increasing employment rate and fast rising education levels, which are improving opportunities in the workplace.[30] Today, one in five fathers is the primary caregiver of preschool-age children who have mothers who are employed full time. In fact, in the last 25 years, the number of fathers who are primary caregivers married to breadwinner mothers has doubled.[31]

Kristin Holter, a 44-year-old director of Global HR Capability at Phillip Morris International, has two sons, a 5-year-old and a newborn, and works full time as a breadwinner mom. She is a graduate of Vassar College and currently lives and works in Lausanne, Switzerland, with her husband Bruce and their two young sons. Kristin grew up in Europe and traveled widely throughout Japan, Korea, China, Tibet, and Nepal before deciding on a career in human resources. She has worked for a number of large organizations including Bain & Company, Deloitte, Bacardi, and now Phillip Morris International.

Along the way, Kristin met her husband Bruce Weber, a former Accenture consultant and CIO. At the age of 39, they had their first child. Kristin says this about becoming a breadwinner mom: "While on a 14 week maternity leave at Bacardi, I was actually promoted to be the global head of change management. While I took my maternity leave when my first son was born, I ended up creating my own roadmap for a re-entry to the workplace. As a family, we decided I would become a Breadwinner mom since my husband was at the end of his corporate career and transitioning into an entrepreneurial role, so it made more sense for him to assume the role of primary care giver for our children."

Bruce Weber has an impressive background. He was a pilot and then a lieutenant in the U.S. Navy; an honors graduate of Georgia Institute of Technology with two master's degrees, one in applied mathematics and a second in physics; a consultant with Accenture; and finally a CIO with a number of privately held companies in Lausanne. Today Bruce manages a number of private investments in restaurants in Switzerland. However, he considers his full-time job as being the primary caregiver for Maxwell and Louis and describes his role as being the "chief household officer," or CHO, for his family.

Bruce relates his decision to become a primary caregiver in the following way: "Kristin and I always believed that at least one parent should be actively involved at home with our children. And we eventually came to the conclusion that it would be easier for me to be the primary caregiver and to continue to manage my restaurants and do some part time consulting, while Kristin continues her career at Phillip Morris International."

Bruce said one of the more difficult aspects of transitioning from CIO to CHO was that "I didn't have any acquaintances in this role so I didn't have much to gauge the transition against, until I thought of this as effectively assuming a new work role when I was at Accenture. There, one of the first things we did when transitioning to a new position was to create an explicit document of new roles and responsibilities, a sort of Playbook for the role. Well, it took Kristin and me about a year to realize we had to apply the same mindset to this role, just as I would have in assuming any new role I had as an Accenture consultant or CIO. Once Kristin and I thought of the transition in this way, I have been able to make it a success, and I am now coaching other dads to do the same."

Kristin and Bruce single-handedly put the pieces together to allow Kristin to work full time, manage a remote team across multiple time zones, and transition Bruce from CIO to CHO. But in speaking to both of them, they made it clear that they believe companies can do more to provide resources and support for families that pursue this path.

Kristin and Bruce suggest companies consider breadwinner moms a distinct segment of the employee population and create a similar set of resources for them as are created for other executives transitioning into a new job or new location. Some of the resources might include an employee affinity group that provides access to local on-site and online childcare resources, a program that brings spouses into the mix to meet other spouses who are primary caregivers, access to services that target the special needs of breadwinner moms such as financial consulting, breast milk shipping for traveling moms, and an employee resource group dedicated to not just working moms but their entire family network.

Unconscious Bias: Companies Take Action Against Hidden Prejudices Directed at Women

When YouTube, owned by Google, launched a video app for iOS users, the app's developers were puzzled by what appeared to be a bug in the code. About 10 percent of the videos uploaded were coming in upside down. Then they realized what happened: the app's coders were nearly all right-handed. The coders hadn't accounted for the fact that phones are usually rotated 180 degrees when held in left hands, and they had designed an app that only really worked for right-handed users.[32]

This was one of the first times that Google realized how unconscious biases can seep unseen into everyday decisions, influencing them without realizing it.

But what exactly is unconscious bias? Catalyst, a nonprofit organiza-tion focused on promoting inclusive workplaces for women, defines uncon-scious bias as an implicit association or attitude about the characteristics of an individual—such as an individual's race or gender—that operates out of our control, informs our perception about a person or group of people, and can influence our decision making and behavior toward a person or group of people—even without us realizing it is happening.

Companies are recognizing that unconscious bias can seep into hiring and promotion decisions, causing roadblocks in diversity and inclusion programs. In May 2014 Google published a report on the demographics of the company. It turns out that 70 percent of Googlers are men, Latinos make up just 3 per-cent of the workforce, and African Americans constitute 2 percent. This disclo-sure set off a wave of similar reports from Facebook, Apple, Yahoo, and others, and plans are under way among these companies to address this issue.[33]

Google, PwC, and Barclays were among the first companies to call out unconscious bias as contributing to the systemic lack of diversity in the technology industry. Google began training its workforce in unconscious bias with 90-minute lectures starting in 2013. Since then, more than half of Googlers around the globe have taken part in these awareness-building workshops, helping to create a culture that calls out prejudice, both blatant and subtle.[34]

Google's former SVP of People Operations, Laszlo Bock, explains Google's point of view: "Our biases are shaped by our experiences and by cultural norms which allow us to filter information and make quick decisions." He writes, "We've evolved to trust our guts. But sometimes these mental shortcuts lead us astray, especially when they cause us to misjudge people. . . . Combating our unconscious biases is hard, because they don't feel wrong; they feel right. But it's necessary to fight against bias in order to create a work environment that supports and encourages diverse perspectives and people. Not only is that the right thing to do, but without a diverse workforce, there's a pretty good chance that our products . . . won't work for everyone."[35]

Moving Unconscious Bias from Awareness to Action

Companies deal with unconscious bias in various ways, from recognizing that it exists and setting goals to change it, to implementing formal training on the topic. But one of the most frequently asked questions is how does an organization move from awareness of unconscious bias to action? Sarah Churchman of PwC explains it this way: "At PwC we have learned everyone finds Unconscious Bias Training fascinating, but the real key is to align this with the talent management process and set targets to hire and promote individuals who are subject to recognizing unconscious bias. For example, if a pool of middle managers is comprised of 50 percent female employees and 50 percent male, then we expect to promote an equal percent of men and women. And if this is not the case, we ask Managing Partners to explain why."

One company that stands out for its commitment to closing the gender gap is Kimberly-Clark Corporation, which since 2009 has seen a 90 percent increase in the number of women holding director-level-and-above positions and received an award from Catalyst for developing diverse talent and creating metrics for this across the globe. It even ties bonus money to it. "To be an exceptional leader at Kimberly-Clark you have to develop talent that looks, thinks, and behaves like the people who use our products," says Sue Dodsworth, chief diversity officer for Kimberly-Clark Corporation.

Recently the company put into place something it calls the Rule of Two: for appointments at the VP level and above, leaders must bring three candidates for consideration, and no more than two of them should have a similar demographic profile. This helps avoid the "just like me" bias that is so prevalent in promotion decisions.

Trevor Gandy, chief diversity officer of the Chubb Group of Insurance Companies, has a long-term perspective on how to close the gender gap. The Women's Development Council at Chubb, an employee resource group, is now 35 years old and was one of the first devoted to furthering women's development. Gandy believes one of the keys to moving from awareness to action in building gender equality is to recruit senior executives into the discussion and planning process for the steps needed to close the gender gap. Ellen Moore, president and CEO of Chubb Insurance Company of Canada, says, "You will not be as successful as you can be if you cling to biases in the workplace." Gandy believes companies not only need to create a governing board including senior executives on the topic of gender gap, but also need to involve them as sponsors of women, not just advocates for them. As Gandy points out, "Just inviting leaders to be mentors of women is really not enough. While mentors talk *with* high potential women, sponsors talk *about them* and advocate on their behalf."

What Can You Do to Move from Awareness of Unconscious Bias to Action?

Organizations need to move beyond building awareness of unconscious bias to taking action against it. But how? Our interviews uncovered seven strategies organizations can consider:

1. Measure.
   - It's hard to know you're improving if you're not measuring. Track gender representation across all standard business activities by job level.

2. Be mindful of subtle cues.

- Who's included and who's excluded? Go further and track the discretionary activities such as your gender representation at conferences, recruiting events and of speakers invited to speak at your larger organizational meetings. In 2013, Googlers pointed out that of the dozens of conference rooms named after famous scientists, only a few were female. So Google changed Ferdinand von Zeppelin Conference Room to Florence Nightingale Conference Room—along with others—to create more balanced representation.[36]

3. If you see something, say something.

- The slogan from the Department of Homeland Security also applies to biases in the workplace. To foster awareness on unconscious bias, encourage a practice of "if you see something, say something." Google created a workshop called Unconscious Bias @ Work to identify and understand the biases employees bring to work. Bias training introduced the language of bias and now it is part of the daily conversation at Google, with employees owning it and challenging each other all the time.

4. Promote employee resource groups (ERGs) to supplement formal training on unconscious bias.

- Think of ERGs in an expansive way and as a supplement to formal training on unconscious bias. Invite not just female leaders but also their networks of support to participate in these groups.

5. Hold yourself and your team accountable for how you source and promote individuals different from yourself.

- Consider recommending that your team set targets to ensure every hiring and promotion panel includes a diverse group of individuals who are part of the decision-making process. Also to further support diversity, some companies are exploring using mobile job matching apps such as Blendoor and GapJumpers in the recruiting process. These apps hide a candidate's name and photo to circumvent unconscious bias during hiring.

6. Create a clear process in advance for making decisions.

- Define criteria to evaluate the merits of each option, and use this consistently. Consider using structured interviews in hiring, applying the same selection and evaluation methods for all. Also to further support diversity, some companies are exploring using mobile job matching apps such as Blendoor and GapJumpers, to counteract bias in the recruiting process. These platforms perform functions like hiding a candidate's name and photo to circumvent unconscious bias during hiring.

7. Pay attention to prevailing gender assumptions.

- When evaluating fit for positions, ask: Would we come to this point of view if the scenario involved someone of a different gender? Sarah Churchman of PwC explains it this way: "At PwC we have learned everyone finds Unconscious Bias Training fascinating but the real key is to align this with the talent management process and set targets to hire and promote individuals that are prone to recognizing unconscious bias. For example, if a pool of middle managers is comprised of 50 percent female employees and 50 percent male, then we expect to promote an equal percent of men and women. And if this is not the case, we ask Managing Partners to explain why."

Female Boomers on the Grid

True to their competitive and live-to-work reputations, female boomers are deciding to stay in the workplace longer. Gallup research shows that nearly half (49 percent) of boomers who are still working say they don't expect to retire until they are 66 or older, including one in ten who predict they will never retire at all.[37] Although boomers first became eligible for social security in 2008, one-third of the oldest boomers, currently aged 67 and 68, are still working in some capacity.[38] While male and female employees both tend to decrease full-time work participation as they age, men stop working full time at a faster rate than women, with larger numbers switching to part-time work.[39] This implies that by age 68, the gender gap in full-time work participation between men and women is 8 percentage points, compared with a gender gap as large as 20 percentage points at younger ages.[40]

While some continue working out of financial necessity, others stay in the workforce because they are highly engaged and enthusiastic about their jobs.[41] One example is Candy Haynes, a managing director at PwC, who is a boomer who wants to continue to work and play hard. Candy calls herself "Grandma on the Grid," and she realizes, looking around her, that she may not be alone! She started her career at Deloitte in 1979 after earning an undergraduate degree in economics from Middlebury College in just three years and then an MBA from Dartmouth. Candy has been a maverick in many ways, from navigating the largely male-dominated accounting world in the 1970s and 1980s to being a breadwinner mom for the past 20 years following the retirement of her husband in 1995 from Deloitte. Now in her fifties, Candy works in an environment where the average age is 27 years old, and she candidly admits to having no intention of retiring. In fact, as Candy says, "I am just getting going, I am motivated at work, love my job, and team members. I also now support my immediate family plus one granddaughter, Riley, who is my best friend and the love of my life."

Candy sees herself continuing in the workforce well into her sixties and challenges employers to think about how to keep boomers engaged in the workplace. One strategy is to devise a new set of benefits to keep highly talented employees working well into their sixties. Consider the new benefits announced by PwC targeting millennials by offering up to $1,200 per year (for up to five years) in student debt assistance. That's great for new entrants into the workforce, but employers should also expand and customize offerings for older workers who want to continue in the workplace. As highly engaged female boomers like Candy elect to stay in the workplace into their sixties, forward-looking companies should understand how to leverage these employees' unique skill sets for mentoring others as well as for inspiration to create customized benefits.

Building Gender Equality Is a Twenty-First Century Challenge

While we have documented the benefits to businesses of closing the gender gap, ranging from improving financial and business performance, to adding diversity of thought in developing new products and services, a gender-based pay gap continues to exist. We believe it is up to countries, companies, and individual *women and men* to create the change they want to see in the workplace.

We can and need to do more. First we should involve men in the discussion to build gender equality. This can start with creating conversations and workshops that build awareness and actions for dealing with unconscious bias in the workplace. Next, we need to encourage the men we work with to move beyond mentoring women to becoming sponsors and advocates for them in the workplace. Third, we must examine the current policy of maternity and paternity leave in our organizations and ask ourselves what more can be done to assist working moms and their families in creating their own personalized path back to work. Finally, we must examine what can be done by our government. Currently, in the United States, maternity and paternity is being handled on a state by state basis with the United States being the only industrialized country that does not mandate paid maternity leave. While we have documented a number of corporations that offer generous paid maternity and paternity leave, and Life Coach services to employees returning to work, this is not the norm. According to the National Center for Health Statistics, only 13 percent of people in the United States have access to paid family leave.[42]

As women in the workplace continue to increase in number and take on leadership roles, it is up to each of us to create a healthy work life integration. We no longer have to choose between the two. Rather, we can change how we think, act, work, develop, and lead, particularly in a workplace where women are projected to account for the majority of the increase in the total labor force growth.

MY ACTION PLAN

Myself

- What is my current situation? Am I a breadwinner mom (or married to one)? A member of a dual career family? A single working parent?
- Am I aware of the vocabulary I use in the workplace? Do we use terms such as *stay-at-home mother* and *stay-at-home father*? Interestingly, men

who identify as chief household officers have expressed the greatest resistance to the *stay-at-home parent* term as they believe this does not capture the important job of childcare.

- Am I aware of the correlation between diversity and profitability for my organization and how this aligns with what is happening at our competitors?

My Team

- Is our team aware of resources for working moms?
- Are my team members aware of our organization's workplace flexibility, maternity and paternity leave policies?
- How could our team start conversations about unconscious bias in the workplace and how do we keep this dialogue going?

My Organization

- How could we create job descriptions that encourage women to apply for traditionally male positions?
- Do we believe our culture is one that is family friendly and offers workplace flexibility?
- How could we organize employee affinity groups and online resources for emerging segments of employees such as breadwinner moms and boomers who want to remain working?

PLAN FOR MORE GIG ECONOMY WORKERS

9

We have entered a new era. Freelancing is changing how we work. In lieu of traditional full-time jobs with a single employer, more Americans are working independently. Instead of working 9-to-5, more are working project-to-project and gig-to-gig.

Sara Horowitz, founder of the Freelancers Union,
"Freelancing in America 2015 Report"

The Growing Market for the Gig Economy Workforce

The workforce of the future won't be all full-time employees. It will be made up of consultants, contractors, freelancers, part-time employees, and other independent workers collectively known as the *gig economy*. The gig economy workforce is growing rapidly. According to a recent study by the Freelancers Union, freelance workers accounted for 34 percent of American workers in 2015, totaling nearly 54 million people and contributing $7 billion to the U.S. economy.[1] By the year 2020, Intuit predicts 43 percent of the U.S. workforce—or 60 million people—will be gig economy workers.[2] This data indicates that HR leaders will need to plan for a shift from managing a workforce of almost all full-time employees to managing a more *blended workforce* of employees and independent, gig economy workers.

Both employers and workers are driving the rise of the blended workforce. Qualified independent workers are now easier to find while workers themselves seek greater flexibility. A study by Ardent Partners found that 95 percent of organizations believe their contingent workforce is important to their company's success and growth. They found that HR leaders are increasingly looking at a mix of contingent workers and full-time employees for talent.[3] A recent survey conducted by Randstad similarly shows that nearly half (46 percent) of HR leaders are including independent contractors as part of their talent acquisition strategy.[4] Our research, conducted with Field Nation, an online platform connecting businesses with freelance workers, for "The Rise of the Blended Workforce in the New Gig Economy" found 58 percent of top-performing firms say that 20 percent or more of their labor force is already composed of freelancers. These freelancers bring valuable skills to companies including: effective teamwork (38 percent), problem solving (36 percent), and self management (32 percent).[5] Companies increasingly are recognizing the value of a blended workforce composed of full timers and contingent workers, and they are building competencies to successfully manage this blended workforce.

The Five Types of Gig Economy Workers

Who are these growing masses of independent workers who move from gig to gig and project to project, eschewing the traditional nine-to-five full-time job? As freelancer and entrepreneur Ritika Puri states: "The old stereotype, that freelancers are just people who can't find full-time jobs, is years—even decades—out of date. The contemporary freelancer is an experienced professional with a specific set of skills, whose track record and personal brand are strong enough to support a thriving business."[6]

Table 9.1 shows that the freelance workforce can be divided into five types of workers. As you can see, independent contractors make up the largest segment. Data on the gig economy workforce indicates that independent workers are mostly self-employed people who take on consulting engagements, contract work, and projects to build a portfolio of gigs.

In 2015, the largest increase in gig economy workers came from the "diversified worker" segment. This increase was driven by workers who have multiple sources of income, from both full- or part-time employment plus freelancing. For example, they may have a 20 hour per week job plus take on gigs sourced

Table 9.1   *Five Freelancer Segments of the Gig Economy*

Segment	Description	Percent	Number of Workers (M)illion	Percent Growth (2014–2015)
Independent contractors	Work project to project. Self-employed.	36	19.3M	−4
Diversified workers	Portfolio of work. Income from both traditional and freelance work.	26	14.1M	+8
Moonlighters	Freelance on the side (often at night) while a full-time employee.	25	13.2M	−2
Temporary workers	Often get work through a temporary staffing agency. Have a single employer.	8	4.6M	−1
Freelance business owners	Self-employed individuals. Consider themselves both a freelancer and a business owner because they have employees.	5	2.5M	0

through online platforms such as Uber, Lyft, or TaskRabbit The number of these diversified workers who earn 10 percent or more of their income from side gigs has increased by over 50 percent in just the past year, from 9.3 million in 2014 to 14.1 million in 2015.[7]

It's important for HR leaders to consider that many of your current employees are likely to already be participating in the gig economy. Workers in part-time, and even full-time, jobs are increasingly taking on side gigs, consulting projects, and contract work in addition to their day job and often without the awareness of their primary employer.

Freelancers and other independent workers are no longer "wannabe employees" who can't land full-time work. Today's gig economy workers are more likely to be highly sought-after workers in the battle for talent, with in-demand skills and expertise. Toptal, a freelance platform, screens software developers and designers from around the world to identify and offer companies the "top 3 percent" of talent. The CEO of Toptal, Taso du Val, notes that "five years ago freelancing was kind of silly, what the hipsters did out of college. Now it's much more of a serious thing."[8]

Miles Everson, vice chair of PwC and creator of *Talent Exchange*, an online marketplace that connects freelancers with job opportunities within PwC, believes mid-career professionals and senior professionals are two segments of workers who can leverage their skills and expertise into independent work. Everson describes the first of these segments as "the mid-career returning women who decide not to pursue full time work and choose freelancing as a way to gain new skills and have greater work-life flexibility." The second segment Everson sees is "retired senior business or military advisors who have amassed specialized skills, certifications and security clearances that are of immediate value to organizations."

The talent and expertise mid-career freelancers bring to organizations is reflected in their relatively high compensation, which is another factor attracting workers to the gig economy. A 2015 study by MBO Partners found that 16 percent of "full-time independents" surveyed earned over $100,000 a year.[9] Compare this figure to the $52,939 figure reported by the U.S Census Bureau as the U.S. median household income for 2013.[10]

Kris Wallsmith, a freelance developer in his mid-thirties based in Portland, Oregon, told the *Wall Street Journal*: "I can make much more money working as a freelancer and picking and choosing my clients around the world and working remotely. Working full time in an office would limit my choices to what we have in Portland."[11]

Millennials are also active participants in the gig economy, but due to their age and experience levels, they tend to have fewer skills and less expertise to offer employers. Millennials work primarily in the on-demand economy, using multiple technology platforms such as Uber, Etsy, Airbnb, and TaskRabbit to find work and sell services.

Benefits of Using Gig Economy Workers

Future Workplace's research for "The Rise of the Blended Workforce in the New Gig Economy" study found 60 percent of HR leaders plan to increase their use of contractors and freelancers the following year with half (49 percent) planning to increase their hiring of freelancers by 30 percent or more.

Figure 9.1   *Top five benefits that HR leaders see in using gig economy workers*

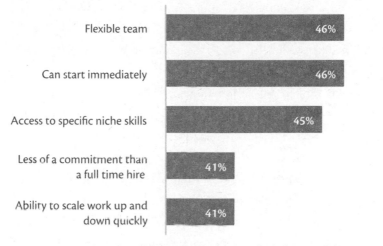

Flexible team	46%
Can start immediately	46%
Access to specific niche skills	45%
Less of a commitment than a full time hire	41%
Ability to scale work up and down quickly	41%

Source: Future Workplace & Field Nation, *Understanding the Gig Economy Worker*

The HR leaders who participated in our research identified several benefits (see Figure 9.1) that companies are realizing by incorporating gig economy workers into their workforce. The top benefits include being able to create flexible teams based on business needs, more immediate availability, and access to niche skills on demand. Managing lower labor costs is also an influencing factor. Since companies don't pay social security or Medicare taxes, make unemployment insurance payments, or provide benefits for contractors, the cost of hiring a contractor is often 30 to 40 percent lower than hiring an equivalent full-time employee.

Billy Cripe, chief marketing officer of Field Nation, an online platform for connecting businesses with freelance workers, says that "contingent workers are becoming a robust segment of the workforce and as important as full-time workers when it comes to meeting critical business initiatives." PwC's Miles Everson notes why gig economy workers are worth pursuing, "From an organizational perspective, we created *Talent Exchange* because we believe figuring out how to engage more contingent workers will give us access to top talent and better serve our client's needs."

It's not just companies driving the growth of the gig economy workforce. Many workers prefer independent work to full-time employment because they value the control, autonomy, and flexibility that working in the gig economy offers them. Gallup's "State of the American Workplace" finds that about 70 percent of employees are disengaged from their jobs—an alarmingly high level that is estimated to cost companies more than $550 billion a year in lost productivity.

Gig economy workers appear to be a happier bunch.[12] Field Nation has found that three out of four freelancers prefer freelancing to traditional employment due to benefits such as "flexible working hours, the ability to be my own boss, and the ability to choose what I work on." Nearly three-quarters (74 percent) of the independent workers surveyed admitted that they had no intention of going back to a full-time job.[13]

Research by Upwork found that the majority (60 percent) of freelancers work by choice today as compared with three years ago. Upwork also found that 70 percent of millennials considered quitting their current job to freelance, listing the flexibility to travel and freedom to set their own schedules as the reasons why.[14] Surveys from the Freelancers Union reinforce how important a sense of control can be for workers, as one of their survey respondents noted, "I find it more rewarding, I work when I want to, I commute only if I choose to and my earnings are dependent on how much I choose to work, not on corporate politics."[15]

With both companies and workers driving the demand for independent workers, we expect to see continued growth in the gig economy workforce.

The Unbundling of a Job

The growth of the gig economy is coming at the same time as a revolution in our thinking about how work is organized. With a highly talented, affordable, flexible, and available workforce only a click away, it is only natural that work is being redefined and organized in ways that aren't a full-time job. A 2016 O'Reilly report notes that everything we think of as a "job"—from finding work to managing income and receiving benefits, training, and social connections—can be unbundled.[16] We don't need a job to obtain the components of a job. Author Nick Grossman describes it this way: "Do people need jobs or can we deliver what jobs provide some other way and in a potentially unbundled fashion? The 'jobs of a job' essentially include income, structure, social connections, meaning, and, at least in the United States today, healthcare."[17]

This great unbundling is now impacting work itself. Freelance work is now easier than ever to find by signing onto one of the online platforms such as Field Nation, Upwork, HourlyNerd, Toptal, Work Market, PwC *Talent Exchange*, and many others. Supporting the unbundling of the job, new options are available for accessing the benefits of a job. The Affordable Care Act makes it possible to find and purchase affordable healthcare insurance as an independent worker. In the United States, there are several options—an individual 401(k), a SEP IRA, and a traditional or Roth IRA—for workers in the gig economy to save for retirement without a job. Coworking spaces like WeWork offer flexible alternatives to the office, as well as social connections.

One example of how organizations are unbundling jobs is in the newspaper industry. This industry has evolved from hiring full-time staff writers to now recruiting freelance journalists. In addition, the organizations have unbundled the writing job and are now predominantly staffing writers externally from the freelance market.

This is happening inside companies as well. Gianpaolo Barozzi, senior director, HR and Leadership and Team Intelligence at Cisco, is one of the HR executives behind the piloting of the Cisco Talent Cloud, an internal "virtual marketplace where assignments and talent can be brokered and screened against each other."

Barozzi explained how it works: "One side of this virtual marketplace provides an opportunity for our business leaders to identify the work that needs to be done using an *assignment profile*. It could be a role for a couple of years, it could be a project, or it could be an assignment for a few months. On the other side, an individual employee completes a *talent profile*. This provides our people with the opportunity to share their aspirations for the next assignment they are looking for, the timeframe they will be available for a new assignment, and the type of assignment they are looking for (e.g., function, location, level, type of work) along with summaries of their professional track record. In total, this creates a picture of their *professional reputation.*"

Essentially, the Cisco Talent Cloud combines the flexibility of the freelance marketplace with the structure of a corporate environment. Cisco's innovation is "taking the control, autonomy, and flexibility of working in the gig economy and combining it with the structure of the corporate world. It's this combination that creates a compelling employee experience. For Cisco, the Talent Cloud initiative provides the company with greater ability to create flexible teams and access specific skills on-demand from internal talent."[18]

With all new markets, there is the proverbial chicken-or-egg question. Which is the bigger challenge, filling the market with assignments or filling the market with the workers seeking assignments? Barozzi responded, "They are very related; you can only fill the market with workers if the manager starts setting them free."

Some will say, "Well, that is exactly what professional services are doing, managing by project." Barozzi states, "Yes, we are trying to insert the best of this into a corporate environment where the work to be done is internal and transparent. The best employees can move from assignment to assignment within our organization, allowing for choice and enabling a 'one company, many careers' journey."

Barozzi foresees the Talent Cloud expanding beyond the organization's employees. "For now, our leaders have access to internal Cisco people only. In the future, we are open to the possibility of opening up access to external assignment seekers."

As an increasing number of workers forgo traditional employment and join the gig economy, both start-ups and traditional companies are stepping in to offer services that make it easier for independent workers to find work, learn on the job, and access a host of other benefits that were previously only available to full-time employees. Today, gig economy workers can pull together the components and benefits of a job customized to their needs, expectations, and desires. It's the ultimate form of personalization: working when, where, how, and with whom you want to!

A recent announcement from Manpower and the Apollo Education Group offers the benefit of tuition reimbursement for contingent workers in a Manpower program known as MyPath. Created by Manpower and Western International University (a subsidiary of the Apollo Education Group), MyPath not only provides tuition reimbursement to Manpower associates who pursue a college degree but also includes many of the benefits of career coaching, assessment, and career guidance, normally only provided to full-time workers. Jonas Prising, CEO of Manpower, and Greg Cappelli, CEO of Apollo Education Group, the company behind this program, believe MyPath allows contingent workers to pursue a degree with the flexibility and support they need as they go through the program. Look for more programs like MyPath where contingent workers can add to their skills and enroll in college while businesses access a wider talent pool. As the gig economy grows, we expect to see more companies emerging to offer support services to workers unbundled from a job. A sample of these new services are outlined in the accompanying sidebar.

Support Services for Gig Economy Workers

- **Finding work.** Job discovery platforms allow contingent workers to search multiple work providers using new platforms and apps like Work Market, Field Nation, Dispatcher, Opus for Work, BlueCrew, and WorkGenius; these platforms also help freelancers manage their time, and in some cases, even provide them with a suite of traditional employment benefits.
- **Managing finances.** The problem of dealing with the administrative burden of managing finances, taxes, and other components of gig work is now solved with services like Even, Hurdlr, SherpaShare, And Co, and Benny.
- **Acquiring benefits.** The Freelancers Union and the Affordable Care Act have been joined by Peers, offering a portable benefits package including health, disability, and retirement and allowing multiple employers to fund a gig economy worker's benefits.
- **Controlling professional identity.** Some start-up platforms such as Karma and Traity are helping workers with their online reputation, giving users the ability to generate and monitor a reputation score.

- **Tapping tuition reimbursement.** Manpower in partnership with Western International University now offers tuition reimbursement for its associates who can combine learning while earning.
- **Finding space.** *Inc Magazine* reported an 83 percent growth in the number of coworking spaces, with memberships increasing by 117 percent year over year. This is a global phenomenon, with the top 10 coworking spaces in the world including WeWork, The Surf Office, The Factory, Hub Impact, B Amsterdam, Hacker Lab, Punspace, BetaHaus, Co+Hoots, and Hacker Lab.

Source: Future Workplace with adaptations from "Serving Workers in the Gig Economy," Nick Grossman and Elizabeth Woyke, and *Ubiq Blog,* 2014.

The Impact of Gig Economy Workers on HR

The growth in the number of gig economy workers is forcing organizations—and HR departments in particular—to reinvent talent management in a way that incorporates a blended workforce of both traditional full-time employees and independent workers. "The Rise of the Blended Workforce in the New Gig Economy" study found that 93 percent of HR professionals see work teams becoming increasingly blended, with full-time employees and freelancers working together to accomplish organizational goals.

As freelancers become an integral part of the workforce, HR departments need to source, develop, and manage them in a way that is consistent with their full time employer brand. We recommend that HR leaders ask their teams to address the following 10 questions about how to source, manage, engage, recognize, and reward the gig economy workers in your company:

1. How are we managing gig economy workers? Manually or via an online platform?
2. Who is responsible for managing gig economy workers? HR? Business unit leaders?
3. How could we onboard and integrate gig economy workers into the organizational culture?

4. How could we reward and recognize gig economy workers?

5. Do gig economy workers receive holidays like full-time workers? What if they earn more than full-time employees?

6. Could gig economy workers take advantage of mentoring, coaching, and career mobility services?

7. What types of training and certification could gig economy workers have access to?

8. What types of benefit or referral programs could gig economy workers have access to?

9. How could we measure the performance of gig economy workers?

10. What criteria could we use to evaluate the various online freelance platforms?

We recommend that HR leaders review their policies on remote and flexible work. HR leaders and employers are slowly coming to recognize that it is no longer necessary to be tied to a single office location or time zone in order to effectively perform one's job duties. Through flexible working arrangements, remote work, and the use of off-site and outsourced contractors, work is being disaggregated from place and time. Research from both Harvard and Stanford business schools shows that workers who are given the flexibility to work where and how they prefer are more productive and more engaged.[19]

HR Strategies to Manage Gig Economy Workers

A workforce that includes steadily rising numbers of gig economy workers will pose both great challenges and great opportunities for leaders. Each organization must sort through options to determine how to best source, develop, manage, and engage gig economy workers. Our suggestion is to take a total talent management approach to the blended workforce. This approach helps HR leaders optimize the supply of independent workers, make faster and better-informed decisions about talent, and reduce the overall labor and infrastructure spend. To that end, we recommend six strategies to help HR leaders on the path to a total talent management approach: Incorporating approach, governance, partnerships, performance, analytics, and compliance.

1. **Develop a strategic approach to sourcing gig economy workers.** With the on-demand workforce already a key part of the talent pool in many companies, this approach begins with having visibility into all the talent your organization has today. What percentage of your workforce are independent? Next, examine how your organization is currently sourcing gig economy workers. Our research has identified multiple approaches, ranging from a centralized approach of posting on a preferred freelance platform to a decentralized approach where hiring managers create their own solution to find contingent workers. Finally, identify how your organization is sourcing and managing to provide clear visibility and data into the skill sets of your gig economy worker pool.

2. **Define governance and success criteria for managing gig economy workers.** The contingent workforce of today resembles the corporate training landscape in 2000. In the last 17 years, corporate training departments have moved from being fragmented and owned by multiple business units to being more centrally managed, usually by a chief learning officer, to maximize the business value of the investment.

   Today we are at a similar juncture with gig economy workers. There is a wide disparity in how companies source and manage their contingent workforce. Some have procurement functions manage these workers; others assign this responsibility to HR or external service providers like temp firms. To avoid inconsistency and fragmentation, organizations should establish clear accountability and management of their gig economy workforce similar to how they manage their investment in other areas.

   As the gig economy workforce grows, some companies may even consider creating new job roles dedicated to overseeing workforce management. Similar to having a chief learning officer, companies might create a chief gig economy officer to manage gig economy workers and develop HR practices targeted to independent workers, including reward and recognition programs, onboarding, and access to specialized skill-building programs.

3. **Build a partnership between HR and IT to support and manage a blended workforce.** Most HR processes involving talent are designed for full-time staffers, not freelancers or contractors. To better reflect the evolving workforce, HR can collaborate with IT to determine how to modify current information systems to support on-demand talent, bring consistency to the process of managing independent workers, and gather data on the characteristics and performance of those workers. According to research by Work Market, 42 percent of its sample of 1,000 companies still use a manual system for independent workers, while the remainder use some combination of vendor management systems, freelance management systems, and a managed service provider.[20]

4. **Develop a range of strategies to ensure the performance of gig economy workers.** Performance of gig economy workers is as important to HR leaders as performance of their full-time employees. "The Rise of the Blended Workforce in the New Gig Economy" study found nearly half the 600 companies we surveyed were incorporating HR practices similar to those for full-time employees to manage the performance of the gig economy workers, including reward and recognition systems, access to special training programs such as company onboarding and certification programs, and performance coaching and mentoring programs. Some companies customized their programs for gig economy workers to reflect the length of their contract, but overall, we found that companies are trending toward offering a set of HR practices for gig economy workers similar to what they offer full-time workers.

5. **Use analytic tools to optimize engagement of gig economy workers.** Managing the supply and availability of a contingent workforce is critical given these workers often work on multiple projects at the same time and have other deliverable and time commitments. It is therefore important for HR leaders to have data and visibility into what the company's needs are in order to accurately source the right number and type of independent workers at the right time. Ardent Partners reports that many companies lack the HR systems that allow them to optimize their freelance workforce, with nearly half of today's organizations possessing only partial visibility into

their current or future total talent pool.[21] Optimizing this more complex workforce requires new data, analytics, and forecasting.

6. **Mitigate legal risk through systematic compliance management of gig economy workers.** Finally, the major risk that companies identify in using independent workers is compliance risk. Because the labor cost savings are so great, companies have to create a rigorous review process to ensure that employees are not misclassified as independent workers. It's important that HR leaders implement clear documentation and manager training to ensure that gig economy workers are both classified and managed appropriately as independent workers, and regularly reviewed.

The Future: What to Expect as the Gig Economy Workforce Grows

The gig economy is rapidly becoming the new normal for how businesses organize work. There are several demographic and technological drivers that are sparking the accelerating growth of the gig economy. First, as we look ahead to what's fueling the expansion of the gig economy, we see increasing demand from companies for independent workers. Gig economy workers are cheaper, are more flexible, provide on-demand skills and expertise, and allow for a dynamic approach to talent management. As long as companies continue to obtain these benefits from adding gig economy workers to their workforce, they will continue to demand gig economy talent.

Shifting values and priorities of the workforce are also contributing to the rise of the gig economy, and it's clear that more workers are seeking the flexibility, control, and autonomy that the gig economy offers. PwC's Everson reveals that "in a study by PwC, the University of Southern California and the London Business School a significant number of employees across sectors and generations feel so strongly about wanting a flexible work schedule that they would be willing to give up pay and delay promotions in order to get it. Sixty-four percent of Millennials say they would like to occasionally work from home, and 66 percent would like to shift their work hours. This is feedback we take to heart at PwC, since almost 80 percent of our more than 200,000 employees globally are Millennials."[22] As millennials become managers and business leaders, their priorities and values will contribute more to shaping how work is organized and done.

Technology is making it easier, more convenient, and increasingly afford-able to find talented, experienced gig economy workers. Leading third-party platforms like Upwork, Field Nation, Toptal, Work Market, HourlyNerd, and many others are another source in addition to traditional temporary staff-ing agencies to help companies identify and recruit independent workers. According to the "Freelancing in America 2015 Report," 69 percent of free-lancers say technology is aiding their ability to do so.[23]

As more professionals switch off the traditional full-time employee track to become gig economy workers, expect additional companies like PwC cre-ating their own platform to source and manage freelance talent. Could this become a movement where certain industries, such as professional services, shift the bulk of their talent to independent workers? Will there be a new breed of Fortune 1000 firm with a core leadership team—a group of lead-ers and team members with specialized skills—and the rest composed of gig economy workers? Consider the high "contractor per employee" ratio at com-panies such as Uber and Lyft. Time will tell, but the growth and benefits of the gig economy point to the rise of a much more flexible and fluid workforce as a way to navigate the changes in the future workplace.

PwC is committed to attracting independent workers as part of its HR strategy because of the company's belief that gig economy workers are the workers of the future. Everson concludes, "At PwC we have launched the *Talent Exchange* as a way to find top talent who want to work on their own terms. We simply cannot walk away from nearly 40 percent of the workforce in 2020!"

Another company that has decided that it can no longer ignore the gig economy is LinkedIn. LinkedIn is offering LinkedIn Profinder, a freelancer-buyer matching service, positioned as "The easiest way to hire top talent" with a menu listing 14 categories of white-collar skill sets ranging from accounting to writing and editing. [24] The LinkedIn platform is one that over 420 million business professionals worldwide are familiar with, so LinkedIn's entry into the gig economy provides a way to explore matching gig economy professionals with employers and test the market for expanding its own services.

Finally, demographics are also a likely contributor to the growth of the gig economy. Many studies have found that baby boomers—who are currently at retirement age—want to keep working well into their golden years. A 2015 survey by The Transamerica Center for Retirement Studies found that nearly two-thirds (65 percent) plan to work past age 65 or don't plan to retire—ever.[25] As older professionals continue to want to work well past the traditional age of retirement, the prevalence of "gray talent" will rise to become an even stronger force contributing to the growth of the gig economy.

While the growth in the gig economy workforce seems certain, what's uncertain is what the legal implications will be of this rise in the gig economy. Courts have already started to wrestle with worker classification lawsuits that are testing the applicability of existing labor laws for contingent workers. While some advocate for a third classification as "dependent contractor," others argue that it's more important to ensure that all workers, regardless of classification, get benefits and protections.

The gig economy landscape is still in flux but growing rapidly. As we move ahead, blended workforces composed of full-time employees and gig economy workers will increasingly become the norm. We may see entire industries, such as professional services and law firms, significantly shrink their full-time workforce as gig economy workers become a more efficient, lower-cost, and flexible option to meet their business priorities. As the rate and pace of change accelerate, organizations will leverage gig economy workers to optimize for increasing uncertainties in the global marketplace.

MY ACTION PLAN

Myself

- If my paycheck were guaranteed, what assignments would I like to take on within the organization?
- What is holding me back from doing so?
- How would I advise a 21 year old about participating in the gig economy?

My Team

- How could we have our HR team review open roles and discuss new ways to fill these roles with gig economy workers?
- What would have to change for us to move from the concept of filling a job to filling an assignment?
- What is our approach for engaging with freelancers and gig economy workers?
- What new platforms, tools, and skill sets are needed for us to create a total talent management approach to the blended workforce?

My Organization

- How could freelance platforms impact our organization's sourcing needs over the next three years?
- What new roles will need to be created to best manage gig economy workers?
- How will teams of stakeholders need to work together to govern and manage our gig economy workers?
- How are our competitors sourcing gig economy workers? For what job roles?

BE A WORKPLACE ACTIVIST

10

It is not the strongest of the species that survive, nor the most intelligent, but the one most responsive to change.

—*Charles Darwin, naturalist and geologist*

In November 2015, an audience of employees, manufacturers, and community members assembled together in Cleveland, Ohio, to celebrate Saint-Gobain Performance Plastics's 350 years of business history. In his opening remarks, Tom Kinisky, president and CEO of Saint-Gobain, framed the key theme of the event as "If we want to survive the next 350 years, what would we need to do?"

Kinisky's question is a provocative one and invites Saint-Gobain employees and customers to reflect on what makes a great future workplace. Saint-Gobain's history began in 1665 when King Louis XIV signed the documents officially establishing the *Manufacture Royale des Glaces de Miroirs* (*The Royal Manufactory of Mirror Glass*) to compete in Europe's mirror glass market. Entering 2016, Saint-Gobain was a $55 billion company, operating in 64 countries with over 180,000 employees. It is one of the leading producers of construction products in the world. Saint-Gobain leaders have a deep sense of pride about how they are part of a legacy of 14 generations of management that have worked in the business over the past 350 years.

Kinisky went on to share the secrets behind being in business for over 350 years: being able to adapt to change, having strong values, and being committed to ongoing innovation. But still Kinisky questions the status quo and invites employees, customers, and partners to be activists in creating the change they know needs to happen. This focus on questioning the present while anticipating the future is what we believe is needed in all organizations. This is the job of a workplace activist, someone who gives a voice to making the changes we all desire in our organization, industry, and workplace.

Workplace activists can lead these changes in three ways:

1. Recognize your job is not your job: Ask yourself, "What really is my job?"
2. Reframe your job description: What do I include to help my organization succeed in a volatile, uncertain, complex, and ambiguous (otherwise known as VUCA) workplace?
3. Rethink how to break HR: Which of our HR processes need to be reimagined for navigating the new world of work?

Recognize Your Job Is Not Your Job

Being a workplace activist requires taking an expansive view of your job in HR or as a business leader. The workplace experience you aspire to is often one that does not exist today in your organization. David Heath, VP of Global Human Resources at Panasonic Avionics, says, "Understanding the type of workplace experience you want to create is a massive opportunity to impact the company and position yourself and your company on the leading edge, ready for the future."

Heath believes that HR will change more in the next 5 years than in the prior 20, and the entire profession has the opportunity to change its mindset, offerings, and value proposition for both employees and business partners.

Given the exponential rate and pace of change, Fred Kofman, philosopher and vice president at LinkedIn, often asks the question, "What is your job?"[1] Kofman wants each of us to think carefully about how we answer this question. Kofman encourages people to try to answer in a concise sentence focusing on the outcomes you are creating rather than your current job title or description. Kofman says, "Think of it this way: Your job is not what you do, but the goal you pursue. So if you are a corporate trainer, instead of saying 'my job is to design and develop learning programs,' you should think of your job as facilitating continuous learning so your company wins in the market-place." Now ask yourself what your job is. Challenge your team members to ask the same question of themselves.

Brendan Browne, vice president of Global Talent Acquisition at LinkedIn, is a convert. Browne says, "For me, I've come to understand, my job is not my job. I'm not in recruiting. Rather I focus on helping the company win. This can mean finding talent in new geographies, sourcing them in new ways or re-thinking the entire candidate experience." Brandon's public profile on LinkedIn says it all—he lists his job, not by his title, but as "Connecting Talent with Opportunity at Massive Scale."[2]

Reframe Your Job Description to Operate in a VUCA World

Consider how differently we communicate with each other today. Five or six years ago we were most likely sending and receiving text messages on our phone to communicate with friends and colleagues. Today, traditional text messaging is on the decline. Americans sent 1.9 trillion texts in 2015, down from a record of 2.3 trillion texts in 2011.[3]

Instead, Americans now increasingly rely on a range of instant messaging apps such as WhatsApp, which had over 1 billion users in 2016. Companies are now struggling to address the challenge of a VUCA world in which consumer messaging apps like Messenger, iMessage, Line, Snapchat, and WhatsApp are entering the workplace and transforming how we communicate.

What does this have to do with the future workplace? Everything. As Kelly Wojda, HR director of Caterpillar, says, "All of us operate in a VUCA world, defined as *Volatile,* having unexpected outcomes, *Uncertain,* where our impact is unknown, *Complex,* with many interconnected components and *Ambiguous,* fraught with unclear information." Wojda uses the VUCA frame as a catalyst to reinvent the Caterpillar succession planning process.

Rather than rely on a static annual process for identifying talent to move into successive positions, Wojda's new succession planning process focuses on answering five questions she poses to her internal business partners:

- **Speed.** How fast and frequently do we have succession planning discussions?
- **Transparency.** How transparent do we want to be with candidates?
- **Visibility.** How do we see around corners, to make sure we are looking far enough and deep enough within the organization?
- **Diversity.** How do we cast our net wider, not just from a demographic standpoint but also to include non-traditional candidates?
- **Agility.** How well do we institutionalize our learning back into the process?

The Caterpillar succession planning process takes into account a challenging business environment characterized by the unexpected and volatile business circumstances such as lower commodity prices and declines in sales and revenues in three of its sectors: energy and transportation, construction, and resources. It's not surprising that managing HR in a VUCA world is a rallying cry for the Caterpillar HR team.

Rethink How to Break HR

In our Future Workplace Forecast survey, we asked HR and hiring managers to rate the ability of HR to attract the best employees.[4] More than half, 53 percent, of HR leaders globally rated themselves as better than the competition. But when we put the same question to hiring managers about the ability of their HR departments to attract the best employees, the response was markedly different. Only 31 percent rated their HR department as better than the competition in attracting talent.

Jayesh Menon, the Singapore-based leader of Global Organizational Effectiveness at Micron Technology, believes the best way to deal with the gap between how HR sees itself and how its clients view HR is to reimagine

HR through the lens of a customer. Menon sees the need for HR to assume the role of a workplace activist, identifying big and small changes that HR can create to develop a more compelling workplace experience. This may range from rethinking performance management, to abolishing rigid guidelines for personal time off and taking vacations, to creating opportunities for employees to learn when and where they desire.

It is important to move outside your comfort zone. As an example, consider expanding your knowledge beyond HR to areas such as wearables and mobile apps. Start a conversation with your team on the impact of wearables and apps on your future workplace. Challenge your thinking in each domain. For example, ask yourself how wearable health devices that track movement and health diagnostics will impact employers and employees. What could employers do with this information? If employers collect employee data that indicates an employee has a serious health condition, should they notify the employee?

Then ask yourself to think about what HR processes could be enhanced or replaced with an app. Is there an app your company could use for time reporting? Corporate campus locations? Employee culture surveys? New hire onboarding? Access to your learning management system? Performance check-ins? Matching coaches to employees? The list goes on. What's on your list?

Next, to develop business acumen, we believe HR professionals should leverage business frameworks to rethink the value of HR. We suggest starting with the simple yet powerful Horizon framework outlined in the book *The Alchemy of Growth*. You can use this to concurrently assess current and future opportunities. The Horizon framework allows you to plot value against time horizon, as shown in Figure 10.1.

We took the liberty of adapting the Horizon model to frame typical HR questions:[5]

- Short term (Horizon 1)
  - What is our current value proposition to the organization?
  - How well are we competing for and retaining talent versus our competitors?
  - How is the composition of our workforce changing?

Figure 10.1   *The three horizons of growth*

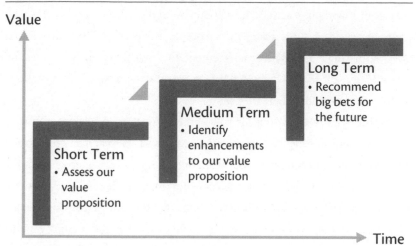

Source: Adapted from The Alchemy of Growth

- Medium term (Horizon 2)
  - How could we compete for talent?
  - Where could we compete for talent?
  - What enhancements could we make to the current value proposition? (How could we create pilots to test new products/processes?)
- Long term (Horizon 3)
  - What is affecting recruiting for everyone?
  - What might be the future challenges for talent engagement?
  - How could we scale any of the piloted enhancements and commit to one or more big bets?

You can apply the Horizon framework to explore what you could do differently to source, orient, develop, and engage multiple generations of workers.

As you continue on your journey to become a workplace activist, you will benefit greatly from thinking, acting and solving for problems from the point of view of the prospective and current worker. After all, your job is not your job and HR is no longer HR! Rather, your job is to help your organization win in an increasingly volatile, uncertain, complex, and ambiguous marketplace and HR is the catalyst to do this.

Anticipating and Navigating the Future Workplace

When we look at organizations that are successful, often the distinguishing characteristic is how well they have responded to change. Consider the situation when Steve Jobs took over Apple in 1997. As he said, "The problem was that Apple stood still. Even though it invested cumulatively billions in R&D, the output was not there. Other companies caught up with it, and its differentiation eroded, in particular with respect to Microsoft." And now consider what happened at Kodak. As computer science pioneer Jaron Lanier explains in his book *Who Owns the Future*, "At the height of its power, Kodak employed more than 140,000 people and was worth $28 billion. They even invented the first digital camera. But today Kodak is bankrupt, and the new face of digital photography has become Instagram." Lanier continues, "Now think about Instagram, a company launched in 2010 as a free mobile app and acquired by Facebook in 2012 for $1 billion. Instagram was acquired by Facebook just three months after Kodak filed for bankruptcy and at the time of acquisition, employed only 13 people."[6]

Our belief is that organizations are identifying the need to nurture workplace activists as one way to prepare for the rapid pace of change. As Salim Ismail, bestselling author of *Exponential Organizations: Why New Organizations Are Ten Times Better, Faster, and Cheaper Than Yours (and What to Do About It)*, says, "If you are not disrupting your business or industry, someone else is." According to Ismail, large corporations are generally ill equipped to identify and harness disruptions for competitive advantage and are thus at serious risk of being disrupted by smaller, nimbler start-ups. Consider the latest report by Citigroup, entitled "Digital Disruption," which projects that up to 30 percent of employees who work in the U.S. banking industry may lose their jobs to new technologies in the next 10 years. And an even sharper drop is predicted for European banks.[7]

What's going on here? The Citigroup report said jobs would be lost to FinTech start-ups taking aim at many different parts of the financial services industry. In the "Be Future Focused" trait of Rule #3, we saw how DBS is creating hackathons for its bankers to build digital literacy skills and empower them to think differently about how to use mobile for the development of new financial service products.

The ability to anticipate the future workplace while looking at the present is what will differentiate winning organizations from the rest. Being an effective workplace activist requires the ability to recognize alternative future states occurring in your workplace. You will also need to become comfortable with working in the unknown and with bringing your best self to work every day on this journey. It's still hard to believe that in 2007 when the iPhone was released, there were no apps as we now know them. The Apple App Store was not launched until 2008. Today on each of the Apple and Android app stores, more than 2 million apps are available for download. The rise of this app economy has massively transformed the behavior of consumers and organizations. Individuals are now accustomed to easily finding an answer to their question via an app. Organizations are taking note and developing Corporate App Stores to manage corporate sanctioned apps. While we have profiled IBM, Qualcomm, and Cognizant Technology in Rule #4, we see the appification of work intensifying as companies in industries as diverse as professional services, financial services, and retail launch corporate app stores to provide employees access at work to similar tools they use in their personal lives.

As workplace activists, we need to consider the convergence of the obvious with the not so obvious trends reshaping our workforces and workplaces.

Disruption presents both opportunities and risks, depending on how prepared we are. Everything we know about why people work, when they work, and where they work is being turned upside down.

Being a workplace activist requires honing our ability to anticipate the future changes to which our organization needs to adapt. While preparedness matters, so too will fostering the behaviors and norms by which we will operate in the the future workplace.

To help our organization win in the future workplace, we need to lead the initiatives to ensure our organization continuously and successfully adapts to change. We must all be workplace activists. This means agitating for change and responding to the volatility, uncertainty, complexity, and ambiguity we see happening around us. Being a workplace activist is both a challenge and an opportunity. Are you ready?

MY ACTION PLAN

Myself

- What is my job?
- Am I passionate enough to agitate for change to help my organization prepare for the future?
- How can I put forward more informed speculations about where our organization should focus? What business frameworks can I use?
- Am I able to competently explain the future to others and engage them to support our mission?

My Team

- Do all the members of the team understand our jobs?
- What changes in our business strategy have we made to get us to where we are today?
- How and when did we recognize these triggers to change our people practices?
- How could we maintain an ongoing practice of revisiting our team's contribution to the future?

My Organization

- What changes do we see coming that we should be preparing for today?
- How could we compete differently for talent?
- What are the assumptions we hold about the future workplace?
- What changes do we see our competitors making to prepare for the future workplace?

LOOKING FORWARD: EXPECT THE UNEXPECTED

To expect the unexpected shows a thoroughly modern intellect.

—Oscar Wilde, playwright, novelist, essayist, and poet

The future is not built on one trend alone. It is the simultaneous convergence of numerous trends, moving at various rates of change and impacting us and our organizations differently depending on our circumstances. Forward-looking organizations tend to have a formal and disciplined process for tracking trends to help them win in the marketplace. When we anticipate the future, we are essentially making assumptions about what will happen. The assumptions we make are our expectations of the trends we expect to see. We need to anticipate both expected and unexpected possible future states and be comfortable not having all the answers along our journey. To bring our 10 rules together, we introduce you to our recommended framework for documenting your assumptions to help you more thoughtfully prepare for your future workplace experience.

Expected Versus Unexpected

The following table outlines each of our 10 rules for navigating the future workplace along with a summary of expected and unexpected assumptions regarding the future of each rule.

The Rule	Expected	Unexpected
Rule #1: Make the workplace an experience	The employee experience continues to mirror the consumer experience	Employee-centric policies go even deeper into the employees' personal lives
Rule #2: Use space to promote culture	A restructuring of how workspace is designed, used, and technologically supported	A further blurring of work and home as companies push to integrate workers even further into the workplace
Rule #3: Be an agile leader	Multifaceted leaders are touted for new levels of leadership agility in producing results	The leadership mantle shifts from "hero leaders" to high-performing teams, with some even hired and compensated as intact teams
Rule #4: Consider technology an enabler and disruptor	Technology enables or disrupts how every employee gets work done	Companies and jobs die off faster as many are caught unprepared for the accelerated rate of business disruption
Rule #5: Build a data-driven recruiting ecosystem	More companies contact job candidates before the candidates start actively job seeking	Recruiting technology enables employees to be hired without ever having been interviewed in person
Rule #6: Embrace on-demand learning	The rate of employee-generated and -curated content grows exponentially	Corporate learning departments expand their capabilities to educate more nonemployees than employees
Rule #7: Tap the power of multiple generations	Workforces continue to diversify in age and culture	Multiple generational and cultural employee resource groups have more strategic influence in the workplace
Rule #8: Build gender equality	Women increase as a percentage of the workforce at all levels but slower at the top	Gender-based labels appear noticeably less frequently in workplace discussions
Rule #9: Plan for more gig economy workers	The workforce is a more blended mix of full-time, part-time, gig, and other non payroll workers	Gig economy workers team up to take on bigger self-organized project leadership roles
Rule #10: Be a workplace activist	More workers become workplace activists, identifying and pushing for the changes they see as needed in the workplace	Workers deeply appreciate the values that do not change, as everything else does

Let's examine each rule and offer an "expected" and an "unexpected" observation for you to consider and discuss with your team. We identify an *expected* future as one that is the probable future we know and may have already experienced in our organization. By documenting and sharing what your team expects, you can ensure that your management teams are building their strategies based on a consistent set of shared assumptions.

An *unexpected* future is relatively more radical and can come about as the result of events, innovations, or societal occurrences that are more difficult to predict and tend to be anticipated by a minority, not the majority. Capturing the unexpected is best done by documenting assumptions made by the minority of people who interpret the direction of trends differently and therefore have different expectations for what will unfold. Celebrate these differences, as they will help you anticipate and accept unfolding trends faster and generate more alternative and thought-provoking outcomes.

To contemplate the implications of the future workplace, we have to be willing to examine potentially conflicting perspectives and, oftentimes, opposing assumptions. To do this, we must develop a framework for making sense of the trends we expect and those that we do not expect. Think about what is expected of yourself, your team, and your organization to navigate the future workplace. Use our framework as a starting point in your journey. Ask yourself: What is expected? What is unexpected?

Rule #1: Make the Workplace an Experience

Expected: The Employee Experience Continues to Mirror the Consumer Experience

The Workplace as an Experience will continue to be carefully orchestrated, where all the elements of work—the emotional, the intellectual, the physical, the technological, and the cultural—are designed to work in concert to create even more memorable employee experiences. The new emphasis on employee experience will create an expanded scope for HR leaders and their teams who will not only focus on traditional HR roles of learning, development, recruiting, and compensation, but they will also assume a new mission for creating a compelling workplace experience, one that will excite employees to work for and be engaged in the company.

Unexpected: Employee-Centric Policies Go Even Deeper into Employees' Personal Lives

The unexpected consequences of enhancing the employee experience are beginning to manifest in unanticipated ways. For example, a growing number of companies enable employees to bring their pets to work. As a result, companies have to now also consider the needs of workers with pet allergies or animal phobias, conditions that HR had no need to previously understand. Pet friendly workplaces have had tremendous appeal to many pet owners across the generational cohorts on selecting or staying with employers. Unanticipated consequences of reinforcing the bond between pet owner and pet have now resulted in the emergence of pet-related benefits that range from offering paid time off in the form of "Pet-ternity" leave (provided by Mars Petcare) when a new pet joins the household, to granting pet bereavement leave (offered by a variety of businesses that include Kimpton Hotels and Restaurants), and free pet health screenings during Pet Parents day (Activision Blizzard) all in recognizing the importance of pets in employees' lives.[1]

Rule #2: Use Space to Promote Culture

Expected: A Radical Restructuring of How Workspace Is Designed, Used, and Technologically Supported

Across many organizations, there has been a steady dismantling of policies that allocate space based on the grade level of employees, and there has been a corresponding increase of interest in designing workspaces to promote an organization's culture, as well as increase productivity and wellness at work. Morris Levy, co-founder of co-working space The Yard, noted that since people can work anywhere, you should provide a space that employees are happy coming to.[2] And as we highlighted in Rule #2, Use Space to Promote Culture, organizations are increasingly taking lessons from co-working spaces and creating lively fun workspaces that can be viewed as workplace experience centers, a place employees want to go to network, collaborate with colleagues, and find a productive spot for their focused work. These workspaces are more than adding Ping-Pong tables or meditation classes. Rather they inspire workers to congregate, network, and connect to each other. The workplace of the future acknowledges a new way of working that is both virtually and physically engaging.

Unexpected: A Further Blurring of Work and Home as Companies Push to Integrate Workers Even Further into the Workplace

Companies are offering new forms of motivation to incentivize employees to integrate their life into work. In fact, some companies are creating new incentives to support "homing from work." Sarah Slater, director of Workplace Strategy, CBRE, talks about employers' efforts to support employees' "second shift" of after-hours work by enabling employees to take care of certain home-life needs from the office. She highlights the emergence and growth of hospitality-minded concierge services (happening beyond Silicon Valley firms) offering employees at work a range of services including shopping, arranging dinner, or collecting the dry cleaning.

But watch for other new incentives such as paying employees a premium to live closer to the office (Facebook) or offering forgivable loans to buy property closer to the office (Quicken). These policies are a substantial pivot from traditional policies of additionally compensating employees who live farther from the office. The trajectory is toward a further blurring of the lines between work and home.

Rule #3: Be an Agile Leader

Expected: Multifaceted Leaders Are Touted for New Levels of Leadership Agility in Producing Results

The permutations of what the agile leader could look like are innumerable. Many of the core characteristics and goals of the agile leader are interwoven. Each agile leader in the making should keep one thing in mind: leadership is about achieving results—while *not* compromising relationships to get those results. The traits of an agile leader fit together in many different ways, with the goal of engaging and mobilizing diverse teams to achieve great things.

Unexpected: The Leadership Mantle Shifts from "Hero Leaders" to High-Performing Teams, with Some Even Hired and Compensated as Intact Teams

"Team lift-out" is the term used to hire an established group of employees who have been working together and then decide to switch to another employer en masse. Traditionally, this has been rare; however, we see large companies acquire small ones specifically for their intact teams. Over time we will see team lift-outs to be an unanticipated consequence of the next-generation economy as the visibility of teams and their accomplishments are seen as the newest type of competency in the workplace.

Rule #4: Consider Technology as an Enabler and Disruptor

Expected: Technology Enables or Disrupts How Every Employee Gets Work Done

Regardless of industry, technology is eliminating, creating, and changing jobs, and the most important lesson is to stay on top of technology shifts in order to avoid skills gaps that leave people and technologies underutilized. The influx of new technologies is changing our behaviors and is altering the way we communicate, collaborate, motivate, and stay productive at work. It's no longer enough for our employees and ourselves to simply be technologically competent—we have to recognize that every job will be enabled or disrupted by technology. It is just a matter of when, what, and how technology gets applied to the job.

Unexpected: Companies and Jobs Die Off Faster as Higher Numbers Are Caught Unprepared for the Accelerated Rate of Business Disruption

No industry will be safe from having its "Uber moment." Former CEO of Barclays Anthony Jenkins said in a speech that banking, as an industry, was facing huge disruption and could be forced to cut jobs and automate operations due in large part to the success of FinTech start ups, displacing and disintermediating the old-world finance via technology. Look for more industries that are upended as technology reimagines entire sectors of business.

Rule #5: Build a Data-Driven Recruiting Ecosystem

Expected: More Companies Contact Job Candidates Before the Candidates Start Actively Job Seeking

The proliferation of apps that proactively analyze and match our online profiles to available openings will continue, enabling everyone to be a continual job seeker. Identifying candidates becomes a lot easier. Successfully hiring candidates becomes a lot harder. Whether a prospect embarks on that proactive opportunity may depend a lot more heavily on the candidate's perception of the employer brand. Forward-looking companies are investing in strengthening their employer brand to influence positive responses from prospects.

Unexpected: Recruiting Technology Enables Employees to Be Hired Without Ever Having Been Interviewed in Person

Conventional recruiting dynamics and assumptions are repeatedly upended by practices previously considered implausible. Conventions used to dictate that employers would schedule a phone chat first, followed by an in person meeting at company headquarters. Some companies are becoming so comfortable with using technology to meet employees they are forgoing the in person meeting and offering a job without an in person meeting or a voice call. This is the case at Automattic, the 400 person firm responsible for the popular blogging platform WordPress. According to Marjorie Asturias, Happiness Engineer at Automattic, the recruiting process includes Skype chats with the hiring manager, and then completing a project for the company while earning $25.00 an hour. Once the applicant sends in the completed work, the hiring manager communicates with the applicant via a private blog. If this all works out, an offer is made without ever having a phone call with the applicant! The recruiting process at Automattic is referred to as "job tryouts" rather than job interviews. Automattic CEO Matt Mullenweg sums up the results this way: "We end up hiring about 40 percent of the people who try out with us. In 2013, we hired 101 people, and only two of them didn't work out. In the entire history of the company we've hired 270 people, and only 40 of them are no longer here."[3] So in this knowledge-based gig economy, powered by data analytics and matching algorithms, it is now reasonable to ask, "How could we reconfigure the recruiting process to hire workers that no one has met in person?"

Rule #6: Embrace On-Demand Learning

Expected: The Rate of Employee-Generated and -Curated Content Grows Exponentially

There is a substantial increase in the content generated by employees to teach fellow employees. As companies reward and recognize employees for sharing knowledge with their peers, organizations are becoming teaching and learning machines. More informal peer-to-peer learning results in more opportunities to empower your learners to be in charge of their own learning and provide them ways to easily contribute learning, find external learning and then tag it, share it, and rate it. Corporate learning is mirroring how we find books on Amazon and movies on Netflix.

Unexpected: Corporate Learning Departments Expand Their Capabilities to Educate More Nonemployees Than Employees

Corporate learning departments may be shocked at how many nonemployees they will be educating in the years to come. Tenaris is already on this path, by opening up Tenaris University to audiences that range from local schoolchildren to global employee prospects. McKinsey Academy offers an immersive platform educating the employees of its clients on methodologies that were formerly reserved for the exclusive and proprietary use of its consultants. McKinsey Academy is now training executives at volumes that exceed many college-based executive education programs. Is it possible that we might see some corporate learning departments spun off as independent learning providers with their host organization as their largest client? We expect so!

Rule #7: Tap the Power of Multiple Generations

Expected: Workforces Continue to Diversify in Age and Culture

The workplace will continue to see multiple generations and cultures working side by side. While the emphasis will be on the similarities across the generations and cultures, companies will recognize the unique behaviors and attitudes of generations and cultures and build inclusive training focusing on developing generational and cultural intelligence. We expect more generational and cultural intelligence training as part of broader diversity and inclusion training programs with the goal of capitalizing upon the business benefit of tapping diverse talent pools.

Unexpected: Multiple Generational and Cultural Employee Resource Groups Have More Strategic Influence In the Workplace

An increasing number of organizations will tap deeper into the diversity of their multigenerational and multicultural workforces and consider this a strategic advantage. IBM is using its Millennial Corps to advise on a range of new products and services that can be developed for millennials and those with a millennial mindset. While leveraging the power of age and cultural diversity can lead to business results, it can also lead to generational conflicts. Businesses must be prepared for increases in younger managers leading older employees as well as Gen Xers and boomers who exhibit resentment about the disproportionate attention on millennials.

Rule #8: Build Gender Equality

Expected: Women Increase as a Percentage of the Workforce at All Levels but Slower at the Top

The proportion of women in leadership roles will slowly increase. March 2016 research from Glassdoor indicated that one of the biggest causes of the gender pay gap is the sorting of men and women into occupations and industries that pay differently throughout the economy, a structural enabler that will take years to change.[4] As women assume more leadership roles, expect more spouses and partners of working women to stay at home. Breadwinner Moms and Chief Household Officers will become more prevalent.

Unexpected: Gender-Based Labels Appear Noticeably Less Frequently in Workplace Discussions

More roles and facilities become delabeled by gender. In the consumer world, companies such as Target are already phasing out gender-based signage in many product categories such as toys and bedding. Some companies proactively push gender relabeling beyond today's boundaries, following the lead of Cooper Union, a college that removed all male and female signs from all of its bathrooms to accommodate both gender-conforming and gender non-conforming people.[5] Expect a significantly lower use of the labels "woman" and "women" in front of roles such as "woman president" or "women leaders," as exemplified by Drew Faust declaring, "I'm not the woman president of Harvard. I'm the president of Harvard."[6]

Rule #9: Plan for More Gig Economy Workers

Expected: The Workforce Is a More Blended Mix of Full-Time, Part-Time, Gig, and Other Nonpayroll Workers

Freelancing "has evolved from what you did between jobs to now it is your job," according to Billy Cripe, VP Marketing of Field Nation, a gig economy platform provider. As more workers choose to join the gig economy, organizations will struggle with the increased complexity of a blended workforce when navigating legal, training, and cultural issues. More assignments within an organization will be filled by contractors from outside the corporation. Blending workers of different contractual status, abilities, ratings, and cost structures will be further enabled with advanced algorithms and platforms.

Unexpected: Gig Economy Players Team Up to Take on Bigger Self-Organized Project Leadership Roles

Gig economy workers will increasingly locate, coordinate, and cooperate with each other and self-organize. The nascent organizing principle for leaders of blended workforces will be to make everybody feel part of the same team regardless of contractual status. And for many gig economy workers—able to set their own hours, balance work with the rest of their lives, and team up with other gig workers—this is being viewed as preferential to being a full-time employee. Dynamo, a virtual forum for freelancers, is already proving that the collective willingness of freelancers to coordinate together is gaining traction.

Rule #10: Be a Workplace Activist

Expected: More Workers Become Workplace Activists, Identifying and Pushing for the Changes They See as Needed in the Workplace

Every people process needs to be a constant target for continual improvement, or the process will be at risk of irrelevancy. Organizations will continue to apply design thinking and agile leadership principles to adopt an iterative mindset as an operating principle. Organizations will be aware of the need for all employees to practice iterative design thinking.

Unexpected: Workers Deeply Appreciate the Values that Do Not Change, as Everything Else Does

Can you and your team members explain the key aspects of your business that *do not change*, regardless of how much your business expands and grows? Organizations that are able to successfully cascade the shared mission and values of the organization to every level without an individual having to pause and think about it are an exception. But this is what is needed, an appreciation for the changes and disruptions, as well as the constants of the business.

Questions Invite Dialogue!

The Future Workplace Experience has presented you with 10 rules to use in navigating the future. We structured each chapter to offer you insights from research, interviews with practitioners, and reflective questions to help you, your team, and your organization prepare for and navigate the future workplace.

Our 10 rules will guide you in rethinking and reimagining your future workplace and in mastering disruptions in recruiting and engaging employees. The questions following each rule will help you start relevant conversations with your peers.

FINAL THOUGHTS

1. What was most useful for me in this book?

2. Who do I initiate a dialog with about shaping our future workplace?

3. How do I start the journey to reimagine our "Future Workplace Experience"?

The ten rules we present in this book are opportunities for you to transform and reimagine your workplace. The future workplace will be shaped by each of you as embark on your journey to become activists and give voice to the changes you see needed, in your organization, on your team and importantly within yourself! We look forward to hearing from you about the ideas, projects and initiatives that you have been encouraged to start after reading our book!

Visit us at www.TheFutureWorkplaceExperience.com to continue the journey!

ACKNOWLEDGMENTS

Our book is the collective insights and contributions of many. We want to express our sincere appreciation and gratitude to the members of the Future Workplace network who were especially generous of your time, expertise, and insights on how you are preparing for the future of learning and working, with a particular call out to those members who hosted peer to peer sharing sessions during our research such as Agilent Technologies, Cisco, GE Crotonville, LinkedIn, MasterCard, and Microsoft.

Our book journey has to begin somewhere, so to Linda and Phil Lader, the gracious hosts of the Renaissance Weekends community, thank you for for inviting us to the weekend where Jeanne and Kevin first met to begin our collaboration of many milestones, including researching and writing this book. To John Willig for your continued support and guidance during our book submission process, thank you as always. To our core McGraw-Hill Education team of senior editor Knox Huston, for your confidence in our abilities to deliver this book and your guidance in seeing us through to our final manuscript, to Patty Wallenburg, for managing our work into a professional product, and to Casey Ebro, for leading us over the finish line for our first printing, thank you. Thanks to all the leadership editors at *Forbes* for allowing Jeanne to test early ideas about the future workplace experience in published articles and to the early adaptors of the concepts contained within *The Future Workplace Experience*, especially to you Mark Levy, one of the first to so explicitly evolve from a chief human resource officer to global head of employee experience and to the team at Cognizant Technology who the shared the why and how of your journey to create millennial friendly learning solutions.

To our Future Workplace colleagues Brianne Helman, David Milo, Dan Schawbel, and Tracy Pugh for your ongoing dedication and daily contribution to our workplace experience, and to Lea Deutsch for your continued support and diligence in managing the many tasks required to complete our book, thank you. And many thanks to the team at IBM, and in particular to you, Diane Gherson, for writing such an insightful forward to this book that shared the IBM journey to creating a compelling workplace experience for your global employees.

Many thanks to Achievers, Callidus Cloud, Catalyst, Degreed, Edcast, edX, Glassdoor, GP Strategies, IBM, NovoEd, PathGather, Pyxera Global, and Zoomi for providing access to your client relationships to uncover many of the best of breed examples we have highlighted in this book.

To our business partners who provide the ideas and resources to shape our ongoing research and discussions, thank you; Gianpaolo Barozzi for helping shape the direction of our Future Workplace Forecast Survey and to Dennis Bonilla, Billy Cripe, Jim Link, Ludo Fourrage, Lydia Frank, Dan Gouthro, Greg Lok, Dominic Lopaco, Yair Riemer, Julie Shenkman, and Ruth Veloria for the opportunities to collaborate together on uncovering new trends in the future of working and learning, thank you.

As we think about who has gone the extra mile (or kilometer) for us, we want to thank our families. From Jeanne, I thank Bob, Danielle, Deborah, and Matt, and even my Havanese dog who sat by my side while I was writing and patiently listened to each book interview.

From Kevin, to you Diane, a very special and loving thank you! To my parents, John and Una, who continue to wonder exactly what it is I do for a living, *go raibh maith agat* (thank you in Gaelic). To my Babson College colleagues, the Babson Alumni who contributed your perspectives to our research study, my MBA students, and BRIC2013 for your community. To AMP189 6B and AMP190 6A of the Harvard Business School, thank you for sharing your leadership journeys during the writing of this book.

Finally, to all HR workplace activists across the HR community helping organizations engage and inspire the incredible talent of the corporate world, thank you all for what you do daily!

Jeanne C. Meister, New York City
Kevin J. Mulcahy, Boston

NOTES

Introduction

1. R. "Ray" Wang, "Disrupting Digital Business: Create an Authentic Experience in the Peer-to-Peer Economy." *Harvard Business Review Press*, May 2015.

2. "Freelancing in America: 2015" study, commissioned in partnership by Upwork and the Freelancers Union, surveyed over 7,000 U.S. workers. See https://www.upwork.com/i/freelancinginamerica2015/.

3. Full quote is: "In your career, knowledge is like milk," says Louis Ross, chief technology officer for Ford Motor Co. "It has a shelf life stamped right on the carton. The shelf life of a degree in engineering is about three years. If you're not replacing everything you know by then, your career is going to turn sour fast" as quoted in *The Lexus and the Olive Tree: Understanding Globalization* by Thomas L. Friedman (1999).

4. https://www.capgemini-consulting.com/resource-file-access/resource/pdf/innovation_center_v14.pdf.

5. "Welcome to the Experience Economy" by B. Joseph Pine II, and James H. Gilmore from the July–August 1998 issue of the *Harvard Business Review*.

6. Glenn Rifkin, "The Future of Work: A Meeting of Minds," December 7, 2015. Quote attributed to Ben Waber, CEO of Humanyze.

7. http://www.apa.org/news/press/releases/2014/04/employee-distrust.aspx.

8. https://www.eiuperspectives.economist.com/sites/default/files/Questfordigitaltalent_0.pdf.

9. Relationship Economics (2014) by Altimeter. http://www.altimetergroup.com/wp-content/uploads/2014/11/Relationship-Economics.pdf.

10. Deloitte, "Global Human Capital Trends 2014 Survey: Top 10 Findings."

11. http://www.industrytap.com/knowledge-doubling-every-12-months-soon-to-be-every-12-hours/3950.

12. http://www.entrepreneur.com/article/232348.

13. http://www.mckinsey.com/insights/organization/why_diversity_matters.

14. http://wpp.com/wpp/marketing/branding/three-lessons-learned-from -the-demise-of-kodak/.
15. Pixel Institute is a fictitious company name, solely used to illustrate this anecdote.

Rule #1

1. The percentage of U.S. workers in 2015 whom Gallup considered engaged in their jobs averaged 32 percent. The majority (50.8 percent) of employees were "not engaged," while another 17.2 percent were "actively disengaged." See http://www.gallup.com/poll/188144/employee-engagement-stagnant-2015.aspx.
2. http://www.gallup.com/businessjournal/183614/employees-responsible -engagement.aspx.
3. http://www.gallup.com/businessjournal/162953/tackle-employees -stagnating-engagement.aspx.
4. http://www.hreonline.com/HRE/view/story.jhtml?id=534358819 June 8, 2015.
5. https://hbr.org/2011/06/how-customers-can-rally-your-troops.
6. http://www.pwc.com/us/en/people-management/publications/assets/ pwc-nextgen-summary-of-findings.pdf.
7. Ibid.
8. Glassdoor US Site Survey, January 2016.
9. http://www.glassdoor.com.
10. Posted anonymously on Glassdoor.com on April 22, 2016.
11. http://monitor-360.com/ideas/making-sure-the-cup-stays-full-at -starbucks.
12. http://www.huffingtonpost.com/sophie-sakellariadis/making-sure-the -cup-stays_b_7935760.html.
13. http://www.forbes.com/sites/jeannemeister/2015/07/21/airbnbs-chief -human-resource-officer-becomes-chief-employee-experience-officer/.
14. Ratings on Glassdoor.com as of April 23, 2016.
15. http://www.csmonitor.com/Business/new-economy/2015/0723/ The-9-to-5-job-is-going-extinct.
16. http://www.nytimes.com/2016/02/28/magazine/rethinking-the-work -life-equation.html?_r=0.
17. Future Workplace "Multiple Generations at Work" survey.

18. http://www.cisco.com/c/en/us/solutions/enterprise/connected-world -technology-report/index.html.

19. Ibid.

20. http://www.forbes.com/sites/jeannemeister/2013/04/01/flexible -workspaces-another-workplace-perk-or-a-must-have-to-attract-top -talent/#55bd9d304382.

21. http://www5.sewanee.edu/business/news/suntrust-chief-outlines-firms -purpose-driven-mission.

22. http://www.aon.com/attachments/human-capital-consulting/2015 -Trends-in-Global-Employee-Engagement-Report.pdf.

23. http://www.independent.co.uk/life-style/gadgets-and-tech/news/there -are-officially-more-mobile-devices-than-people-in-the-world-9780518 .html.

24. https://blogs.adobe.com/digitaleurope/digital-marketing/adobe-digital -roadblock-report-2015/.

25. http://www.forbes.com/sites/chriscancialosi/2016/08/01/digital -communication-in-the-workplace-is-no-longer-optional/ #1d4170a11b0e.

26. http://www.huffingtonpost.com/2015/02/11/office-of-the-future_n_ 6649574.html.

27. Gensler "2013 U.S. Workplace Survey: Key Findings."

28. Ibid.

29. http://www.wired.com/2014/12/airbnb-invents-call-center-isnt-hell -work/.

30. https://www.steelcase.com/insights/360-magazine/steelcase-global -report/.

31. http://www.cisco.com/c/en/us/solutions/enterprise/connected-world -technology-report/index.html.

32. http://www.slideshare.net/joannapena/presentation-io-tdesignv5.

33. http://www.glassdoor.com/Reviews/Airbnb-Reviews-E391850.htm.

34. Ibid.

35. Ibid.

36. Charlene Li, *The Engaged Leader, A Strategy for Your Digital Transformation*. (Philadelphia: Wharton Digital Press, 2015), p. 65.

Rule #2

1. Thomas J. Peters, *Liberation Management: Necessary Disorganization for the Nanosecond Nineties* (New York: A. A. Knopf, 1992).

2. From a presentation by Kurt L. Darrow to the Michigan Colleges Alliance "Roundtable on Talent," Mackinac Island, Michigan, June 2015, and post-presentation conversation with author Kevin Mulcahy.

3. Sourced from an on-site interview between Lea Ann Knapp and Tony Geflos of the Action News team of WTVG TV of Toledo, Ohio, in June 2015.

4. A British BBC/University of Chester study found that both heart rate and energy expenditure were raised significantly by standing work and that sit-stand desks were effective in generating more favorable movements in blood glucose, calorie expenditure, and heart rate metrics.

5. Interesting data to suggest that pets improve productivity, http://www.entrepreneur.com/article/237982.

6. Susan Cain, "The Power of Introverts," filmed February 2012, http://www.ted.com/talks/susan_cain_the_power_of_introverts.

7. Vanessa Van Edwards, a behavioral investigator, who asserts that many people are actually ambiverts, in that they are both introverts and extroverts depending on the situation they find themselves in or the people they are surrounded by. In a LinkedIn article by Van Edwards, titled "Ambivert: The New Introvert?" December 9, 2014, she encouraged readers to find their nourishing locations in their personal lives based on the responses to three questions: "Where are you your best self?" which she labeled as "Thrive" locations; "Where are you indifferent?" which she labeled as "Neutral" locations; and "Where do you dread going?" which she labeled "Survive" locations. Inspired by the direction of these questions, we proposed three parallel questions to encourage employees to explore their connections to their workspace.

8. "The Quiet Ones," by Tim Kreider, published in the *New York Times Sunday Review* on November 17, 2012, provides entertaining insight into the norms and expectations of Amtrak's northeast corridor "Quiet Car." http://www.nytimes.com/2012/11/18/opinion/sunday/the-quiet-ones.html?_r=2.

9. Similar tools like Toggl, Loggr, Reporter, Gyroscope, Exist.io, and Zenobase are apps that can collect and aggregate employees' fitness tracking, location, mood, habit, and productivity data to discover correlations between specific workspaces and employee productivity.

Useful resources on this topic can be found on "A List of Life Logging/
Quantified Self Apps," http://lifestreamblog.com/lifelogging/. Another
list of time-tracking apps can be found on https://zapier.com/blog/
best-time-tracking-apps/.

10. A great graphical representation of the difference between "morning
bird/night owl" and "traditional nine-to-five/alternative work hours"
productivity can be found on http://thefuturebuzz.com/2013/03/28/
the-cost-of-interruption-visualized/.

11. "Top Considerations When Planning Strategic Workplaces," June 2,
2015, by Petra Geiger: "Too often in the open plan office more attention is paid to facilitating collaboration. The noise level, distractions and
constant interruptions are causing high amounts of stress in the workplace—in fact 61 percent say they go home to get work done." http://
www.red-thread.com/blog/top-8-considerations-when-planning
-strategic-workplaces/.

12. https://drive.google.com/file/d/0BzJ27RjmQhGZOHcyZFFwSF9BQmM/
view.

13. "The Human Era @ Work" study. Findings from The Energy Project and
Harvard Business Review, 2014 available at https://theenergyproject.com/
landing/sharehumanera.

14. "Sedentary Time and Its Association with Risk for Disease Incidence,
Mortality, and Hospitalization in Adults: A Systematic Review and
Meta-analysis," By Aviroop Biswas, BSc; Paul I. Oh, MD, MSc; Guy
E. Faulkner, PhD; Ravi R. Bajaj, MD; Michael A. Silver, BSc; Marc S.
Mitchell, MSc; and David A. Alter, MD, PhD available at http://annals
.org/article.aspx?articleid=2091327.

15. "The Sedentary Office: A Growing Case for Change Towards Better
Health and Productivity," expert statement commissioned by Public
Health England and the Active Working Community Interest Company,
March 2015, provides a great synthesis of insights on standing and sit-
ting for those that wish to read more. http://www.getbritainstanding
.org/pdfs/BJSM_Expert percent20Statement percent202015_06.pdf.

16. The International WELL Building Institute is a public benefit corporation. Public benefit corporations are an emerging type of U.S. structure
for corporations committed to balancing public benefits with profitability. This form of corporate structure was signed into being in Delaware
on July 17, 2013. Directors of public benefit corporations are legally

obliged to balance "the pecuniary interest of stockholders, the best interests of those materially affected by the corporation's conduct, and the identified specific public benefit purpose." While out of the scope of our focus for this book, public benefit corporate structures have the potential to have much greater appeal to a more socially conscious and purpose-driven employee.

17. http://www.WellCertified.com.

18. http://www.cnn.com/2011/LIVING/02/08/shrinking.american.cubicle/.

19. Ann Bamesberger directs work environment strategy, planning, real estate, and design and construction of the South San Francisco headquarters for 10,000+ Genentech and Roche employees. She is a recipient of the CoreNet's Global Innovator's Award and Sun's HR Leadership Award for innovation in workplace effectiveness strategies.

20. The initial discussions about the configuration of the new space involved improving from 60:40 standards (60 percent cubes:40 percent offices) to 70:30, a way of thinking that Ann advocated as dated.

21. "In mid-June 2013, we did a bunch of utilization studies for a series of weeks to understand the level of use of the offices as well as workstations, and it was 35 percent," reported Jamie Moore, IT program manager, Neighborhood Environments Team of Genentech, at the Future Offices Conference, held in New York City in January 2016.

22. Whitepaper titled "Network The Future Workplace" (2012) by Judith Heerwagen, Daniel Anderson, and William Porter, commissioned by Allsteel. Fourth places share a number of physical and social characteristics including flexible and informal seating arrangements, sociability in working in proximity to others, connectivity through virtual technologies, and individuality as workers engage in activities unrelated to one another and often from different departments or organizations.

23. Global Coworking Unconference Conference, May 6–8, 2015, Berkeley, California.

24. Todd Sundsted, Drew Jones, and Tony Bacigalupo, "I'm Outta Here! How Coworking Is Making the Office Obsolete." NotanMBA Press, October 27, 2009.

25. Extracted from "The History of Coworking," presented by *deskmag*, the coworking magazine, http://www.tiki-toki.com/timeline/entry/156192/ The-History-Of-Coworking-Presented-By-Deskmag#vars!panel =1512900.

26. http://www.deskmag.com/en/2500-coworking-spaces-4-5-per-day-741.

27. According to Cat Johnson, a blogger on freelancing, coworking, and thriving in the new economy, http://www.shareable.net/blog/coworking-visionaries-weigh-in-on-the-future-of-the-movement-0.

28. Brad Neuberg is said to have borrowed the term *coworking* from author Bernie DeKoven, who first used the term in 1999 to describe "working collaboratively" in an online space. http://www.deskmag.com/en/has-coworking-replaced-the-incubator-175.

29. The original blog posting for what is regarded by the coworking community as the first promotion of a "coworking" space. http://codinginparadise.org/weblog/2005/08/coworking-community-for-developers-who.html.

30. From an article by Elizabeth Segran in The Atlantic.com, February 27, 2015, http://www.theatlantic.com/business/archive/2015/02/as-coworking-spaces-scale can they-keep-their-communal-vibe/385653/.

31. http://workdesign.com/2015/09/what-to-look-for-in-your-next-community-manager/.

32. 2015 GCUC/Emergent Research Coworking Survey Results, presented at the Global Coworking Unconference Conference in May 2015 by Jacob Sayles (@jacobsayles) of Office Nomads.

33. http://workdesign.com/2015/09/what-to-look-for-in-your-next-community-manager/.

34. In 2006, Mark Fields of the Ford Motor Company attributed this quote to Peter Drucker. The quote is rumored to hang in a "war room" at Ford.

35. Inspired by Pico Iyer, in a talk titled "Where Is Home?" at TEDGlobal 2013, where he said that "home has less to do with a piece of soil than a piece of soul."

Rule #3

1. Our firm, Future Workplace, in partnership with Cisco, conducted a survey entitled the Future Workplace Forecast to uncover the discrete practices that organizations put into place to navigate the disruptions of technology, workplace mobility, and changing demographics in the workplace. The survey was conducted among 2,147 global human resource and business leaders across seven countries, with the top five industries represented including financial services, technology, manufacturing, professional services, and healthcare. The leadership skills

question we asked was "Thinking about the next three years, what are the top leadership capabilities an employee will need to possess to be promotable to a leadership role in your organization?"

2. The authors wish to acknowledge the contribution from the LMAP 360 Assessment, the work by Psychologist Ronald Warren, PhD and his colleague Brian Connelly, PhD for inspiring the macro frame for categorizing our seven dimensions of the agile leader into the two macro dimensions of "the ability to produce results" and "the ability to engage people." Their extensive studies with the LMAP 360 demonstrated how leadership and overall effectiveness are tied to both Task Mastery and Teamwork Traits. Task Mastery traits are the best predictors of leaders' "ability to produce results," while Teamwork traits tend to be the scales most predictive of "getting along with others." Kevin Mulcahy has used the LMAP 360 Assessment (Leadership Multi-Rater Assessment of Personality) in coaching executives on identifying actions to improve their leadership effectiveness. Warren and Connelly's statistical studies from samples of tens of thousands of leaders are outlined in a white paper, "Methods and Statistical Summary," June 2013, available on http://www.lmapinc.com/uploads/LMAP_Methods_&_StatisticalSummary.pdf.

3. http://www.nytimes.com/2016/02/15/technology/atts-strategy-is-one-part-innovation-one-part-inspiration.html?_r=0.

4. https://slashdot.org/story/14/02/07/1659232/how-adobe-got-rid-of-traditional-stack-ranking-performance-reviews.

5. http://www.forbes.com/sites/danschawbel/2013/09/09/why-companies-want-you-to-become-an-intrapreneur/#401f5ab24d31.

6. http://www.forbes.com/sites/davidkwilliams/2012/06/25/growing-a-company-qa-with-brad-smith-intuit-ceo-remove-the-barriers-to-innovation-and-get-out-of-the-way/#aa054af47382.

7. http://chapmancg.com/news/podcasts/2015/08/the-emergence-of-the-digitally-minded-leader.

8. https://www.dbs.com/newsroom/print-news.page?newsId=i7u1lx0y&locale=en.

9. https://medium.com/@HappyDaysInBali/the-five-most-influential-people-in-the-future-of-banking-65f4ddf40e34#.5zczut8pa.

10. http://www.mckinsey.com/global-themes/leadership/why-leadership-development-programs-fail.

11. Future Workplace Forecast Survey, 2015. "How important is it to you that your senior leaders model your organizational culture?" (5: Extremely Important; 4: Very Important; 3: Somewhat Important; 2: Not Very Important; 1: Not at all Important). Responses for Extremely Important and Very Important were aggregated.
12. Results from Future Workplace Forecast Survey.
13. Steve Gruenert and Todd Whitaker, "School Culture Rewired: How to Define, Assess, and Transform It," January 2015).

Rule #4

1. From the novel *A Man Without a Country* by Kurt Vonnegut (New York: Seven Stories Press, 2005).
2. http://www.gartner.com/binaries/content/assets/events/keywords/digital-workplace/pcce10/evtm_294_06_digitalworkplacepcc2015_infographics_emea.pdf.
3. http://www.forbes.com/sites/jeannemeister/2015/03/30/future-of-work-using-gamification-for-human-resources/#2d54bd0a32ba.
4. The name *Multipoly* is a play on the popular board game Monopoly. http://www.multipoly.hu/.
5. http://www.forbes.com/sites/jeannemeister/2015/03/30/future-of-work-using-gamification-for-human-resources/#2d54bd0a32ba.
6. Identified in 1885 by the German psychologist Hermann Ebbinghaus, the Ebbinghaus forgetting curve leads to a decline of memory retention over time since learning. The retention percentage lowers significantly—with individuals shown to retain 100 percent immediately, 58 percent after 20 minutes, 44 percent after 1 hour, 36 percent after 9 hours, 33 percent after 1 day, 28 percent after 2 days, 25 percent after 6 days, and only 21 percent after 31 days.
7. "Driving Innovation," November 2015, Badgeville and Booz Allen Hamilton. https://badgeville.com/driving-innovation-across-the-enterprise/.
8. The authors met with one Cognizant employee who completed all his "paperwork" for his move from India to the United States using a series of apps; this included filling out his visa application, completing cultural and etiquette training on U.S. office customs, navigating international relocation logistics, booking travel, and completing his transfer to the U.S. payroll system. He never actually spoke to anyone in HR during the complete process.

9. http://venturebeat.com/2016/02/10/the-app-economy-could-double-to
   -101b-by-2020-research-firm-says/.
10. http://www.cio.com/article/2980242/wearable-technology/how-hr-uses
    -fitness-trackers-to-increase-company-wellness.html.
11. http://www.fastcompany.com/3058462/how-fitbit-became-the-next-big
    -thing-in-corporate-wellness.
12. The Health Enhancement Research Organization (HERO), "Exploring
    the Value Proposition for Workforce Health Business Leader Attitudes
    about the Role of Health as a Driver of Productivity and Performance,"
    February 2015.
13. http://www.wired.com/insights/2015/02/the-future-of-wearable-tech/.
14. http://www.bloomberg.com/news/articles/2015-08-07/wearable
    -technology-creeps-into-the-workplace.
15. Ibid.
16. http://www.meddeviceonline.com/doc/fda-clears-first-ingestible-device
    -for-medication-adherence-0001.
17. http://futurism.com/researchers-develop-a-sensor-that-can-monitor
    -vital-signs-from-the-inside/.
18. The Liberty Mutual Workplace Safety Index ranks the top 10 causes of
    disabling work-related injuries and their direct costs. The "Overexertion
    Involving Outside Sources" event category includes injuries related to
    lifting, pushing, pulling, holding, carrying, or throwing objects. https://
    www.libertymutualgroup.com/about-liberty-mutual-site/research
    -institute-site/Documents/2016 percent20WSI.pdf.
19. http://www.ibtimes.co.uk/exoskeleton-boots-leapfrog-evolution-by
    -making-walking-more-energy-efficient-1494683.
20. http://www.ibtimes.co.uk/panasonic-mass-produce-alien-style-robot
    -exoskeleton-suit-help-workers-heavy-lifting-1509593.
21. http://www.just-auto.com/analysis/bmw-group-prioritises-factory
    -digitalisation-and-ergonomics-as-workforce-ages_id167978.aspx.
22. An optical head-mounted display is a wearable device that has the capa-
    bility of reflecting projected images as well as enabling the wearer to see
    augmented reality through it.
23. http://expandedramblings.com/index.php/pokemon-go-statistics/.
24. We encourage readers to visit DAQRI's home page (http://daqri.com)
    and view the videos demonstrating the sensory-enhancing immersive
    experience provided to the wearer.

25. Definition by Kevin Mulcahy, Future Workplace.
26. Enables users wearing a connected VR headset to paint life-sized, three-dimensional brush strokes and to then navigate digitally in and around their creations.
27. As of January 2016, Google shipped more than 5 million Cardboard VR viewers. http://www.androidcentral.com/more-5-million-google-cardboard-viewers-have-shipped-over-25-million-cardboard-apps-downloaded.
28. https://www.vrfocus.com/2016/05/google-daydream-launch-date-confirmed/.
29. http://jobsimulatorgame.com.
30. The organization looked at 15 companies and more than 300,000 hires in low-skilled jobs and compared the tenure of those hired via an algorithm with those chosen by hiring managers. The algorithm ranked the candidates into "greens," the high-potential candidates; "yellows," those with moderate potential; and "reds," the lowest potentials. On average, greens stayed in the job 12 days longer than yellows, who stuck around 17 days longer than reds. That showed that the algorithm worked. http://www.bloomberg.com/news/articles/2015-11-17/machines-are-better-than-humans-at-hiring-top-employees.
31. https://www.technologyreview.com/s/519241/report-suggests-nearly-half-of-us-jobs-are-vulnerable-to-computerization/.
32. http://www.socialmediatoday.com/social-networks/messenger-bots-what-are-they-how-do-they-work-and-why-should-you-care#sthash.iTwKHjKu.dpuf.
33. http://www.bloomberg.com/news/articles/2016-05-05/chatbots-are-your-newest-dumbest-co-workers.
34. Google Assistant is also built into Allo, a Google chatbot app, as well as Google Home. Google Home and Amazon Echo are shaping the market for voice-activated home products, further raising expectations for increased voice-activated experiences in the workplace.
35. Correspondence by e-mail between Kevin Mulcahy and Dr. Bernard S. Meyerson, May 25, 2016.
36. https://hbr.org/2012/10/data-scientist-the-sexiest-job-of-the-21st-century/.
37. This quote is credited to both Abraham Lincoln and Peter Drucker.

Rule #5

1. "78 percent of Candidates Would Apply to Jobs from Mobile," *Indeed. com Blog*, September 18, 2014, http://blog.indeed.com/2014/09/18/78-of -candidates-would-apply-to-jobs-from-mobile/.

2. Josh Bersin, "Culture: Why It's the Hottest Topic in Business Today," *Indeed.com Blog*, March 13, 2015, http://www.forbes.com/sites/ joshbersin/2015/03/13/culture-why-its-the-hottest-topic-in-business -today/2/#2715e4857a0b4fdfba5cf4de.

3. Emily Smykal, "Net Promoter Score: What Recruiters Need to Know About It," *Jibe*, July 29, 2015, https://www.jibe.com/ddr/net-promoter -score-what-recruiters-need-to-know-about-it/.

4. http://knowledge.wharton.upenn.edu/article/should-hiring-be-based -on-gut-or-data/.

5. "The Impact of Successful Employee Referral Programs," iCIMS Hire Expectations Institute, 2015, https://www.icims.com/sites/www.icims .com/files/public/The percent20Impact percent20of percent20Successful percent20Employee percent20Referral percent20Programs percent20 FINAL.pdf.

6. Ibid.

7. Jeff Schwartz, Josh Bersin, and Bill Pelster, "Global Human Capital Trends 2014: Engaging the 21st-Century Workforce," Deloitte Consulting, LLP, and Bersin by Deloitte, 2014, http://www2.deloitte .com/hr/en/pages/human-capital/articles/human-capital-trends-2014 .html.

8. Jim Whitehurst, *The Open Organization: Igniting Passion and Performance* (Boston: Harvard Business Review Press, May 12, 2015), https://books.google.com/books?id=nHsyBgAAQBAJ&lpg=PA42&ots =IBADXQp-XZ&dq=when percent20did percent20red percent20hat's percent20ambassador percent20program percent20began&pg=PA42# v=onepage&q=when percent20did percent20red percent20hat'spercent 20ambassador percent20program percent20began&f=false.

9. Reid Hoffman, "Four Reasons to Invest in a Corporate Alumni Network," September 1, 2014. Mary Lorenz, "Creating a Successful Corporate Alumni Program," CareerBuilder, April 3, 2014.

10. Lydia Dishman, "What Glassdoor Has Learned from Seven Years of Studying Other Companies," *Fast Company*, July 17, 2015, http://www

.fastcompany.com/3048590/lessons-learned/what-glassdoor-has
-learned-from-seven-years-of-studying-other-companies.

11. Ibid.

12. Steven Loeb, "How Does Glassdoor Make Money?" *VatorNews*, June 20, 2015, http://vator.tv/news/2015-06-20-how-does-glassdoor-make-money.

Rule #6

1. http://www.nytimes.com/2016/02/14/technology/gearing-up-for-the-cloud-att-tells-its-workers-adapt-or-else.html?ref=technology&_r=1&mtrref=www.nytimes.com.

2. http://www.businessinsider.com/people-who-dont-spend-5-hours-a-week-online-learning-will-make-themselves-obsolete-says-att-ceo-2016-2.

3. Jam session with Tim Ferriss and Josh Waitzkin http://fourhourworkweek.com/2016/03/23/josh-waitzkin-the-prodigy-returns/.

4. Louis Ross, Ford Motor Company in a speech to a group of engineering students http://it4b.icsti.su/1000ventures_e/business_guide/crosscuttings/tbt_whitepaper_4individuals.html.

5. http://www.industrytap.com/knowledge-doubling-every-12-months-soon-to-be-every-12-hours/3950.

6. Todd Tauber and Dani Johnson, *The Next Evolution of Learning Content*, Bersin by Deloitte, December 2014.

7. Universum, "Generation Z Grows Up," October 2015, p. 9.

8. PwC, "Millennials at Work, Reshaping the Workplace," p. 14.

9. The authors thank Jamie DePeau for her thoughtful contributions to our book while fighting cancer. Jamie passed away just three months following our book interview.

10. Todd Tauber, November 3, 2015, http://www.clomedia.com/articles/6547-the-missing-ingredient-for-innovation-you.

11. "Global Human Capital Trends Report 2015," Bersin by Deloitte, p. 27.

12. http://www.clomedia.com/articles/6593-mckinsey-is-moocing-on-up.

13. http://www.forbes.com/sites/joshbersin/2014/02/04/the-recovery-arrives-corporate-training-spend-skyrockets/.

14. http://www.fastcompany.com/3007369/heres-google-perk-any-company-can-imitate-employee-employee-learning.

15. Ibid.

16. Laszlo Bock, *Work Rules! Insights from Inside Google That Will Transform How You Live and Lead* (New York: Grand Central Publishing, 2015), p. 213.

17. https://www.td.org/Publications/Blogs/Learning-Executive-Blog/2014/11/What-Ceos-Want-and-How-to-Give-It-to-Them.

18. Simon Sinek, *Start with Why: How Great Leaders Inspire Everyone to Take Action* (New York: Portfolio, 2009), p. 228.

Rule #7

1. Lailah Gifty Akita, *Think Great: Be Great!* (CreateSpace, 2014).

2. https://www.ssa.gov/planners/lifeexpectancy.html, accessed May 27, 2016.

3. "The Multi-Generational Leadership Study," November 2015, sponsored by Future Workplace and Beyond.com—5,771 respondents, https://workplacetrends.com/the-multi-generational-leadership-study/.

4. Ibid.

5. Ibid.

6. Ibid.

7. http://www.bls.gov/opub/mlr/2012/01/art3full.pdf.

8. http://usnews.nbcnews.com/_news/2013/06/13/18934111-census-white -majority-in-us-gone-by-2043.

9. http://www.npr.org/sections/thetwo-way/2015/03/04/390672196/for-u-s -children-minorities-will-be-the-majority-by-2020-census-says.

10. http://www.huffingtonpost.com/2012/07/12/more-than-half-american -women-breadwinners_n_1668140.html.

11. http://www-935.ibm.com/services/us/gbs/thoughtleadership/millennialworkplace/.

12. Of course, there will be individuals who behave differently from their generational peers, as we have seen how generational affinity groups at companies such as IBM now include anyone with a millennial mindset.

13. "Get Ready for Gen Z," a report of a Robert Half Company survey on attitudes and behaviors of generation Z at work, July 2015, More than 770 college and university students between the ages of 18 and 25 in the United States and Canada were surveyed.

14. Deep Focus interviewed a nationally representative sample of 902 gen Z respondents, ages 7 to 17. In compliance with COPPA (Children's Online Privacy Protection Act), all 7- to 12-year-old respondents were

recruited through one of their parents and fielded from December 18
through December 29, 2014. "Winter/Spring 2015 Cassandra Report,"
http://www.deepfocus.net/press/deep-focus-cassandra-report-Gen-Z
-uncovers-massive-attitude-shifts/.

15. Ibid.
16. Ibid.
17. http://finance.yahoo.com/news/study-universum-details-gen-zs
    -060000284.html;_ylt=A0LEVvXSEqxWIykA7R0nnIlQ;_ylu=X3oDM
    TByNXM5bzY5BGNvbG8DYmYxBHBvcwMzBHZ0aWQDBHNlYwN
    zcg--.
18. http://www.forbes.com/sites/micahsolomon/2014/12/29/5-traits-that
    -define-the-80-million-millennial-customers-coming-your way/
    #3aa449792a81.
19. Sylvia Ann Hewlett, Laura Sherbin, and Karen Sumberg, "How Gen Y
    & Boomers Will Reshape Your Agenda," *Harvard Business Review*,
    July–August 2009.
20. Jeanne C. Meister and Karie Willyerd, "Accelerate Your Development:
    Tips for Millennials Who Need Mentoring," in *HBR Guide to Getting
    the Mentoring You Need* (Boston: Harvard Business Publishing, 2012),
    chapter 12.
21. http://www.pwc.com/gx/en/services/people-organisation/publications/
    nextgen-study.html, p.8.
22. Personal interview with Johanna Soderstrom CHRO, Dow Chemical.
23. http://www.wsj.com/articles/squeeze-the-parents-new-student-loan
    -goes-straight-to-mom-and-dad-1459205216.
24. http://www.nytimes.com/2016/03/26/your-money/medical-dental
    -401-k-now-add-school-loan-aid-to-job-benefits.html?_r=0.
25. http://www.forbes.com/sites/jeannemeister/2012/08/14/job-hopping
    -is-the-new-normal-for-millennials-three-ways-to-prevent-a-human
    -resource-nightmare/#570b720f5508.
26. http://www.businessinsider.com/5-reasons-why-gen-x-workers-quit
    -their-jobs-2012-11.
27. https://hbr.org/2014/09/4-ways-to-retain-gen-xers/.
28. https://www.capgemini-consulting.com/the-innovation-game.
29. Gallup, http://www.gallup.com/poll/168707/average-retirement-age-
    rises.aspx.
30. AARP 50 Best Businesses.

31. http://thehiringsite.careerbuilder.com/2012/09/13/ younger-bosses-the-new-normal/.
32. https://hbr.org/2015/10/when-your-boss-is-younger-than-you.
33. https://www.mainstreet.com/article/retirement-impossible.
34. http://www.thestreet.com/story/13152984/1/boomers-biggest-retirement -regret-they-didnt-work-longer.html.
35. David Hole, Le Zhong, and Jeff Schwartz, "Talking About Whose Generation: Why Western Generational Models Can't Account for a Global Workforce," *Deloitte Review*, 2010, issue 6, p. 91.
36. https://www.youtube.com/watch?v=aXV-yaFmQNk.

Rule #8

1. Sheryl Sandberg, *Lean In: Women, Work, and the Will to Lead* (New York: Knopf, 2013).
2. Ibid., p. 36.
3. https://www.linkedin.com/pulse/know-your-value-mika-brzezinski.
4. https://s3.amazonaws.com/s3.documentcloud.org/documents/1350163/ women_education_workforce.pdf.
5. http://www.sciencemag.org/news/2016/02/even-ebay-women-get-paid -less-their-labor.
6. Andrew Chamberlin research briefing provided by Glassdoor, March 23, 2016.
7. http://www.mckinsey.com/insights/organization/women_in_the _workplace.
8. Ibid.
9. http://www3.weforum.org/docs/GGGR2015/cover.pdf.
10. https://www.weforum.org/agenda/2016/02/where-is-the-best-country -to-be-a-working-woman/.
11. http://www.theatlantic.com/business/archive/2015/10/japan-woman -pay/408790/.
12. http://www.cnbc.com/2015/10/15/closing-the-global-gender-gap -commentary.html.
13. http://www.huffingtonpost.com/entry/gender-equality-at-work_ 560b00a4e4b0af3706de64c4.
14. http://readwrite.com/2014/09/02/women-in-computer-science-why-so -few/.

15. "Next Generation Diversity: Developing Tomorrow's Female Leaders," PwC, p. 3.

16. Claire Cain Miller, "Men Do More at Home, but Not as Much as They Think," *New York Times*, November 12, 2015.

17. http://www.nytimes.com/2015/07/31/upshot/millennial-men-find -work-and-family-hard-to-balance.html?_r=0&abt=0002&abg=0.

18. Published in the *American Sociological Review*, vol. 80, issue 1, 2015, p. 131.

19. http://www.gallup.com/poll/175286/hour-workweek-actually-longer -seven-hours.aspx.

20. https://hbr.org/2014/12/rethink-what-you-know-about-high-achieving -women.

21. https://www.shrm.org/hr-today/trends-and-forecasting/research-and -surveys/Documents/2015-Employee-Benefits-Tables.pdf (page 14).

22. http://time.com/money/4098469/paid-parental-leave-google-amazon -apple-facebook/.

23. Ibid.

24. https://www.oecd.org/els/soc/PF2_1_Parental_leave_systems.pdf. (Table PF2.1.A. Summary of paid leave entitlements available to mothers).

25. http://www.theatlantic.com/magazine/archive/2014/01/the-daddy -track/355746/.

26. http://www.bloomberg.com/news/articles/2015-04-30/the-10-u-s -companies-with-the-best-paternity-leave-benefits.

27. http://www.nytimes.com/2016/07/23/your-money/why-companies -have-started-to-coach-new-parents.html?_r=0.

28. http://www.pewsocialtrends.org/2013/05/29/breadwinner-moms/.

29. Ibid.

30. Ibid.

31. https://www.whitehouse.gov/sites/default/files/docs/nine_facts_about _family_and_work_real_final.pdf.

32. http://bits.blogs.nytimes.com/2014/09/26/the-business-case-for -diversity-in-the-tech-industry/.

33. http://www.usatoday.com/story/tech/2015/05/12/google-unconscious -bias-diversity/27055485/.

34. http://www.nytimes.com/roomfordebate/2014/10/29/reversing -gender-bias-in-the-tech-industry/fighting-unconcious-bias-at-google.

35. https://googleblog.blogspot.ie/2014/09/you-dont-know-what-you-dont
    -know-how.html.
36. Ibid.
37. http://www.gallup.com/poll/166952/baby-boomers-reluctant-retire.aspx
    ?utm_source=babypercent20boomers&utm_medium=search&utm_
    campaign=tiles.
38. http://www.gallup.com/poll/181292/third-oldest-baby-boomers
    -working.aspx.
39. Ibid.
40. Ibid.
41. http://www.gallup.com/poll/166952/baby-boomers-reluctant-retire
    .aspx?utm_source=babypercent20boomers&utm_medium=search&utm
    _campaign=tiles.
42. http://www.nationalpartnership.org/issues/work-family/paid-leave
    .html?referrer=https://www.google.com/.

Rule #9

1. https://www.freelancersunion.org/blog/dispatches/2015/10/01/
   freelancing-america-2015/.
2. http://qz.com/65279/40-of-americas-workforce-will-be-freelancers-by
   -2020/.
3. https://www.fieldnation.com/the-state-of-contingent-workforce
   -management-2015-2016-the-future-of-work-is-here-part-7.
4. https://www.randstad.cn/FileLoad/Attachment/20150814164313626.
   pdf.
5. "The Rise of the Blended Workforce in the New Gig Economy" study,
   May 2015. A Future Workplace research survey of 600 HR decision
   makers and 959 freelancers, conducted in partnership with Field
   Nation, a provider of a Freelancer Management System for companies
   and freelance work opportunities to over 70,000 service providers.
   https://www.fieldnation.com/the-rise-of-the-blended-workforce-in-the
   -new-gig-economy-3.
6. http://www.forbes.com/sites/sage/2014/02/11/why-the-new-freelance
   -economy-is-great-for-your-small-business/#2ccc4a7960d7.
7. https://www.freelancersunion.org/blog/dispatches/2015/10/01/
   freelancing-america-2015/.

8. http://www.wsj.com/articles/companies-find-tech-talent-in-robust
   -freelance-market-1453941466?cb=logged0.4658805225044489.

9. https://www.mbopartners.com/state-of-independence.

10. The U.S. Census Bureau reported in September 2014 that U.S. real
    (inflation adjusted) median household income was $51,939 in 2013
    versus $51,759 in 2012, statistically unchanged.

11. http://www.wsj.com/articles/companies-find-tech-talent-in-robust
    -freelance-market-1453941466?cb=logged0.4658805225044489.

12. http://www.forbes.com/sites/victorlipman/2013/09/23/surprising
    -disturbing-facts-from-the-mother-of-all-employee-engagement
    -surveys/#1d24cfc71218.

13. "Future Workplace Forecast" study by Future Workplace, November
    2016.

14. http://www.elance-odesk.com/millennial-majority-workforce.

15. http://www.slideshare.net/upwork/2015-us-freelancer-survey
    -53166722/1.

16. http://www.oreilly.com/iot/free/oorving-workers-gig-economy.csp.

17. Nick Grossman and Elizabeth Woyke, *Serving Workers in the Gig
    Economy* (O'Reilly Press, 2015), p. 3.

18. G. Barozzi and T. Lamberty, "Cisco Talent Cloud," Internal HR White
    Paper, January 2016. Confidentially shared with the authors for back-
    ground context only.

19. https://hbr.org/2014/01/to-raise-productivity-let-more-employees-work
    -from-home; https://www.gsb.stanford.edu/insights/researchers
    -flexibility-may-be-key-increased-productivity.

20. https://blog.workmarket.com/workforce-managers/new-research-27
    -million-people-part-corporate-on-demand-economy.html.

21. https://www.fieldnation.com/the-state-of-contingent-workforce
    -management-2015-2016-the-future-of-work-is-here-part-7.

22. https://www.linkedin.com/pulse/tapping-freelance-economy-brian
    -snarzyk?trk=prof-post.

23. http://www.shrm.org/hrdisciplines/technology/articles/pages/2016
    -tech-predictions.aspx.

24. Visit https://www.linkedin.com/profinder. The professional services
    categories listed as of June 1, 2016, were accounting, business consult-
    ing, coaching, design, financial services, home improvement, insurance,
    IT services, legal, marketing, photography, real estate, software develop-

ment, and writing and editing. The Profinder service is currently free for both freelance professionals and potential buyers. Customers describe the assignment, and the platform will offer a short list of proposals from potential matches, along with their LinkedIn profile.

25. http://www.transamericacenter.org/retirement-research/15th-annual -retirement-survey.

Rule #10

1. Fred Kofman asks this in a presentation segment titled "Your Job Is Not Your Job," https://www.youtube.com/watch?v=6OI7REyatq4, delivered as part of a LinkedIn speaker series. Kofman is the author of *Metamanagement and Conscious Business: How to Build Value Through Values*, published in 2006 by Sounds True. LinkedIn applies this expansive thinking to state its vision to win as "to create economic opportunity for every member of the global workforce," as mentioned by Fred Kofman and reinforced by Allen Blue, VP Product Management and cofounder of LinkedIn, in a March 2016 blog, https://blog.linkedin .com/2016/03/17/how-linkedin-is-helping-create-economic -opportunity-in-colorado-and-phoenix.

2. https://www.linkedin.com/in/brendanbrowne, as of July 20, 2016.

3. http://www.wsj.com/articles/global-telecoms-struggle-to-answer -challenge-from-messaging-apps-1464038370.

4. The precise question we asked was "As an HR leader, how would you rate the ability of your Human Resource Organization to attract the best employees?"

5. Adapted from *The Alchemy of Growth* by Mehrdad Baghai, Stephen Coley, and David White (New York: Perseus, 1999).

6. http://wpp.com/wpp/marketing/branding/three-lessons-learned-from -the-demise-of-kodak/.

7. http://www.nytimes.com/2016/03/31/business/dealbook/FinTech -startup-boom-said-to-threaten-bank-jobs.html?_r=0.

Looking Forward

1. http://www.hrgrapevine.com/markets/hr/article/hr-software-firm-to -offer-pet-bereavement-leave#.VuyxzD6WW_Q.mailto. Also, http://fortune.com/2016/03/08/here-are-the-12-most-pet-friendly -companies/.

2. http://www.businessnewsdaily.com/7456-workspace-design-productivity
   .html#sthash.Eq5vyqgA.dpuf.
3. https://hbr.org/2014/04/the-ceo-of-automattic-on-holding-auditions
   -to-build-a-strong-team.
4. "Demystifying the Gender Pay Gap" by Dr. Andrew Chamberlain, chief
   economist, Glassdoor, March 2016.
5. Cooper Union Pioneer Blog, http://pioneer.cooper.edu/2015/10/12/
   genderneutral-facilities-announced/.
6. Faust famously said this during a press conference in 2007 regarding
   her appointment as the twenty-eighth president of Harvard University,
   http://www.washingtonpost.com/wp-dyn/content/article/2007/02/12/
   AR2007021200075.html.

INDEX

ABOUT THE AUTHORS

Jeanne Meister is a founding partner of Future Workplace, an HR executive network and research firm. Jeanne is the author of three previous books. She is the coauthor of the bestselling book *The 2020 Workplace: How Innovative Attract, Develop & Keep Tomorrow's Employees Today* and previously, *Corporate Quality Universities* and *Corporate Universities*. Jeanne's name is synonymous with the establishment and institutionalization of global corporate universities.

Jeanne is a regular contributor to Forbes and the recipient of the Distinguished Contribution in Workplace Learning Award, given by Association for Talent Development (ATD) to one executive each year honoring their body of work. Jeanne regularly speaks on how companies are preparing for the future of work and appears frequently on CNBC Power Lunch, Fox Business, CNN, WPIX, New York, and NPR Market Place sharing best practices on the future workplace. Jeanne has been named to the Top 50 Influencers in Human Resources.

Previously, Jeanne was Vice President, Market Development, Accenture. She is a graduate of University of Connecticut and Boston University. Jeanne serves on the Board of Advisors for Kronos Workforce Institute and on the edX Corporate Advisory Board and lives in New York City and Columbia County, New York.

Follow Jeanne on Twitter: @jcmeister
Email Jeanne: jeannemeister@futureworkplace.com
Connect with Jeanne on LinkedIn:
    https://www.linkedin.com/in/jeannemeister

Kevin Mulcahy is a partner with Future Workplace and the cohost of The Future Workplace Network, a membership community for HR executives. He is a champion of framing trends that shape the future of work. Organizations regularly engage him to facilitate corporate workshops on "future proofing" their business and HR strategies.

Previously, Kevin has served as the practice head of a research consulting firm, in several executive roles at Sprint and as the CEO of an international telecom business. He coaches on leadership effectiveness at the Harvard Business School and promotes entrepreneurial thought and action as an adjunct faculty member at Babson College.

Kevin is a graduate of Trinity College Dublin and Boston College. He serves on the board of the Irish International Immigration Center and lives in Boston, MA.

Follow Kevin on Twitter: @KevinMulcahy
Email Kevin: KevinMulcahy@Futureworkplace.com
Connect with Kevin on LinkedIn:
    https://www.linkedin.com/in/kevinmulcahy1

About Future Workplace

Future Workplace is an HR Executive Network and research firm dedicated to providing insights on the future of learning and working. The firm operates the Future Workplace Network, a consortium of senior HR, Talent and Learning leaders from Fortune 1000 organizations who regularly convene to discuss, debate and share "next" practices on the future of work. The firm also operates WorkplaceTrends.com, a comprehensive repository of curated HR tools and research summaries. To learn more about becoming a member of the Future Workplace Network and WorkplaceTrends.com, email us at info@futureworkplace.com.

Follow Future Workplace on Twitter: @FutureWorkplace
Follow on LinkedIn: https://www.linkedin.com/company/future-workplace